BEST OF

Home Grown

1977–1981

An anthology of art and articles from Europe's first magazine devoted to cannabis and the psychedelic experience.

Edited by

Lee Harris and Chris Render

To Mal Burns,
Who was always there.
Thanks for all your
love + energy,
Stay High!
Lee Harris

RED SHIFT BOOKS

Lee Harris would like to dedicate this book to his family,
Brigitte, Amira, Deben and Edana.
Also special thanks to Henk Targowski and Gerry Coughlan.

Chris Render would like to thank Sue Render, Diana Gravill,
Anne Shepherd, Tony Bennett, Don Skirving and Pete Gotto.

Front cover design executed by Gregory Sams at CHAoS WORkS (Tel. 0181-459 5002) based on a joint session with Lee Harris and Chris Render.

First published by Red Shift Books, London 1994
Box 10, 234 Camden High Street, London NW1
ISBN 0 9524350 0 4
Printed in Denmark

CONTENTS

Colour Pages

INTRODUCTION
THE HOME GROWN YEARS

High,
Welcome to Home Grown, Europe's first dope magazine. In this premiere issue we present the most authoritative writers on dope-oriented subjects and an array of fine graphic art.

Thus began the editorial to *Home Grown,* No. 1, published in June 1977. In that first editorial I stated that *Home Grown* would aim at presenting an enlightened and informative, as well as entertaining, attitude to its subject — views and approaches not expressed by the popular media. It was produced as a celebration of 10 years of alternative culture. The flower children of that Summer of Love had grown up and most of the culture they spawned had been assimilated into the wider society. Cannabis, which was once something the hippies took, was used and accepted by people in all walks of life. Like many others, I believed that the laws on cannabis were immoral in principle and unworkable in practice. Cannabis has been illegal in Britain since 1928, and by the mid-seventies over 100,000 persons had been convicted of cannabis offences.

Looking back over the yeas it is hard to believe the furore that first issue caused. It received widespread publicity with reports appearing in many parts of the world. The press had a field day. "DANGER OF THE DRUG MAGAZINE. This bookstall horror is a nasty threat to your children" ran the lurid headline of a Sunday tabloid. "SHOCKING DISCOVERY IN GLASGOW RECORD SHOP" and "POLICE KEEP EYE ON DRUG MAGAZINE", were some of the responses of the provincial press. In a thumbs-down review in an underground paper I was called a 'crypto-fascist' for signing off with the words, "Into the New Age".

As the dust settled, and the threat of writs from a seed and tobacco company receded, the headline "BAN THIS NEW DRUGS MAG, DEMANDS MP", appeared in the popular press. A long-forgotten Labour member of parliament, Peter Hardy, had written to the then Home Secretary, Merlyn Rees, asking him to ban the magazine and prosecute us for "inciting people by implication to break the law". The press reported that the Home Office were "taking a keen interest" in the magazine and had asked to be sent future copies. So the Home Office's Dangerous Drugs Branch became one of our first subscribers.

After all the hue and cry it became increasingly difficult to find distributors and stockists brave enough to take further issues. To top it all, our first distributor went bankrupt owing us money, and making our hard sacrifices seem fruitless. But somehow, by sheer dint of determination, we overcame the various hurdles in our path, and with scant financial resources continued to publish two issues of *Home Grown* each year, for the next five years, improving and learning as we went along. In the ten issues we published over 150,000 copies of the magazine, reaching many parts of the world. Today copies of *Home Grown* are much revered collectors' items; a complete set being valued at $200 in an American catalogue of rare drug and counter-culture works.

Being the publisher and erstwhile editor of *Home Grown*, as well as advertising manager, street-seller and general dogs body, was a labour of love. Out of painful and difficult experiences often come rich rewards. One of them was the privilege of meeting and working with an interesting group of writers, illustrators and photographers, whom I shall call the *Home Grown Generation.*

In the Ladbroke Grove area of West London in the late seventies there existed a high society of writers, poets, visionaries, artists, thinkers, musicians, performing artists, and street-hustlers. A creative community of counter-culturists, a veritable bohemia of activity that thrived through a stagnant cultural climate of collectivism and conformity.

This Ladbroke Grove renaissance took place in the wake of the serious demise of the underground press of the late sixties, which left a lot of nurtured talent high and dry. In the charged atmosphere of repression and censoriousness, a small number of radical publication emerged and flourished for a time, like beacons in a dark landscape.

Notably, there was *The Fanatic,* an anarchic journal put out by Richard Adams and Heathcote Williams; *The Beast,* the first animal liberation magazine, published and edited by John May, who was an associate editor of *Home Grown*; *The Index of Possibilities,* by the collective from the last days of *Frendz* magazine, which included Michael Marten, John Chesterman, John Trux et al; *Bananas,* a literary magazine edited by Emma Tennant; Michael Horowitz's poetry journal, *New Departures*; and John Michell's *Radical Traditionalist Papers.*

It was a very productive time. Andy Leighton and later

Max Handley, an associate editor of *Home Grown,* and Chris Saunders revived that old stalwart of the alternative society, *International Times (IT)*; Tony and Carol Bennett began publishing Gilbert Shelton's underground comix, *The Fabulous Furry Freak Brothers,* and the work of Hunt Emerson. In the years preceding *Home Grown,* I published the *Brainstorm Comix* series, which featured the then unknown Bryan Talbot's trilogy, the adventures of Chester P. Hackenbush, the psychedelic alchemist. The Sams family, Ken, his sons Gregory and Craig, put out *Seed,* the journal of organic living. Amon Saba Saakana (Sebastian Clarke) published *Frontline* on black politics and culture. And Georgina Downs published *Alternative London.*

In this cauldron of creativity there were community presses run by Mike Braybrook and Colin Bennett; and Tony Allen's *Corrugated Times.* Writers and artists of calibre like Mick Farren, Ed Barker, Michelle Mortimer (Mikki Rain), and the photographer Ron Reid. There were the typesetters Caroline McKechnie and Dark Moon's Helen Lowe and Ann Lewis. There was also the explosion of punk fanzines that emanated from the presses of Jolly's Better Badges in the Portobello Road.

I lived and worked in the Grove amidst this creative hub of people, many of whom contributed to the magazine. It was a coming together of many interesting characters, what Ram Dass might call "the most exquisite rascals of our age". Some were luminaries of the underground and my culture heroes from the early days of psychedelia, such as Michael Hollingshead, who wrote *The Man who Turned on the World*; George Andrews who co-edited with Simon Vinkenoog *The Book of Grass*; and David Solomon, author of *The Marijuana Papers* and *LSD, The Consciousness Expanding Drug,* published in 1964.

Heathcote Williams, the poet, playwright and polemicist of the free state of Albion, introduced me to David Solomon just two weeks before he was arrested on LSD conspiracy charges in March 1977, in the biggest bust ever mounted in this country, code-named Operation Julie. The gentle 52 year old writer, who had cycled to my flat, was made out to be 'Mr Big' in the show trial that followed and sentenced to ten years imprisonment, and later deported to America. Such was the spirit of the time.

There was Steve Abrams, founder of SOMA, and initiator of the full-page advert in *The Times* in July 1967, which called for the decriminalisation of cannabis. And Brian Barritt, author of *Whisper,* a former merchant seaman and dope smuggler, who was back in the Grove, writing "loon-time scripts as a method of getting high".

We highlighted the plight of prisoners in foreign jails, publishing the moving letters of Danny de Souza, from Ladbroke Grove, who was busted in Turkey in 1975 for importing five kilos of hashish, and sentenced to 30 years in jail, later reduced to eighteen. Danny de Souza served twelve years of his sentence, and I had the pleasure of eventually meeting him in the Grove in 1990.

As time passed new talent appeared and made their mark on *Home Grown,* like Tim Malyon, broadcaster, photographer and founder member in 1978 of the Legalise Cannabis Campaign, which had an office in the area; Don Irving, photographer and writer, an associate editor and art director of the magazine; Harry Shapiro, author of books such as *Jimi Hendrix: Electric Gypsy,* whom we first published; Jan Pawlowicz, art teacher, who designed some of the issues; and Chris Render, bookseller and photographer, who is co-editor of this anthology.

The list of featured contributors to *Home Grown* over the five years, some commissioned, others reprinted from their published work, is voluminous, and, in retrospect, quite impressive. Besides those already mentioned, we published work by Timothy Leary, George Melly, Patti Smith, Julie Burchill and Tony Parsons, Anthony Henman (Antonil), Simon Vinkenoog, William Levy, Dr Fred Hickling, Alexis Korner, Peter Stafford and Bruce Eisner, Paul Krassner, Simon Gandolfi, Siva Kalki Swami, Laurence Cherniak, Peter Tosh, Mim Scala, Mervyn Harris, Freddie Venn, Dr Max Arbesfeld, Sean Sprague and many others too numerous to mention here. I proffer my sincere apologies to them and hope they will forgive me.

Taking on the task of publishing the magazine, often sailing close to the wind and against the prevailing tide, was a bracing experience that I can now look back on with warm affection, like rediscovering an old friend. In the winter of 1981 we published the tenth and final issue of *Home Grown,* though we reprinted a limited edition of the first issue at the end of 1982, and decided that the time had come to stop.

The chill winds of Thatcherism were blowing and there was a climatic change. A new ethos of greed and individuality, at the expense of community and caring, rent the social fabric asunder. There were riots by unemployed black youths in the front-line urban waste-lands of our inner cities. The issue of ganja smoking was at the barricades of the political scene, inextricably wound up with racial and social tensions. The War on Drugs was hotting up.

Lee Harris
August 1994, East Anglia

Timothy's Declaration

When, in the course of organic evolution, it becomes obvious that a mutational process is inevitably dissolving the physical and neurological bonds which connect the members of one generation to the past and inevitably directing them to assume among the species of earth the separate and equal station to which the Laws of Nature and Nature's God entitle them, a decent concern for the harmony of species requires that the causes of the mutation should be declared.

We hold these truths to be self-evident that all species are created by God different but equal, that they are endowed, each one, with certain unalienable rights, that among them are freedom to live, freedom to grow, and freedom to pursue happiness in their own style.

That to protect these God-given rights social structures naturally emerge basing their authority on the principles of the love of God and respect for all forms of life.

That whenever any form of government becomes destructive of life, liberty, and harmony, it is the organic duty of the young members of that species to mutate, to drop out, to initiate a new social structure laying its foundation on such principles and organising its power in such form as seems most likely to protect the safety, happiness, and harmony of all sentient beings.

Genetic wisdom, indeed, suggests that social structures long established should not be discarded for frivolous and transient causes. The ecstasy of mutation is equally balanced by the pain. Accordingly, all expierence shows that members of a species are more disposed to suffer, while evils are sufferable, rather than to right themselves by discarding the forms to which they are accustomed. But when a long train of abuses and usurpations, all pursuing invariably the same destructive goals, threatens the very fabric of organic life and the serene harmony upon the planet, it is the right, it is the organic duty, to drop out of such morbid covenants and to evolve new, loving social structures.

Such has been the patient sufferance of the freedom-loving people of this earth; and such is now the necessity which constrains us to form new systems of government.

The history of the white, menopausal mendacious men now ruling the planet earth is a history of repeated violation of the harmonious laws of nature, all having the direct object of establishing a tyranny of the materialistic, the aging over the gentle, the peace-loving, the young. To prove this, let facts be submitted to a candid world.

They have maintained a continuous war against other species of life: enslaving and destroying at whim fowl, fish, and animals, and spreading a lethal carpet of concrete and metal over the soft body of earth.

They have maintained a continual state of war among themselves and against the coloured races, the freedom-loving, the gentle, and the young. Genocide is their custom.

They have instituted artificial scarcities denying peaceful folk the natural inheritance of earth's abundance and God's endowment.

They have glorified material values and degraded the spiritual.

They have claimed private, personal ownership of God's earth, driving, by force of arms, the gentle from their passage on the land.

In their greed they have erected artificial immigration and customs barriers preventing the free movement of people across the land.

In their lust for power they have set up systems of compulsory education to control the minds of the young and to destroy the wisdom and innocence of playful children.

In their lust for power they have controlled all means of communication to prevent the free flow of ideas and to block loving exchanges among the gentle.

In their fear they have instituted great armies of secret police to spy upon the privacy of the people.

In their anger they have coerced the peaceful young, against their

Leary's of Evolution

will, to join their armies and to wage murderous wars against the young and gentle of other countries.

In their greed they have made the buying and selling of weapons the basis of their economies.

For their own profit they have polluted the air, the rivers, the seas.

In their impotence they have glorified murder, violence and unnatural sex in their mass media.

In their aging greed they have set up an economic system which favours impotent age over the living young.

They have in every way attempted to impose a robot uniformity and to crush variety, individuality, and independence of thought.

In their greed they have instituted a political system which guarantees rule by the aging, and forces youth to choose between plastic conformity or despairing alienation.

They have invaded the privacy of the young, the coloured, the dissident, by illegal search, unwarranted arrest, and contemptuous harassment.

They have sown distrust by enlisting an army of informers.

In their greed they sponsor the consumption of deathly tars and sugars and initiated draconian punishments for the possession of life-giving alkaloids and acids.

They never admit a mistake. They unceasingly trumpet the virtue of greed and war. In their advertising and in their manipulation of information they make a fetish of blatant falsity and pious self-enhancement. Their obvious errors only stimulate them to greater error and noisier self-approval.

In their greyness they force the gentle to wear uniforms and to look the same.

They are bores.

They have taken leave of their senses and become prudish machines.

They have no sense of humour.

They hate beauty.

They hate sex.

They hate creativity.

They hate life.

We have warned them from time to time of their inequities and blindness. We have used every available appeal to their withered sense of justice and righteousness. We have tried to make them laugh. We have prophesied in detail the terror they are creating. But they have been deaf to the weeping of the poor, the anguish of the coloured, the rocking mockery of the young, the warning of the poets. Worshipping only force and money they listen only to force and money. But we shall no longer talk in these grim tongues.

We must, therefore, acquiesce to genetic necessity, detach ourselves from their uncaring madness, and hold them, as we hold the rest of God's creatures, in harmony, life-brothers: in their excess, menaces to life.

We, therefore, God-loving, peace-loving, life-loving, fun-loving men and women, appealing to the Supreme Judge of the Universe for the rectitude of our intentions, do in the Name and by the Authority of all sentient beings who seek to gently evolve on this planet, solemnly publish and declare that we are free and independent and that we are absolved from all Allegiance to the United States government and all governments controlled by the menopausal, and that grouping ourselves into tribes of like-minded fellows, we claim full power to live and move peaceably on the land, obtain sustenance with our own hands and minds in the style which seems sacred and holy to us, and to do all Acts and Things which independent free men and women may of right do without infringing on the same rights of other species and groups to do their own thing.

And for the support of this Declaration of Evolution with a firm reliance on the protection of Divine Providence, and serene confidence of the approval of generations to come, in whose name we speak, do we now mutually pledge to each other our Lives, our Fortunes, and our Sacred Honour.

LEGALISE IT

'There is probably one thing, and one thing only, on which the leaders of all modern states agree ... That thing is the "scientific fact" that certain substances which people like to ingest or inject are "dangerous" both to those that use them and to others ... However, there is little agreement — from people to people, country to country, even decade to decade — on which substances are acceptable and their use considered a popular pastime, and which substances are unacceptable and their use therefore considered ' "drug abuse" and drug addiction.'
THOMAS SZASZ—*Ceremonial Chemistry*

In 1973 when Nelson Rockefeller was Governor of New York State, he delivered a tough speech in which he outlined his plans for a war against the drug problem. He painted a graphic picture of a society "terrorised" by crime and claimed: "We the citizens are imprisoned by pushers. I want to put the pushers in prison so we can come out, ladies and gentlemen."

At the same time that he ushered in the strongest anti-drug penalties in the country, a committee was set up in order to study the performance of the new laws. They reported recently that by mid-1976, the State had spent $76 million on hiring 49 new judges, plus prosecutors, defence counsels and support staff in order to handle the new legislation.

'Yet', the report claimed, 'there were fewer drug cases processed per year by the courts than there were under the old law.' The tougher penalties simply meant that defendants fought their cases harder and the courts began to bog down. By mid-1976 the backlog of cases in New York City alone had reached 2,600, a year's workload for the courts.

The new penalties had been publicly announced via a $500,000 advertising campaign but its deterrent effect did little. There was an initial drop in drug cases and dealers began hustling from doorways rather than the pavement, but within a few months an improvement was blown away. The law had to be altered.

This method of drug control, the Rockefeller syndrome, was clearly defined in a UNESCO seminar on 'Youth and the Use of Drugs in Industrialised Countries' which pointed to 'The increasingly political use of the "drug bogey" by the public authorities in order to influence public opinion and validate forms of action which are completely out of proportion to the problems involved.' Making a mainline out of a roach clip, you might say.

This general attitude towards "the drug problem" is exemplified by the official stance on cannabis, a relatively mild plant drug — one among thousands — which has been hogging the public limelight for more than a quarter of a century.

Now it seems, in America at least, that the facade of cannabis control and the myths surrounding it, are breaking down. Lenny Bruce rightly pointed out that when the lawyers started to smoke then things would change. Even he couldn't forsee the possibility of the son of a Republican President openly admitting to the media that he turned on.

Official statistics now claim that 45 million Americans have tried it and 11 million are regular users out of total population of 216 million. Cannabis has ceased to be an exotic herb smoked only by blacks, Jews and radicals and is now a national pastime of the middle class. This in turn has stimulated the growth of a huge paraphernalia industry with its own bible, *High Times,* and a new breed of hip entrepreneurs like Burt Rubin.

Rubin, a one-time metals salesman, now heads Robert Burton Associates which last year grossed $5 million from selling rolling papers. Rubin was 24 when he had the idea which was to change his life: "Everywhere I went, I noticed that people always stick two pieces of rolling paper together to roll a joint. So I figured why not make the paper wide?" E-Z Wider Rolling Papers were launched into a national market which consumes 150 million packets a year, and are now racked in supermarkets.

Of course it must be remembered that America had Prohibition to look back on as a prime example of what happens when you try and stop the people getting what they want. Marijuana's prime identification with the youth revolt in the '60's did little for its legal chances but, once the cordite fumes had cleared, the authorities were under increasing pressure to adopt more reasonable attitudes.

Decriminalisation became the marching watchword and changes arrived thick and fast. Oregon was the first state to go in 1973 and nine others have followed its example with 30 bills pending. Public attitudes combined with a large-scale, influential lobbying campaign by the Playboy-financed organisation NORML did the trick. Cops began carrying scales next to their nightsticks to weigh your stash to see if you were under the legal limit.

Of course this is still a long way from the utopia envisioned by psychedelic radicals of the '60's. As Dr Robert duPont, a leading drug expert points out, decriminalisation "need not be viewed as a stepping stone to legalisation," but rather a "rational step that takes into account the realities of mass use, while at the same time attempting to make clear that such use is both undesirable and without social approval."

This shift in emphasis was echoed by President Carter's speech in which he announced plans to reduce Federal penalties. He said, "We can and should continue to discourage the use of marijuana, but this can be done without defining the smoker as a criminal." He pointed out that 90% of deaths from drug abuse are related to heroin, barbiturates and other sedative-hypnotic drugs. His conclusion is important: "Penalties against possession of a drug should not be more damaging to an individual than the use of the drug itself."

Meantime, back in Blighty, we're still in the Dark Ages. In 1978 it will be fifty years since cannabis was first banned in this country purely, it now seems, as a kind of diplomatic backhander to keep friends and neighbours happy. It seems that the majority of our lawmakers still tend towards Rockefeller's end of the spectrum and there is little public incentive to change this. Only a kamikaze candidate would risk his political career for such an issue.

A series of campaigns, spearheaded by Release, have attempted to enlighten public opinion and lobby in the corridors of power. As a result minute concessions have been granted while the whole issue has been quietly defused, its very real political nature masked by a mass of jargon until it can be safely handled by experts in the art of technicalities. How can you rally round the call "Let's kick out Sub Paragraph 3(b)"?

Meantime the situation remains that if you smoke the stalk and tops of a cannabis plant it's a Class B offence, while leaf smokers are classified up there among the Main Offenders in Class A. In addition a considerable number of people still get sent down for simple possession charges while the drug laws in general are used to discriminate against certain bolshy sections of the community.

Prime bone of contention is the power the police have under the drug laws to stop and search. In 1975 there were 14,000 reported "stops" and only in 24% of cases were drugs found. When you consider that the number of searches recorded can only be a fraction of the total carried out, this "success" percentage is even lower.

On the one hand the authorities bemoan the financial pressure placed on courts and prisons while on the other official figures show that 80% of all drug prosecutions are for simple cannabis possession.

The UNESCO report mentioned earlier fingers the root of the problem. "Legislative, judiciary, penitentiary and police systems, just like medical, psychiatric and educational systems, which in various capacities are concerned with the drug problem, constitute so many cogs in the social mechanism which move only when changes occur in public opinion, which is itself conditioned by the evolution of systems of representation."

In other words, it's all one big ball game conditioned by the PUBLIC IMAGE. Change that, and everything else will follow. The blame for the current situation lies with the media's constant campaign of misinformation which is largely designed to perpetuate old myths and untruths — what used to be termed 'yellow journalism'. Propaganda masquerades as fact, ignorance as informed opinion. Meantime hundreds of young people each year discover what the inside of a cell looks like, have their fingerprints taken, are fined in court and pilloried in public as a result.

On the scale of things of course, the cannabis issue is a fleabite on an elephant. There are many more dangerous threats to civil liberties. Presley is dead and pollution is spreading. Europe is racked by terrorism and punks and teds fight it out in the streets. But even fleabites have a tendency to keep on itching.

So let's celebrate the new year by making it a real Golden Jubilee Anniversary. Let's write the obituary for the cannabis laws.

You know what they say. The only problem about cannabis is getting busted.

THE EDITORS

A JAZZMANS VIEW
OF DOPE: by
George Melly
BLUEBIRD
Electrically Recorded
PHONOGRAPH RECORDS
Not Licensed for Radio Broadcast
ST. LOUIS BLUES-Fox Trot
(W. C. Handy)
Louis Armstrong and his Orchestra
Trumpet solo by Louis Armstrong
Brunswick
MADE IN UNITED STATES OF AMERICA
Not Licensed for Radio Broadcast
WISHED ON THE MOON
TEDDY WILSON and his ORCHESTRA
7501
BRUNSWICK RECORD CORPORATION
Fox Trot
Vocal Chorus by
Louis Armstrong
I HOPE GABRIEL LIKES
MY MUSIC
(DAVE FRANKLIN)
LOUIS ARMSTRONG and his
ORCHESTRA
672 A
B 1023
I Couldn't Hear Nobody Pray
—Arr. by Bradford—
Cotton Belt Quartet
MANUFACTURED BY
THE BRUNSWICK-BALKE-COLLENDER CO.

"Gage is more of a medicine than a dope. But with all the rigmaroo going on, no-one can do anything about it. After all the vipers during my heyday are way up there in age – too old to suffer those drastic penalties. So we had to put it down. But if we get as old as Methusela our memories will always be lots of beauty and warmth from gage. Well that was my life and I don't feel ashamed at all. Mary Warner, honey, you sure was good . . . . "

Louis Armstrong
(Extract from "Louis" by Max Jones and John Chilton : Studio Vista)

Thus, and much more from the late Louis Armstrong, a much more courageous man than the young firebrands of a later generation gave him credit for. As for *"putting it down"* there a certain doubt creeps in. I suspect that until the end of his life, when everything was *"cool"*, Louis didn't refuse a joint, but as he says he was *"way up there in age"* and not prepared to make an open stand, attend smoke-ins or light up on the stand. He didn't however deny *"the beauty and warmth"*. He never denounced *"Mary Warner"*.

From the earliest days dope was Black Jazz's secret, but things were always difficult for Black Jazz musicians. There were so many pressures and the use of dope was yet another weapon that could be used to harass the jazz man. Louis' one bust for instance was, according to the policeman who arrested him, because a bandleader up the road, probably a user himself, got jealous at Armstrong's greater success and "dropped a nickel" on him. For jazzmen, of necessity, dope was an hilarious secret.

Around it arose an elaborate slang. Most people know, and now laugh at as old-fashioned, the word "reefer" meaning a joint, but less familiar are the disused words for the weed itself: "muggles", "Mary Jane (or Warner)", "gage", "shuzzit". A regular user was known as a "Viper", and the object of smoking was to get either "high" (still in use) or "tall" (archaic).

As however dope was mostly confined to Blacks or those white jazz musicians who admired or hung out with Black jazzmen after hours, it was ignored as a general problem, and throughout the twenties and thirties it was possible for jazz and swing musicians to put out a large number of celebratory records knowing that either they would be largely ignored by the white record buying public or that the argot would conceal the meaning. Comparatively recently Stash Records, (ST 100) issued an L.P. called *"Reefer Songs"*, sixteen cheerful tracks describing the pleasures of dope, all of them issued between 1932 and 1944.

On Bessie Smith's *"Gimme a Pigfoot and a Bottle of Beer"*, the Empress of the Blues herself demands *"a reefer and a gallon of gin"*, a mixing of intoxicants that would appal the more puritanical devotees of *Home Grown* perhaps, but for such a full-blooded hedonist as Bessie would seem no conflict. Amusingly enough Bessie's niece, Ruby while being questioned by Chris Albertson for his fine biography, became impressively indignant when Albertson asked if her aunt indulged in dope or shit. *"No, Bessie never touched nothin' like that – just regular reefers."* A classic example of linguistic confusion.

It would seem logical that, following the revival of interest in early jazz in Britain towards the end of the forties that those of us involved would have taken up dope as well, but in fact this didn't happen for a number of reasons which I shall try to explain here.

This revival coincided with the Bebop explosion; a rival school for whom, with very few exceptions, the music began with Charlie Parker and Dizzy Gillespie. This initial antagonism, later much resolved, was so extreme that it went far beyond the music itself and dictated two entirely separate life styles. Revivalists were studiously scruffy so Modernists were sharp. Modernists were cool, so Revivalists were extroverts. Modernists were known to smoke dope, so Revivalists confined themselves to alcoholic excess.

But why, as the heroes of the Revivalists had also smoked, did this taboo remain? Well for one thing it was not generally known. The records on the subject, with the exception of Bessie's one refer-

ence, were unobtainable, and none of the earlier jazzmen had come out front. Then, whereas the Bebop musicians were mostly professionals who had crossed the Atlantic playing on the boats, met their idols and observed and copied their habits, the Revivalists were largely semi-pros and, due to the embargo on American jazzmen coming over, hadn't even heard a jazz giant in the flesh, let alone spoken to one. Finally it was Bebop which attracted the still sparse West Indian immigrant population with their tradition of smoking and in consequence access to the weed. During the fifties a few British Modernists were bust and given fairly Draconian sentences. This strengthened the Revivalists reluctance to try it. What you've never had you don't miss.

Towards the end of the decade, with the gradual breakdown of hostility between the two schools we'd become more tolerant. We'd smelt it, and seen it smoked, but few of us had crossed the barrier. It was associated with flattened fifths, sharp suits and turning your back on the audience. Then came the sixties, rock burst in, jazz, whether Bebop or Traditional was swept out of the way, and dope became, not a minority pleasure but a crusade and a cause.

or a jazzman the sixties were professionally a disaster, but for someone interested in general in social development they were a fascinating if at times infuriating decade. The principal development was the sudden elevation of youth into a religion. Youth itself was not just a stage between childhood and adulthood, but the only virtue, and dope was one of the ways it cut itself off from anyone over thirty. Dope was no longer the modern jazz world's secret, or the American and West Indian Black world's relaxation. It was a provocation, a sign of belonging, a means to distinguish "them" from "us". I must admit I found the free-masonry of dope as irritating as I was intended to. (I was around 38 in 1964.) Those beatific smiles which were so exclusive, those endless discussions as to quality and source, that deliberate rejection of language as a form of communication. On the other hand I tried it and found it pleasantly relaxing, dream-inducing, the reverse of aggressive. I preferred and still prefer alcohol, but could see little harm in it, certainly no more harm, and probably less, than in whisky. The law however thought otherwise, using its illegality as a stick to beat the young. Thus long hair equalled dope, and the police took to stopping young haired boys in the street to search them and were frequently rewarded. The point was that long hair like dope was a cause, a fairly negative one in my view, but not to long-haired dope smokers. Caution was frowned on. As a result dope could be planted and no magistrate would believe that any long-haired hippy wasn't guilty. Dope could be used, and was, to harass anyone with unpopular views; the Oz defendants for example. I had no hestitation

in signing the advert in *The Times.* While whisky and cigarettes are advertised everywhere, it seemed to me insane to single out marijuana as a criminal substance, and nor did the escalation theory seem in anyway convincing. Of course most heroin addicts probably started on dope. So most alcoholics, dying from cirrhosis, started with a glass of beer. On the other hand it seemed to me by making marijuana illegal you linked it with other illegal and undoubtedly dangerous drugs, equating the young man with more than he needed for his own use and selling some to a friend, with the dealer, usually far more cautious, who made his living pushing addiction and despair. My wife's work for *Release* revealed to me what I might otherwise have never believed without witnessing it; the lengths the law would go to bust those whose life style, as a whole, they disapproved of. The extraordinary witch hunt against the Beatles and the Stones were of course widely publicised and raised doubts and misgivings even in the august columns of *The Times* but no such publicity was afforded the thousands of kids on the street or in squats who were equally at threat.

Nor, by that curious double-think which comes into play the moment money is involved, was anything done to suppress all those overt references to dope in Rock music. *"Smoke dope"*, sung the superstars. *"Turn on! Drop out!"* and the kids did, and got busted.

owever, during the seventies much of the steam has gone out of the issue. Dope, while still much smoked by all classes and age-groups, is no longer a cause celebre, nor even especially fashionable. Playing as we do at universities we notice, it may be partially economic of course, that whereas five years ago you could get a contact high simply by breathing in and out, there is much more drinking and far less smoking. The press no longer raise their hands in horror. There are other, more serious problems around and the age-group split has in part healed.

Yet this doesn't mean there are no more arrrests, doesn't rule out the possession of however small a quantity of hash or grass as a way to pin down those considered to be trouble-makers or anti-social. In a way the general public tolerance is a danger. *"Nobody care anymore do they?"* is the general attitude, but that's just because the news value has gone out of it. Its still as unfair as it ever was – perhaps more so. The young doctor or schoolmaster who enjoys a joint to relax at home in the evening will probably suffer no consequences. The working-class kid on the streets is statistically likely to be less secure. All strength to the campaign to legalise the use of this comparatively harmless narcotic not, in my view, because of its positive or beneficial qualities if such they be, but because its illegality is partial, unjust, and hypocritical.

"Dreamed about a reefer five feet long" sang the irrepressable Fats Waller.

"Mighty mezz but not too strong.
You'll be high, but not for long,
If you're a viper."

I'll light up to that!

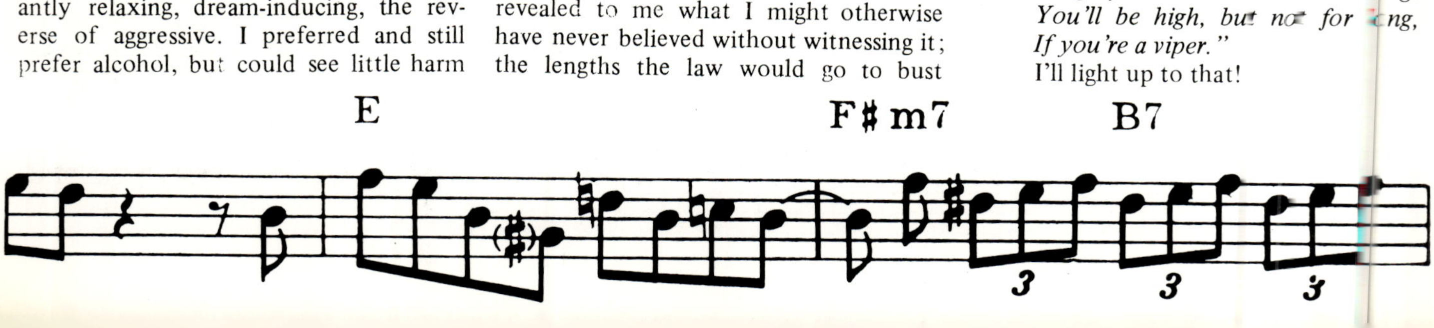

SMOKEY BEARS
"The law against cannabis is immoral in principle and unworkable in practice"
DRING
WHO'S THERE?
WAIT A SEC!
RAYMOND? IT'S ONLY US!
CLUNK
BAH GUM
CLANG
CLANK
KLIK
KLIK
CLUNK
CHESTER!
LYDIA!
COME IN!
LATER..
THANKS FOR THE GRASS - IT'S GREAT.
THAT'S O.K.
WE'VE GOT LOTS OF IT*
HEH HEH
Y'KNOW JAMES WAS UP IN COURT YESTERDAY? IT WAS SIMPLE POSSESSION UNTIL THEY HUNG AN 'INTENT TO SUPPLY' RAP ON HIM TOO...
* SEE LAST ISSUE
...THEY SENT HIM DOWN FOR THREE YEARS!
SWEET JESUS!
THAT'S TERRIBLE! PRISON'LL MURDER HIM.
THA' KNOWS TONY? - TH' MILKMAN? THEY RAIDED HIS HOUSE TWO WEEKS AGO... RANSACKED THE PLACE, SMASHED THINGS - EVEN DRAGGED HIS KIDS OUT OF BED TO LOOK UNDER TH' MATTRESSES.
DID THEY FIND ANYTHING?
NO - HE STOPPED SMOKIN' YEARS AGO - 'COS HE'S ASTHMATIC. SO THEY PLANTED SOME AN' BUST HIM ANYWAY!
STANDARD PRACTISE.
HANG ON!
SCREECH!!
A CAR'S JUST PULLED UP OUTSIDE...
IT'S ALRIGHT.
IT'S ONLY THE NEXT DOOR NEIGHBOURS.
ER... WE'LL BE OFF NOW...
RIGHT. I'LL BURN THESE JOINT-ENDS
MIND IF I USE YOUR LOO?
GO AHEAD - IT'S A FREE COUNTRY!
THANX & A TIP OF TH' HAT TO ERIC PRESLAND
BRAINSTORM STUDIOS
©1979 BRYAN TALBOT
FREEZE SHOT & FADE OUT...

Calligraphy by Richard Adams.
THE
PSYCHEDELIC
POGROM
HEATHCOTE WILLIAMS
O-LEVEL ACID
A twice-told tale, but
"lest we forget....."

"FROM THE POINT OF VIEW OF ENTRENCHED SOCIAL ESTABLISHMENTS, IT IS PERHAPS LEGITIMATE TO CLASSIFY THE PSYCHEDELICS (LITERALLY, MIND-MANIFESTING OR CONSCIOUSNESS-EXPANDING COMPOUNDS) AS DANGEROUS SUBVERSIVE AGENTS. BY THEIR ACTION OF FLINGING WIDE "THE DOORS OF PERCEPTION", THE INSIGHTS THEY POTENTIATE FREQUENTLY ENABLE ONE TO SEE THROUGH THE MYRIAD PRETENSIONS AND DECEITS WHICH MAKE UP THE MYTHOLOGY OF THE SOCIAL LIE. THUS, TO THE EXTENT THAT POWER STRUCTURES RELY UPON THE CONROLLED POPULAR ACCEPTANCE OF THE LIE TO SHORE UP AND STABILIZE THEIR HEGEMONIES, PSYCHEDELIC SUBSTANCES DO INDEED REPRESENT A KIND OF POLITICAL THREAT.

MOREOVER, I BELIEVE THAT THE ASTONISHING HUMAN BRAIN IS MAN'S MOST INALIENABLE POSSESSION, HIS INTELLECTUAL BIRTHRIGHT. NO PERSON OR INSTITUTION HAS THE MORAL RIGHT TO MUFFLE OR INHIBIT ITS DEVELOPMENT. NO SOCIAL AUTHORITY CAN SUCCESSFULLY ARROGATE UNTO ITSELF THE RIGHT TO DICTATE AND FIX THE LEVELS OF CONSCIOUSNESS TO WHICH MEN MAY ASPIRE, WHETHER THOSE STATES ARE INDUCED PHARMACOLOGICALLY OR OTHERWISE. *DIE GEDANKEN SIND FREI."*

DAVID SOLOMON, LSD, THE CONSCIOUSNESS EXPANDING DRUG, PUTNAMS 1964.

David Solomon, a friend of the author, was sentenced to ten years imprisonment in 1978 for his involvement in the acid conspiracy, popularly known as "Operation Julie". The following is from the first chapter of a forthcoming book about it.

WHO? WHERE? WHEN? WHY? & WHAT

What we arrogantly call 'human consciousness" – meaning something that we feel allows us to cock a snoot at the 'beasts' – came not from the mutation of a crooked thumb, but from our merely being drawn to a different drug from those that the other 'beasts' chose for their enlightenment.

Koala bears are addicted to eucalyptus leaves. The exhilarating effects of coffee were legendarily discovered by an Abyssinian goat-herd who noticed his flock prancing around the pasture after eating the fruit of that glossy, green tree. The Indian mongoose, when bitten by a cobra, crawls into the jungle to nibble mungo root as an antidote. Cows everywhere love loco-weed (datura). Cats gobble cat-nip. Reindeer munch mushrooms (amanita muscaria). Rabbits prefer belladonna (atropine)., or wild lettuce, which contains opiates. Songbirds and mice thrive on hemp-seed. Elephants are passionately fond of certain palm fruits that produce a strongly intoxicating liquor, and after ingesting it make antic hay. . . . . .

"I said, Ye are gods,
"And all of you sons of the Most High." Psalm 82, verse 2

"We have drunk soma, have come immortal.
Gone to the light have we, the gods discovered.
What can hostility do against us?"
Rig Veda, c.1000 B.C.

"Helen, the child of Zeus, had a happy thought. Into the bowl in which their wine was mixed, she slipped a drug that had the power of robbing grief and anger of their sting, and banishing all painful memories. No one that swallowed this dissolved in wine could shed a single tear that day, even for the death of his mother or father, or if they put his brother or his own son to the sword and he were there to see it done. This powerful anodyne (nepenthes) was one of many useful drugs which had been given to the daughter of Zeus by an Egyptian lady, Polydamna, the wife of Thon. For the fertile soil of Egypt is most rich in herbs, many of which are wholesome in solution, though many are poisonous. And in medical knowledge the Egyptian leaves the rest of the world behind."
Homer, The Odyssey, 4.221 c.900 B.C.

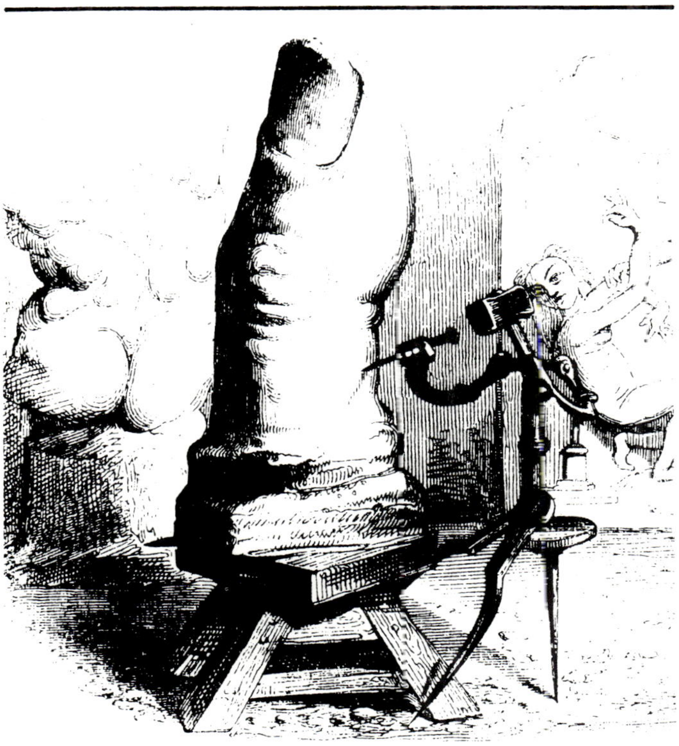

"The cumulative evidence in such books as Dr. Andrija Puharich's **The Sacred Mushroom**, *John Allegro's* **The Sacred Mushroom and the Cross**, *R. Gordon Wasson's* **Soma: Divine Mushroom of Immortality**, *Robert Graves' revised fourth edition of the* **White Goddess**, *Professor Peter Furst's* **Flesh of the Gods**, *Dr. Weston Labarre's* **The Peyote Cult and Ghost Dance: Origins of Religion**, *Margaret Murray's* **The Witch Cult in Western Europe** *etc., leaves little doubt that the beginnings of religion (awareness of, or at least belief in, High Intelligence) is intimately linked with the fact that shamans – in Europe, in Asia, in the Americas, in Africa – have been dosing their nervous systems with metaprogrammed drugs since at least 30,000 B.C.*
Robert Anton Wilson, Cosmic Trigger, 1977.

Recent carbon dating of rock-shelter sites in Texas and Mexico confirm that hallucinogenic red mescal beans were certainly used well over 10,000 years ago by prehistoric buffalo hunters. Our theo-botanical brain-buster was more than likely an hallucinogen which made the first transitional ape hold his head in his heads, and then move his hands away from his head with pulsating, palpitating gestures, as if indicating that he or she was now in charge of a staggering device, turned to quite novel frequencies.

"Woe to the man who tries to stretch the imagination of man. He shall be mocked, he shall be scourged by the blinkered guardians of morality." Marat Sade.

Word perhaps spread of the first ape's curious ecstasies, and others quietly dared to explore their source, ensuring their safety by conspiring

 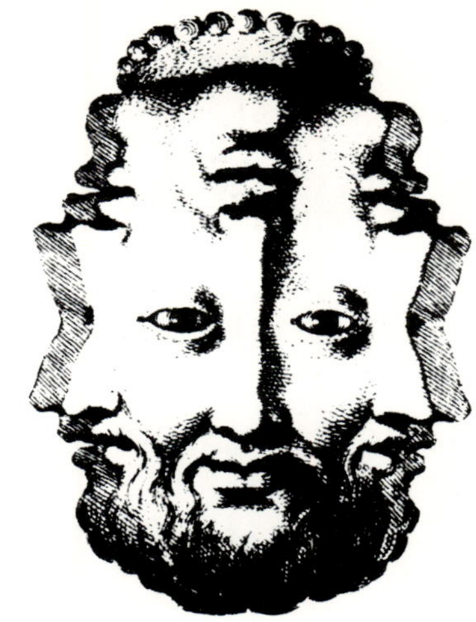 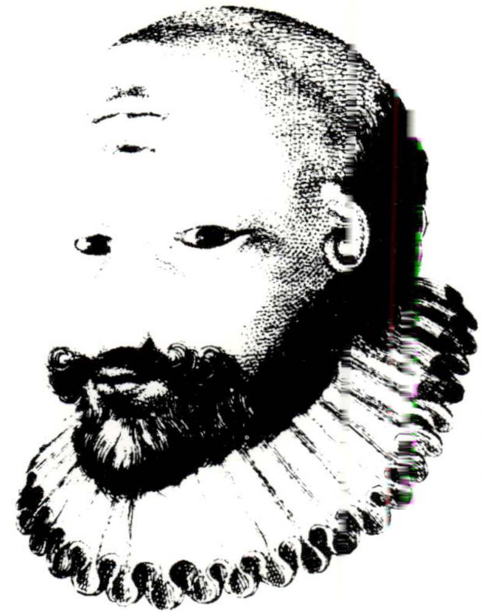

with a few friends first.

They popped the pod. The algebra of need suddenly had a non-local factor. Events were not merely here or there, but both. Space and time were perceived as real only to our mammalian sense organs. Global glue was traded in at a discount for cosmic glue, and our visions became our evolutionary back-packs.

The psychic spores were laid. The trail was on.

Fade a few slithers of an aeon . . . .

THE D.N.A. REFEREE STEPS IN AT MOMENTS OF CRISIS

At the height of World War Two, just four months after the first artificially created nuclear reaction was released in a pile of uranium ore in Chicago, an 'accidentally' absorbed trace of a semi-natural rye fungus derivative, occultly exploded in the brain of a 37 year old Swiss Chemist in Basel, thus producing an antidote of equivalently apocalyptic dimensions.

"Nature is often hidden, sometimes overcome, seldom extinguished."
Francis Bacon, Essays, 1625.

" . . every lack of integration in the human sphere simply asks for the appearance, somewhere in space and time, of the missing opposite. And the personification, the embodiment of that predestined antagonist will inevitably show its face."
Heinrich Zimmer,
The King and the Corpse.

This is not merely a hippy, dippy, trippy fantasy from the Yin, Yang, Jung Show. Such psychedelic synchronicity is authenticated by other cultures. Amongst the Menomini Indians it is believed that peyote is a gift of the Great Spirit, given at a time of great tribal and internecine strife, to teach the basic lessons of peace.

"To live without killing is a thought which could electrify the world, if men were only capable to staying awake long enough to let the idea soak in."
Henry Miller,
Reunion in Brooklyn, 1959.

Dr. Albert Hofmann called the compound in question LSD-25, simply because it happened to be the twenty-fifth compound of lysergic acid, the child of ergot, that he'd worked on.

"I know who I was when I got up this morning, but I must have been changed several times since then."
Lewis Carroll,
Alice in-Wonderland.

After he had absorbed a tiny, dose, on April 19th, 1943, Dr Hofmann began to notice that reality had a 'pleasant, fairy-tale quality.' He left Sandoz laboratories and went off on his bike, looking all the while through a window on the virtual infinity of intracellular lines of communication.

"... a sense sublime
Of something far more deeply interfused,
Whose swelling is the light of setting suns,
And the round ocean and the living air,
And the blue sky, and in the mind of man:
A motion and a spirit, that impels
All thinking things, all objects of all thought,
And rolls through all things."
William Wordsworth,
Tintern Abbey.

In an interview last year, with Sphinx magazine, of Basel, over a quarter of a century afterwards he had this to say: "From my LSD experiments, I have received knowledge of not only one, but of an infinite number of realities. Depending upon the condition of our senses and psychic receptors, we experience a different reality. I realized that the depth and richness of the inner and outer universe are immeasurable and inexhaustible, but that we have to return from these strange worlds to our homeland and live here in the reality that is provided by our normal, healthy senses. It's like astronauts returning from outer space flights: they must readjust to this planet."

"In some of my psychedelic experiences I had a feeling of ecstatic love and unity with all creatures in the universe. To have had such an experience of absolute beatitude means an enrichment of our life."

The interviewer asked him how he would like future ages to remember him and his discovery. Hofmann replied:

"Perhaps the image of a chemist riding along on a bicycle on the very first LSD trip will change to the Old Man of the Mountains."

He continues: "Another reason for the incidence of religious experiences in the LSD state is the fact that the very core of the human mind is connected with God. The deepest root of our consciousness which in the normal state is hidden by superficial rational activities of the mind, may become revealed by the action of the psychedelic drug."

Interviewer: "Is LSD an evolutionary agent?"

Hofmann: "Possibly. In the LSD state we may become conscious, in the words of Teilhard de Chardin, of the 'entire complex of interhuman and intercosmic relations with an immediacy, an intimacy, and a realism.' that otherwise happens only in spontaneous ecstatic states and to a very few blessed people. Agreement exists among spiritual leaders that the continuation of the present development, characterised by increasing industrialisation will result in the exhaustion of natural resources and destroy the ecological basis for mankind's existence on this planet. This trend to self-annihilation is reinforced by international politics based on 'power trips and the preparation of

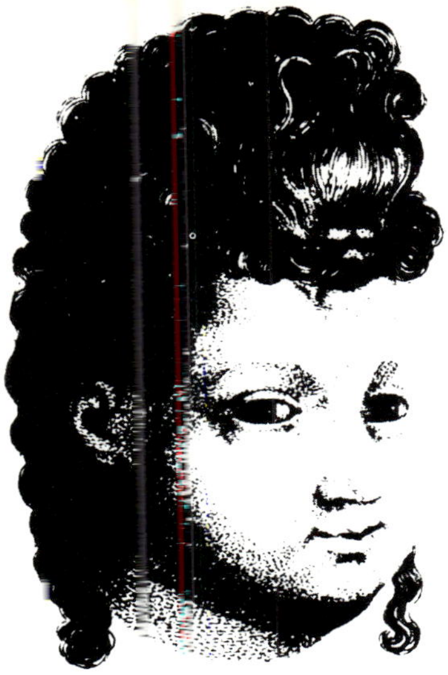

weapons of apocalyptic potential.

"This development can be stopped only by a change in the materialistic attitude that has caused this development. This change can result only from insight into the deepest spiritual roots of life and existence, from comprehensive use of all forces of our intelligence and all resources of our knowledge.

"This intellectual approach, supplemented by visionary experience, could produce an alteration of the consciousness of truth and reality that could be of evolutionary significance. LSD selectively and wisely used could be one means of supplementing intellectual with visionary insight and helping the prepared mind become conscious of a deep reality."

What psychedelic sleuths have enveigled from its hidden inter-actions in the green room behind the cranial stage is that something chemically very similar to one of the active ingredients of acid, called adrenochrome, already exists in the human brain, producing in many people the hypnagogic state – a whim-wham, crinkum-crankum, rhapsodic extravaganza, with a direct line to Erewhon, Happy Valley, the land of Cockaigne, Shangri-La, Atlantis, and all points perpendicular to Soul Central, many not yet pin-pointed by beatific Baedekers. It's simply the state between sleeping and waking induced by the above-mentioned substance adrenochrome seeping uncensored into a multiplicity of cranial nooks and fissures producing a valuable state: the world marinated in a particle accelerator fuelled by neurones sparking as they wish, and glia putting on a startling show of chemical insight.

MOLOCH WAS THREATENED

"Pot is walking a foot off the ground; LSD is leaving the earth entirely and zooming across the galaxy at the speed of light."

Baba Ram Dass,
Be Here Now, 1971.

"The psychedelics are the strongest tools ever dreamed of for man's betterment."

Dr. Duncan Blewett,
Macleans, 1967.

"Chemistry is applied theology,"

August Stanley Owsley III.

Acid is a contraceptive against planetary ruin, but as popular as a durex in the Vatican. Losing height for a moment, in order to fly back onto the rung more firmly, the press hyped LSD murders, orgies and riots consistently for about ten years. A few unscrupulous medical researchers announced that LSD caused people to go blind from staring into the sun (an admitted hoax), and that pregnant women who used LSD could bear deformed babies. The mud from this last, the most serious, stuck longest, though it was proved shortly afterwards that aspirin, coffee and measles jabs caused far more chromosomal damage than LSD, if indeed, as it was later proved, LSD caused any at all. In all cases the leucocytes remained intact.

"In regard to chromosome damage, we designed experiments to find out if there was any. These turned out to be completely negative. Even though the evaluation of the damage was done by a man who was quite set against the taking of LSD, he could not find any chromosome damage due to LSD per se.

"I am reminded of a cartoon that appeared in Cavalier magazine at that time, during the height of the public controversy: A long-haired boy is looking up at a poster, and says "They're grasping at straws." The poster is a picture of an adolescent with a big sign across it saying "LSD causes acne."

"In regard to the possible damage to children conceived during an LSD trip and to a pregnant mother taking LSD, we had lots of examples of people in the early days who were on psychotherapeutic regimes with LSD and who conceived and produced babies while taking LSD. I know of these children today, and they are really delightful people. There is no sign of damage whatsoever. If you wish to check out these points, look at the papers published from Spring Grove Hospital by the LSD research group, and papers by Drs Walter Pahnke, Stanislaf Grof, Charles Savage and Albert Kurland from the Maryland Psychic Research Centre, Caton-ville, Md."

John C. Lilly, M.D.,
The Centre of the Cyclone,
1972.

Its criminogenic qualities had to be inculcated. The man in the street was quickly persuaded that 'LSD drove you crazy.' The zeitgeist rape was on. "Enough LSD could be carried in a two-suiter piece of luggage to temporarily incapacitate the entire population of the United States." Sidney Cohen reported in the The Beyond Within: LSD Story, Secker & Warburg, 1965, "Illuminate" might have been a happier choice of word than "incapacitate", however his assessment of the dosage necessary to achieve this end has never been contradicted – two suitcases.

Moloch was threatened. The flying fox was set amongst the dodos.

However, almost all the research indicates that LSD induces entirely opposite qualities from the rumoured scenario of mayhem. A Canadian Government's Commission of Inquiry, for example, into the non-medical use of drugs concluded that where arrests were associated with LSD, the evidence showed them to be 'disturbance of the peace' type of offences, with "little or no data to indicate that LSD plays a significant role in the commission of major crimes."

Apart from alleging that

each tablet had *KILL*: osmotically imprinted on it (most West Coast blotter acid had a picture of Robert Crumb's Mr. Natural stamped on it with food-dye, pointing upwards – to Heaven), it was also claimed by opponents of the psychedelic prototype, that it induced either schizophrenia or psychosis, or both.

"As to the question of whether the LSD state is identical with schizophrenia, we have it "from the horse's mouth" that it is not. A group of schizophrenic patients given LSD declared the two states dissimilar. With this verdict, many scientific investigators are in accord, noting important differences between schizophrenic and drug-state symptoms."

REL Masters and Jean Houston, The Varieties of Psychedelic Experience, Blond, 1966.

Psychosis, the total dissolution of the reasoning self in a chaotic manner, is rare on acid, but one commentator even felt that this unusual symptom was more fruitful than not:

"The most important effect of the drug for me was directly experiencing a psychotic state. I look on the experience as having been a provocative, rich source of data for speculation – richer, I am embarrassed to say, than much of my formal scientific research and study."

E. Robert Sinnett. Experience and Reflections, 1970.

"In my opinion every discovery in the field of natural science is to be positively viewed, and thus also the discovery of LSD. . . . There are no forces in the universe that are bad in themselves. It is always up to man whether he will make good or bad use of them."

Dr. Albert Hofmann, in correspondence with William Braden (op.cit.)

Nevertheless, "rumour doth double, like the voice and echo, the numbers of the feared," and the forces of awe and boredom, acting on information received, opted for prohibition. The two suitcases were held up briefly at the psychic customs.

"I hear man cry: 'Would there be no wine! O folly! O madness!' Is it wine that causes this abuse? No. For if you say: 'Would there be no wine!' because of drunkenness, then you must say, going on by degrees, 'Would there were no night! 'because of thieves. 'Would there were no light!' because of the informers, and 'Would there were no women! because of adultery.' "

St. John Chrysostom (345 to 407 A.D.), Bishop of Constantinople.

A fine argument, though a little flawed: "Would there were no nuclear power stations because of meltdowns?" Answer: yes!

Here is a better one, though less obvious:

"I am out beyond our galaxy, beyond galaxies as we know them. Time is apparently speeded up 100 billion times. The whole universe collapses into a point. There is a tremendous explosion and out of the point on one side comes positive matter and positive energies, streaking into the cosmos at fantastic velocities. Out of the opposite side of the point comes antimatter streaking off into the opposite direction. The universe expands to its maximum extent, recollapses, and expands three times. During each expansion the guides say, "Man appears here and disappears there." All I can see is a thin slice for man. I ask, "Where does man go when he disappears until he is ready to reappear again?" They say, "That is us."

During this experience I was filled with awe, reverence, and a fantastic feeling of smallness, of not amounting to very much. Everything was happening on such a vast scale that I was merely an observer of microscopic size, and yet I was more than this. I was part of some vast network of similar beings all connected somehow or other responsible for what was going on. I was given an individuality for temporary purposes only. I would be reabsorbed into the network when the time came.

After this experiment, word came that LSD was no longer to be used and each of the investigators was to send his supply back to Sandoz. New laws came into effect, making it illegal to use LSD any more, except under strictly limited conditions. Now I could understand why people were frightened of LSD; now I could understand why it seemed necessary to stop the legal use of LSD."

John C. Lilly M.D. The Center of the Cyclone, The Julian Press, 1972.

We can't have people feeling smaller than we can make them feel – the world as we know it would disappear up its own arsehole . . Or larger even . . . Nothing wrong with our spectacle, is there?

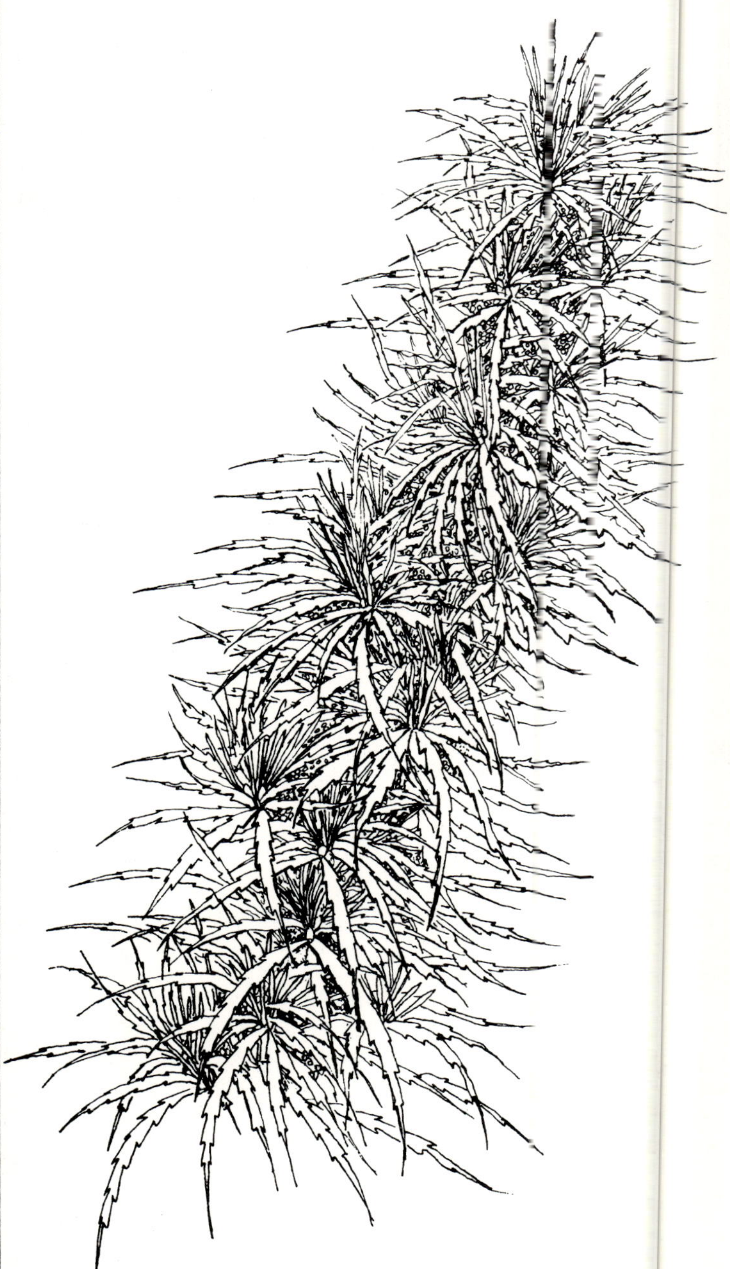

HEMP HARVEST

photo-story by Don Irving

France, as well as Britain, was a traditional major producer of hemp fibre with more acres under cultivation than ever before in the Nineteenth century. Although hemp fibre production disappeared from the British countryside in the 1920's it has continued in areas of Northern France and has recently enjoyed a significant revival. In fact, since 1968 the total land area under cultivation has increased by almost 50 times for seed and fibre production. Most of the fibre goes to produce high quality paper, especially cigarette papers — JOB for example.

The French government operates strict control over hemp cultivation. Farmers need a licence from the Ministry of Health and Agriculture, seeds must be obtained only from the Federation Nationale des Producteurs de Chanvre (national Federation of Hemp Farmers) and they must have a contract with a processing mill to whom they sell their fibre.

Since the 1940's the Federation has been developing monoecious varieties with mature plants containing much more CBD (Cannabidiol) than THC (Tetrahydrocannabinol). The major commercial varieties; Fibrimon 24, Fedrima 74, and Fibrimon 56 all originated from a German stock. Federation farms that produce seed are required to grow a small amount of marijuana for assay at government laboratories in Paris. The definition of 'hemp' is quite clear. If a sample has a THC content of less than the CBD content then that sample qualifies as hemp. If the THC content is greater than the CBD content then that sample is Marijuana.

At the farm shown here, they were engaged in an ongoing seed breeding programme. One small field was sown with seeds from Polish, Hungarian, Bulgarian, Italian and Turkish origin. Each variety and cross-breed was carefully labelled and coded. Qualities most

Marijuana grown for assay only

sought after are height, disease resistance, high fibre yield. At the same time, varieties that grow rapidly and mature early are of special importance. One variety that caused considerable interest reached full maturity in only 68 days.

Since all the plants are monoecious; that is, both male and female flowers occuring on the same plant, each plant is self-pollenating, producing fields of uniform height and maturation time. This is particularly important where cutting is mechanised and harvesting of fields is staggered.

During the winter the fields are dressed heavily with a 1-1-2 mix of Nitrogen, Phosphorous and Potassium at the rate of 30 to 50 tonnes per hectare. By late April to early May the soil should be warm enough for sowing (12–14°C). Seeds are sown by converted corn-hopper about one inch apart in rows 7 inches apart at the rate of 55–70 kilogrammes per hectare. This ensures a high density of stalks with little branching to maximise fibre yield.

The commercial varieties mentioned earlier mature from 100 to 120 days after sowing and are harvested from August 15–20, and September 5–10 for the later varieties. The 7 to 8 foot high plants are cut and left on the ground for 7 to 10 days to dry. The stalks are then separated from the seed and superfluous vegative matter by machine and packed into bales which are later sent to the processing mill. Under normal conditions the farmer expects from 7 to 9 tonnes of raw fibre from each hectare. All waste vegetative matter is discarded.

Where seed production is the primary concern, seeds are collected, graded, packed with fungicide, coded and latter distributed to other farms by the Cooperative Centrale des Producteurs de Semences de Chanvre (Central Cooperative of Hemp Seed Producers).

On the trail

"Wherever Particular People Congregate"
-- Pall Mall Packet.

Like any Maverick in any game the first few sniffs of a fresh city told me where the playground was this year, but it might be hard to crack an opening. All I had was a couple of vague leads. But, once you sniff hard enough and get the taste, and keep your nostrils flared and primed, the old hooter may lead you anywhere. From my previous experiences of San Francisco and the surrounding Bay Area, not only is it exciting and constanly surprising but can give you what you seek if you look hard enough,or just be damn lucky! With a couple of weeks of sponsored business coming to an end I shifted thoughts to my own trail. Top of my calling list was Fred who I had just heard was away in New York, so I scrubbed his name off. Then walking through an associate's office in Berkeley, I came face to face with him so promptly arranged a rendezvous. I'd waited quite awhile for this. A break at last!

to Oakland

Next day I found my way up to the first floor of a large old red brick warehouse close to the Bay. After several knocks Fred opens up and leads me into his office and through to a large concealed room which contains his hydroponic culture experiments, then proceeds to explain what he's up to. Fred's pretty serious about his work and tolerates me taking photos and asking questions as he prepares the evening meal for his plants. After discussing technical details and a bit of topical scandal we move back to the office and smoke some. An associate will be coming by in half hour to collect several bags of homegrown tops so I snap away while I can. The transaction

Homegrown sinsemilla ready to smoke.

completed we leave the building and I follow him in my hire-car into the freeway madness. Fifteen minutes of stoned rush hour traffic and at last we leave the daily drole behind. A few twists and turns and we park in front of Fred's place high up in Oakland overlooking the Bay. The house is a large Victorian wooden building standing alone on one side of dirt dead-end. Fred introduces me to his partner Kim who's sitting beside a kindling fire in the grate. Grey clouds have settled over the city and a chill is in the air so we go out back for a tour of the green-house before the light gets too bad. Fred unlocks the door and we enter a bright building with solid wooden walls and a trans-lucent plastic roof. In one corner Fred has four different hydro-ponic systems on the go. The rest of the space is shared by Kim's young plants started this Spring and his mature plants sown last November. Most of the mature plants are thickly budded with glistening white-cream flowers or older deep red flowers surrounded by a mass of tight bright green leaves. Each plant is labelled with its parentage on the container. There are Afghanis, Africans, Nepalese, Thais, Columbians, Mexicans and various crosses and hybrid strains, both sativas and indicas.

Kim is an experimental marijuana breeder and has several hundred labelled specimens in his seed collection. He is just one of the many California seed breeders, but what makes him special (like some of the others) is his uncompromising dedication to his craft. His seed collection is meticulously marked to identify each variety by their parental origin, cross-breed or hybrid history with his own special coding system. When Cannabis is legalised and the tobacco companies are scouting for the best 'established brains', Kim could easily find himself in the high places if he wished, responsible for the genetic origin of varieties of the new commercial homegrown in the USA.

After dinner Kim takes me upstairs to show me his seed collection. It's housed in four deep drawers in a chest. He selects varieties and crosses he thinks will be suitable for the British

* *

CALIFORNIA

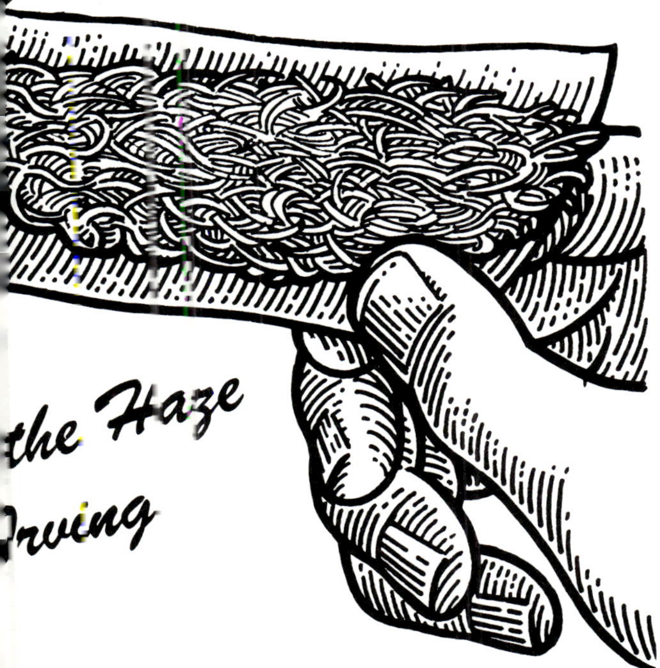

the Haze

Irving

* *

latitude and climate, particularly those which tend to flower early, a necessary attribute for maturing marijuana in Britain. This selection included Kush, Kush and Afghani crosses, Afghanis, Afghani hybrids, African and Afghani crosses, Southern Indian and an intriguing Californian Sinsemilla – a cross of Nepalese and Haze. I was to learn more about the elusive Haze later on the trail. With a wad of seed packets safely bequeathed, Ken disappeared to a date in SF. By the time we got to the movie house a little later, the evening's toking had rendered me oblivious to anything except that moment in time. Stoned again! Yes! Plants in the garden, plants in the attic and now plants in the bedroom. Deep breathing, yeah, that'll do the trick!

Kush & Haze

Homegrown California Sinsemilla, particularly from Humboldt and Mendecino counties, is fast becoming as much a legend as the best Thais, Hawaiians, and Afghanis. California has a climate ideally suited to producing high quality marijuana, but any experienced pot farmer will tell you that high potency primo sinsemilla can be grown anywhere in the world. OK, so you'll have to increase environmental control the further north you are located. Beyond 50 degrees you'll have to think about protective measures (greenhouses) from September onwards, and perhaps supplementary lighting for full flowering and maturity. However, over fifteen years of experience in CA have shown that the introduction of simple breeding techniques can produce selected varieties that will flower early and be fully mature by the end of August or early September; will be acclimatized to local weather conditions and still retain the potency and flavour of the original exotic parents. In fact many connoisseurs believe some varieties of Californian Sinsemilla, Haze and Kush for example, to be the finest anywhere.

to Santa Cruz

The next day starts with a big pipe of Nepalese hash (not so rare in Cal.) and then I set off south to Santa Cruz. I'd planned to visit friends there and had arranged to contact number two on my list. Jingles was someone I knew nothing about apart from his name and an article he'd written about seed breeding, so it could be hit or miss. An hour of easy cruising from San Francisco and you hit Skyline Boulevard. This is the highest point of the peninsular. To the east Santa Clara and San Jose, to the west the Pacific. You descend south, then down Route 9 and through 30 miles of Redwood forest to mellow Santa Cruz; broadwalk, mall, flea-market, and Sun State Beach 15 miles south. Later that evening I found myself sleeping with several hundred pounds of imported Columbian in large plastic bags and a couple of large bales. Jake obliged by opening the bales. He'd got into dealing. After a phone call Jingles arrived the next day about noon bearing a carton full of marijuana impedimenta. He energetically got down to straight talking right away and suggested we begin the afternoon by tasting several varieties of California finest. He explained that he was keeping the last of his stash for a special time such as this. The opener was to be the Queen of the crop, a large gleaming bud of sativa. Jingles was adamant about his preference for sativa. The indica he said, was overrated and was a heavier smoke better associated with a high quality Humalayan hash; whereas sativa was light and psychedelic and at best trippy. An opinion I still had to test fully. From his carton he produced a selection of packaging labels from past illicit sales of home-grown. Talk inevitably came round to the Haze. He gave me a photo of a poster of 'The Original Haze' brand. (For technical reasons the photo is impossible to reproduce here).

The poster is headed by a piece of beautiful artwork with the words THE ORIGINAL HAZE emblazoned over a stoned

Sativa sinsemilla showing extended flowering.

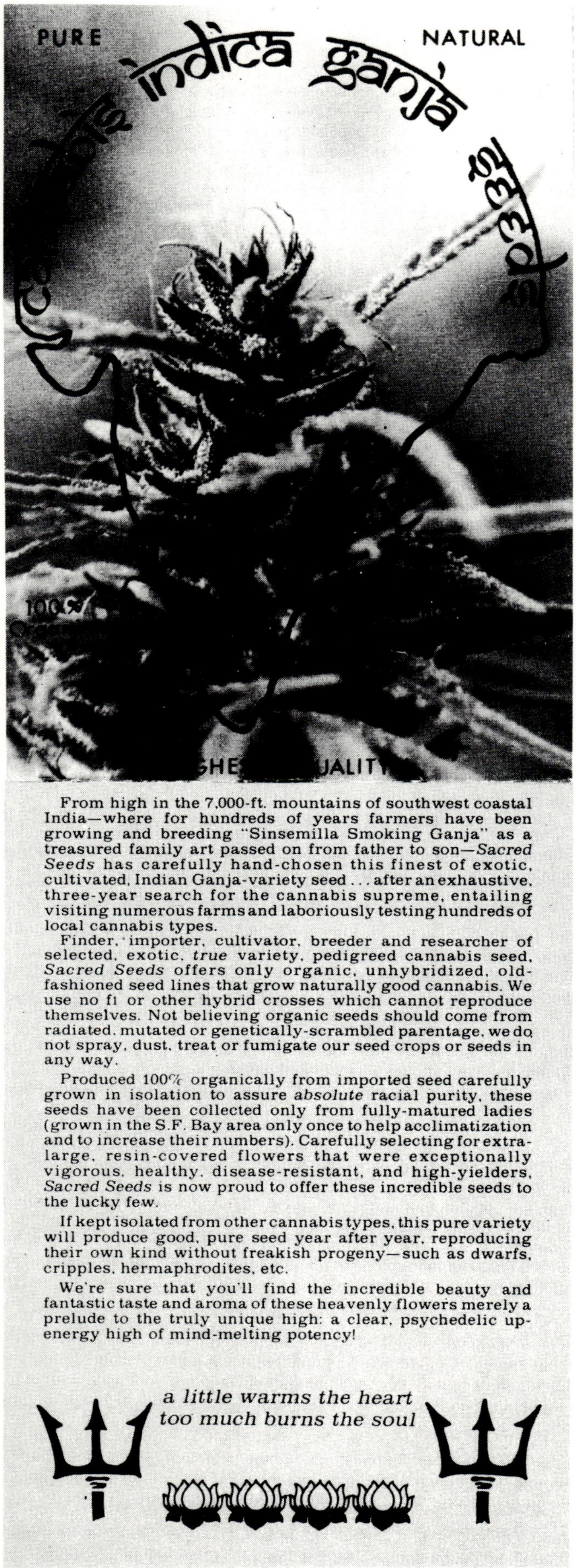

From high in the 7,000-ft. mountains of southwest coastal India—where for hundreds of years farmers have been growing and breeding "Sinsemilla Smoking Ganja" as a treasured family art passed on from father to son—*Sacred Seeds* has carefully hand-chosen this finest of exotic, cultivated, Indian Ganja-variety seed . . . after an exhaustive, three-year search for the cannabis supreme, entailing visiting numerous farms and laboriously testing hundreds of local cannabis types.

Finder, importer, cultivator, breeder and researcher of selected, exotic, *true* variety, pedigreed cannabis seed, *Sacred Seeds* offers only organic, unhybridized, old-fashioned seed lines that grow naturally good cannabis. We use no f1 or other hybrid crosses which cannot reproduce themselves. Not believing organic seeds should come from radiated, mutated or genetically-scrambled parentage, we do not spray, dust, treat or fumigate our seed crops or seeds in any way.

Produced 100% organically from imported seed carefully grown in isolation to assure *absolute* racial purity, these seeds have been collected only from fully-matured ladies (grown in the S.F. Bay area only once to help acclimatization and to increase their numbers). Carefully selecting for extra-large, resin-covered flowers that were exceptionally vigorous, healthy, disease-resistant, and high-yielders, *Sacred Seeds* is now proud to offer these incredible seeds to the lucky few.

If kept isolated from other cannabis types, this pure variety will produce good, pure seed year after year, reproducing their own kind without freakish progeny—such as dwarfs, cripples, hermaphrodites, etc.

We're sure that you'll find the incredible beauty and fantastic taste and aroma of these heavenly flowers merely a prelude to the truly unique high: a clear, psychedelic up-energy high of mind-melting potency!

a little warms the heart
too much burns the soul

Cover of seed packet.

Afghani, Mexican, and Kush seeds
(in clockwise order).

looking Eagle with outspread wings, perched on the American flag. A scroll cicles the eagle with the announcement; 'Connoisseurs Choice Cultivated California Cannabis'. Beneath the eagle, a sub-inscription 'Organically Grown Acclimatised'. The text under the picture is titled 'The Cosmic Boogie 1976'

This is the entire text:

THE COSMIC BOOGIE 1976

In clandestine locations sparsely scattered throughout California, a few dedicated farmers cultivate the herb cannabis as a way of life. Any one can grow weeds and see the virgin greens, but to cultivate the exotic queens beyond your dreams, you should have dedication, sensitivity to plant life, consistency, a little basic knowledge, Good Karma, and a great desire to find harmony with Mama Nature.

The basis for any strong healthy plant is the soil it growns in. Resin producing herbs grow best in soil that is neutral to semi sweet. The larger the bush or tree, whatever it may be, the larger the root structure needed to support it.

Roots develop most freely in a loose, rich soil. Mix one yard of soil composed of 30% mushroom compost, 30% redwood sawdust, 40% sandy loam topsoil. Mix organic nutrients: three pounds of hoof & horn meal, five pounds of rockphosphate, four pounds of kelp, one pound natural compost, one pound soil iron, five pounds of gypsum, and five pounds of dolomite.

Mix soil and minerals thoroughly and let sit for at least a week, then check the soil with a soil-testing kit for pH and add agricultural lime to bring the pH to 7.5 - 8.5 range, semi-sweet for the connoisseurs treat.

Spring arrives, and with it comes new life, fresh spirit, and new hope for the new crop. Plant your favorite seeds on the 6th or 7th of April: the moon is in Cancer. Best sign for planting above ground herbs. In May, the 3rd, or 4th and 5th are good. If you're still not together, try June 8th and 9th while the moon is in Scorpio.

When you irrigate make sure that the moon is in one of these signs (when possible); Cancer is the most excellent time to irrigate; Taurus, Scorpio, and Pisces are also good

* *

Four different hydroponic systems

Hydroponic plants (indica in foreground).

for irrigation. Pruning should be done only in the third quarter.

Patience is the real secret and the true test. Try to make it until December 10th or 11th when the moon is in Leo and harvest conditions are perfect. So, if you can dig it . . .

After the Indica, Jingles rolled another spliff-sized Sativa, and gave me one of his seed packets of 'Cannabis Indica Ganga' (fig. 1). On the reverse side of the card is advice on how to store the seeds, and precise planting instructions including soil mix. We finished up with a fourth spliff of the Queen California Finest and then he showed me a selection of his seed jars that filled the bottom half of the carton. A little later, Jingles gave me a copy of his latest soil recipe, and left. Hours afterwards my friends and I were still sitting around in the same places. Another time, another space. The Haze was found.

Cannabis indica.

Haze 'el Primo'

Anyone can grow sinsemilla. Not everyone can grow 'el Primo'. Care, patience, and dedication are required to produce a high that people will delight in, rave about, travel thousands of miles to taste and indulge, spend enormous sums of money on, go to jail for, and occasionally dedicate their lives to. 'El Primo' (or more correctly 'Prima') is many things; is Shiva, is Kali. It is a serious affair. No laughing matter. SHe slaps you on the back then there is too much to laugh about. You crash about in hilarious fits, almost gagging and gasping for air. Then there is silence and calm and pure light. Everywhere. Yes, this is a serious affair. Once SHe has grabbed you by the short and curlies SHe rarely lets go. You're spell-bound and you're had for good. The 'Cosmic Blackmail'. You're bled dry, drained of life: of everything, of soul, of spirit. Your breath is drawn – you die, you are consumed and consummated. Your ashes are scattered to the end of the Universe, and return. Your rebirth is complete. To test your love, SHe pits you against your greatest opponent – yourself. Again and again SHe teases and toys with you. In return for your faithfulness SHe gives you all. SHe gives you Love more perfect than any other. SHe has you forever. But beware! 'El Primo''s Love is not always what it seems.

SPACED-OUT in AMSTERDAM
BEING A COLLECTION OF SUBJECTIVE IMPRESSIONS
THE FLIGHT OVER
MY BRAIN'S FLOATING
ISN'T IT DINGY!
I WONDER HOW OLD IT IS
ENGINES SOUND FUNNY
FINANCIAL TIMES
I WONDER IF THAT STEWARDESS IS IN TH' MILE HIGH CLUB
I WONDER IF THE CAPTAIN'S DRUNK
ARRIVAL AT THE HOTEL – "WASTED TOWERS"
HI KEVIN
JUST GOT HERE? MELLOW OUT WITH SOME DURBAN POISON!
I'M SURE IT'S ALONG HERE SOMEWHERE..
LIDS?
WE WERE SO MELLOW IT TOOK US 1½ HOURS TO FIND THE 'KOSMOS'
MY GOOD FRIEND, 'HOME GROWN' SUPREMO LEE HARRIS:
BRYAN! GLAD YOU COULD MAKE IT!
ENTRY INTO THE KOSMOS
AT FIRST, AN ATMOSPHERE OF STRANGENESS
THE FRIDAY NIGHT PARTY
JUMPIN' JACK FLASH AND IT'S A GAS GAS GAS!
GERMAN HOME GROWN
THE RITUAL ECSTASY COULD BE HAPPENING TEN YEARS AGO. I REALISED HOW MUCH I'VE CHANGED.
SAUNA
GIRLS

WELCOME GENTLEMEN TO THE RED LIGHT DISTRICT!
IT WAS LIKE AN EROTIC FAIRYLAND. THE CANAL GLOWED RED WITH THE REFLECTION OF THE FLUERESCENT STRIP LIGHTS. IT WAS MARVELLOUS.
THE CHIPS & MAYONNAISE WERE GOOD...
...THAT WAS THE ONLY THING I COULD AFFORD.
THE KOSMOS LOUNGE AREA
KOOS SWART–THE GUY WHO USED TO READ OUT WEEKLY DOPE PRICES ON HIS SATURDAY MORNING D.J. RADIO SHOW
HOME GROWN ART AUCTION
T-SHIRTS
BIBLIOTHEEK
THE REV. WILLIAM DEANE OF NORML
ALEXIS KORNER
SIMON VINKENOOG POET
COME SUNDAY, WE VOTED FOR VARIOUS PROPOSITIONS
WOULD ANYBODY LIKE TO ADD ANYTHING AT THIS JUNCTURE?
THIS EVOKED SOME MEMORABLE RESPONSES...
AHEM!
SHIVA IS WITH US!!!
ER... THANK YOU! ANYBODY ELSE LIKE TO COMMENT?
YES
LADIES & GENTLEMEN - I JUST WANT TO TAKE THIS OPPORTUNITY TO SAY TO YOU ALL, FRIENDS...
THANK YOU FOR POT SMOKING
THANK YOU FOR POT SMOKING!

ER ... ANYBODY ELSE?
YEAH! WOW! FAR OUT!
HEY PEOPLE!! LISSEN T' ME!!
I'M RILLY COSMIC Y'KNOW!
YEAH! RILLY!
Y'KNOW SOMETHING?
YEAH!
FOR THE PAST FOUR MONTHS I'VE BEEN HOLDING A MIND-BEAM ON AFGHANISTAN!
...AND I'M KEEPIN' IT ALL TOGETHER THERE Y'KNOW! WOW!
SUNDAY NIGHT - THE GAY TIMES PARTY
PANAMA RED
5000 KILOS
J
...OF COURSE I'LL INTRODUCE YOU TO SHELLEY
ER..'SCUSE ME - IS THERE ANY BIER LEFT?
BYZANTIUM
JESUS
JEEZ
...A WHOLE DRIED SINSEMILLA FLOWERTOP
WHAT AN ASSHOLE
ZIPPY
I'M A VIPER
URP
...COST EFFECTIVENESS
WOW
COKE?
THE TEENAGE PINHEAD
YEAH SURE! HEH HEH! IN THE REFRIDGERATOR DANS LE KITCHEN! HEH!
THESE PEOPLE DON'T FUCK AROUN
BEST Afghani
SNORT?
2·30 AM - LOOKING FOR A CAB WHEN...
SCREECH!
SIE!!
KOMMEN SIE HIER! HERÜBER!
SCHÜCHTERN SIE NICHT!
AS THE GIRLS GOT MORE INSISTENT...
ER... I THINK WE'D BETTER START WALKING!
KOMMEN SIE HIER!!
MONDAY 4·00 PM - DAM SQUARE
GRASS?
HASH?
END
WALKING PAST THE ROYAL PALACE WITH THE SUN SHINING AND BEETHOVEN'S 9TH PLAYING IN THE CLOCK TOWER - NOT THE SORT OF PLACE YOU EXPECT RIOT

Brew Your Own Homegrown!

The Brewer reveals all!

Nowadays most of the beers we buy and drink are made with hops and malt as the main flavouring agents; the bitterness of the hops conteracting the sweetness of the malt. But many other plants can be used, and have been for thousands of years; not only for their flavour but their stimulant or soporific effects, e.g. spruce, liquorice, wormwood, nettles, ginger, burdock and sarsaparilla.

Hops have a bitter taste due to resins and oils secreted in the flowers and also have soporific and antibiotic effects. Hops (Humulus lupulus) belong to the family Cannabinaceae, which only contains two genera, the other being Cannabis which is also eminently suitable for brewing.

The alcohol in beer is produced by fermentation. This is the action of yeast living and multiplying, using the sugar we feed them for energy and raw materials, and producing alcohol and carbon dioxide as waste products. As the concentration of alcohol in a fermenting liquid gradually increases it poisons and eventually kills the yeast; so there is a limit to how strong (alcoholic) you can make a beer without distilling it.

Malt is made by roasting barley; like coffee it can be roasted either light or dark. To the brewer it supplies colour, taste and sugar. This sugar is in the form of maltous, which like glucose is a single sugar, and the yeast can digest these more readily than the larger molecules of ordinary sugar (sucrose). For this reason glucose is often used for brewing as it ferments faster and more completely than common sugar.

Recipe

To make 35–40 pints of Herb Beer.

4lbs glucose
2 teaspoons yeast
3½lbs malt extract
4ozs hops/2ozs flowertops
or 2ozs hops/8ozs bottom leaves

Method

Take two large saucepans (8 pints). Put 5 pints of water in each and place them on the stove to boil. While the water is heating up there are two things to do. Wrap the hops loosely in a piece of muslin, and start the yeast fermenting. This is done by mixing the yeast and a small amount of ginger (2-3 teaspoons) in ¼ pint of luke warm water (70-90F). Set this yeast aside until later. In one pan put the glucose to dissolve. After it has dissolved put in the bag containing the hops and herbs. Tip the malt extract into the other pan of boiling water, and simmer both pans for 40 minutes.

Take the bag containing the hops and herbs out of the pan and put it into a basin of cold water.

Pour the contents of both pans into a large bucket (5-6 gallons, white or black plastic — not yellow or red). Squeeze the muslin bag into the bucket. Add enough cold water to make the temperature in the bucket fall to about 80F, (this usually brings the total volume in the bucket up to 40 pints). Finally add the yeast. Set the bucket aside somewhere warm to ferment it. At 70F it will take about 6-10 days. You can lag the bucket with blankets or a quilt to keep it warm; the yeast generates its own heat.

The beer is ready for bottling when the surface clears of bubbles only little patches of bubbles remaining about ½cm in diameter). Clean and sterilize the bottles. Put ½ teaspoon of sugar in each bottle and fill with beer to the base of the neck. This sugar is fermented by residual yeast to produce carbon dioxide (under pressure) which makes the beer fizzy and stops it going bad.

Leave it to settle for two weeks, then drink it.

REMEMBERING JOE SCHLEPP

by

HAL MUSIN

There was a time when people smuggling hashish never longed for company. They had their own travellers' guide, about a dozen hangouts between the old Taj in Bombay to the Hotel Stella in Paris. They all were polarised by the same force. They all drifted in and out of the same harbours: Mazzar-i-shariff, Baalbek and Adana.

Do you remember the scene, Joe Schlepp, the Super Smuggler of a decade ago, slipping through customs with twenty kilos of prime smoke in his bag and and nothing more to conceal it than a change of underwear.

The year is 1969. Joe Schlepp and his old lady, Carrie, are at the immigration counter at Kennedy airport. Both are wearing dark glasses and are dressed entirely in leather. The immigration goon leers as Joe slips a gloved hand into his breast pocket and produces an old, mangled passport. The pages are festooned with weird stamps, oriental markings, cryptic scrawling, smeared and blotted with grease, sweat and saliva from the thumbs of hot climate fuzz. The goon takes out a big magnifying glass and begins peering at each visa, page by page.

Minutes tick by.

Joe rolls a twenty dollar bill and snorts a line of coke off his old lady's pocket mirror.

The goon begins to drool* over the passport. Beyond him Joe can see the customs agents. They are prying open his luggage, breaking it apart with crow bars, axes, sledge hammers. The heady smell of rich Baluchistan hashish seeps into the air. Pollen fills the terminal like a thick, sticky fog. Everywhere the fuzz and incoming passengers are freaking out, wailing, rolling on the floor, stripping naked, groping blindly.

Joe and Carrie quickly don gas masks and race through the terminal to safety outside.

Times have changed and Joe hasn't been on the scene for years now. Nowadays one would have to be an amateur or simply insane to do a *Kamikazi* run through Kennedy International. It would probably be easier to drive a straw through a brick wall.

When the U.S. customsmen made suitcases unpopular, stash cars came into style and with them came the Big Money. Hashish started coming into any one of a number of ports on the Atlantic Seaboard and the Gulf in lots of fity to a hundred kilos at a time. By the time the DEA stepped in there was enough money around to expand the operation still further and it wasn't long after before dope from Morocco and the East wás being dumped on the U.S. market by the boatload.

The result was inevitable: the little guy got squeezed out, good hash became scarce and the "nickle bar" became a memory as nostalgic to some as five-cent beer.

As for Joe Schlepp, no one really knows what became of him. Some say he's making oil from Thai weed in Bangkok; others say he is smuggling diamonds from Istanbul under the name of Stanislaus the Greek; he has been seen cheffing opium in Calcutta and dealing cocaine in Bogota. He could be anywhere; but I do believe he is living in Morocco, somewhere up in the Rif. I am almost certain that I saw him myself – in Tangier

– since he has dropped from the scene.

The year is 1974. I am buying a honey cake in the shade of a stall in the Socco Grande. It is high noon and behind me I can hear the murmur of the mob pressing in and out of the bowels of the medina, a faceless crowd shifting like bundles of tattered rags under the glaring sun.

I am turning to leave when I feel a hand tugging at my sleeve. A beggar? I am facing a toothless, bearded Berber, hunched and nearly hidden within the folds of a threadbare, grease-stained *jaleba*. Is he asking for a handout? No. Instead he presses a small lump of hashish into my hand, quickly slips into the flowing crowd and is gone.

It had to be Joe Schlepp, for when I look at the hashish I know it is his. No one except Joe ever made smoke like that.

Joe Schlepp. He was a one-man band, so dedicated to making good smoke he would fade into the boondocks for months while he put his number together: selecting the weed, collecting the pollen, doing his own press, making a stash, then hiking it alone, from Bombay, from Beirut, from Kabul, Instanbul or Tangier into New York – six or seven kilos of dynamite hash.

Joe Schlepp claimed he made the best dope money could buy and sometimes not even money could buy it. Not just anyone could cop from Joe Schlepp. If you didn't dig his trip, he would tell you he wasn't holding. He was proud of his product but he was also honest, for he did admit that there was once one person who had made better hash than his own, A.R. Schlubb, the German-Lebanese hemp beetle expert.

Schlubb at one time headed a U.S. sponsored programme that sought to develop a hybrid of this beetle, a bug which could ravage the world's grass crops overnight.

Hemp beetles had never been a threat to cannabis growers. Most beetles got too stoned to do much crop damage and growing good quality grass was a sure way of keeping destruction to a minimum.

Schlubb was imported secretly into the U.S. to direct the programme on an Agricultural Department range station laboratory in southwestern New Mexico. Using outlawed, sophisticated growth hormones, Schlubb produced a one inch ravenous being that could munch within hours through a half acre of rich grassland before expiring in drugged ecstasy.

All too late Schlubb learned that in the process the new beetle left hundreds of droppings which were almost pure cannabis resin and fortified in some unexplained way by the bug's digestive process. Secret agents had deposited thousands of these beetles on the cannabis fields of Asia before the mistake was discovered. The research programme was cancelled and Schlubb has not been heard from since but now and again the fruits of his folly appear like rare gems on the dope markets of the world.

The year is 1972. I am sitting in Handsome Tony's apartment overlooking the waterfront on the island of Ibiza. It is a dull, hazy day. The harbour traffic is nearly still. The Barcelona ferry arcs gently around the long breakwater, spilling a white wake into the flat, grey sea.

Joe Schlepp and Carrie are there along with two freaks from London whose names I don't recall.

Joe is rolling one of his super joints and Tony is rapping about a gimmick called a "smuggler's flap", a plastic surgery technique that creates a pocket of skin that can be closed to look like a healing incision. Joe lights the joint and passes it to Tony who goes on with his rap, explaining how the technique was developed for use by German espionage agents during World War II and later adopted by old time coke runners who learned about it from Nazi surgeons living in exile in South America.

We smoke another joint. Tony drops a tape into his new cassette player and one of the English freaks pulls out a matchbox and shows it to Joe and me. Inside are two crusty balls about the size of pepper corns.

"Dig it, man," says the English cat.

"Hemp beetle shit," says Joe.

"Far out," says Tony, "where'd you score it?"

The freak doesn't say but splits off a tiny piece with his thumb nail and presses it into a small pipe. Immediately we smell the resin from the broken ball. Tony lights the pipe and passes it to me. I decline. Joe's old lady takes a poke and swoons before she can finish dragging. The rest of us are already spinning in a wave of euphoria from the escaping fumes.

Epilogue

How did a nice kid like Joe Schlepp ever get involved in a gig that could so easily land him in jail? Some people, and especially his parents, I suppose, found it ironical that a kid from a middle class home should turn to dealing drugs. What was it? Easy money? Social protest? A deep-rooted death wish?

On the other hand there is a possibility that the real Joe Schlepp never existed at all. He always was bigger than life and the contradiction between his life style and his background have led some to believe that he was really an undercover agent working for the DEA. If that theory is true then there is no doubt that Joe was an "identity subject", a bonafide graduate of the Yankowitz Institute.

The institute, of course, is little known. It's existence has been revealed from time to time by it's failures – agents who have dropped their cover under severe nervous stress.

The institute's programme was developed by Dr. Rudolf Yankowitz, a Lithuanian nationalist who defected to the United States fifteen years ago with a Sino-Soviet system for inducing personality changes in certain psychiatric cases.

The system was adopted by the CIA and modified to programme undercover agents for work in the field. Candidates for the programme are screened for several years before admission. They must be so loyal and so dedicated they are willing to sever all memory of their former life. They graduate with their personalities totally changed, unaware they are secret agents working for the federal government.

Although they are trained by the CIA, identity subjects are often put at the disposal of other federal agencies. Those under the supervision of the DEA are so programmed they eventually fall to the law. The arrest is real. It is impossible to return an agent to his former life role. Instead he is debriefed unknowingly by sodium pentathol or other hypnotic methods, usually convicted, imprisoned, then returned to his role in the field.

Except in unusual circumstances, these people are retired with a government pension at the age of 65. At that time, however, those with repeated narcotic convictions are expected to be serving long prison terms.

Footnote:

* *Drooling is sometimes a symptom of the Borden Syndrome, a rare but fatal degenerative disease of the olfactory ganglia with other symptoms such as snarling and an uncontrolled appetite for raw meat. Victims become highly excited by the smell of filth and in later stages of the disease develop a compulsion to commit obscene acts in public.*

The malady was first isolated and reported in Neadle *(Vol. IX, June 1969) by Sir Malcolm Borden, a British pathologist and the foremost expert on diseases of the olfactory nervous system. Borden revealed that the disease reached near endemic proportions among members of the United States Immigration and Customs Service working in the New York area between the years 1968 and 1969.*

Autopsies showed that the victims had received injections of a canine pituitary extract in an experiment to heighten nasal sensitivity.

The article precipitated a series of secret investigations in which it was learned that the injections were given to help agents sniff out hidden caches of the drug cannabis. In view of the hazards the federal government resorted to the use of dogs for detection purposes.

Sir Malcolm Borden emigrated to Bangladesh in 1974 after he was convicted by a British court of possessing two grammes of hashish.

BONNE CHANCE
SLIM-HIPPED GAMBLER
BY BRIAN

BLAM BLAM AMSTERDAM! Seaport in cold January, wind hustling the stricken streets, lace-work of canals and little bridges, a bruised and blackened sky thunders down at us from a great height. "Welcome to the Nether Lands!"

We came from the heights of Switzerland to damp, underwater Amsterdam in twelve hours train ride – from riches to rags in half a day, from acid to smack at the turn of a wheel – and began looking for somewhere to live among the boats moored along the canals that squirm between the tall, narrow houses. There are around two thousand houseboats in A'dam and over a thousand are unregistered and therefore illegal. Add together all the illicit people that live on the boats and a floating civilisation of land-locked flotsam emerges, washed up from all over Europe, along with false passports and criminal records, all eking a dodgy living.

Liz and I, broke and homeless, looking for a friendly omen, see a playing card face down in the street. "Bet that's a Joker?" Bingo! – just round the corner is an empty boat called the Joke. 'Joke,' pronounced Yo-ka in Dutch, is a girl's name; apple-cheeked maid in a print dress and yellow clogs holding a tulip. We slap a sticker of Barbarella on the door and a week later I find £150 in the back of a taxi. So we rented the floating love-nest, lazing on its tree-lined canal, and leaned into the volume of the Sony, until shortage of bread again began inhibiting our style.

Superimposed on the big blatant blat that Amsterdam sells to the tourists advertising Dutch cheeses, Amstel Bier, Ann Frank's Hideout and the house in Rosengracht where Rembrandt went broke, is another city, a subterrania of drugs, boats and Underground Comix. Beneath the surface of commercial awareness lies the zone of monstrous joys and gigantic depressions, realm of archetypal deals and mythological busts, Submarine City – the lost Atlantis.

Looked at through the eyes of the Joke the streets of Submarine City open out like strip cartoons. The Furry Freak Brothers peer suspiciously round every corner, Stella Stardust juggles used cars outside the American Express, Wyat Winghead sells hash-oil ice-lollies on the steps of the Moses and Aaron church. The sub- and super-minds of Amsterdam mingling in the bars, cafes and night-time pinball arcades, all acting as relay stations for the transmission of dope.

Our first flash of Submarine City was a huge pulsing brain with each person a neuron, wired in to every other neuron in the drug consciousness. The law of the neuron is all or nothing, when it fires it goes full out, all the way. Just like acid, Sub. City will take you any place you choose, as far as you dare to go.

Rollicking, rollicking sailors with big beards and sea-boots pitching and rolling across the street, drunk, loud and belligerent, guffawing at the size of the dildos in a sex-shop window. Birdman fluttering against the glass, every peek at the cunt books followed by a nervous glance over his shoulder. One of the sailors speaks to him and laughs. He scuttles off on thin legs, threatening to peck them under his breath.

A'dam has a rhythm all of her own, a hop, skip and jump, easygoing quick and lazy at the same time. If you catch the tempo the city looks after you, if you lose step she waits for you to pick it up again; but if you can't jive she beats you up, rips you off and busts you just for being there. Amsterdam, the world's Western dope centre where drug laws are liberal compared with the rest of Europe, and the solid Dutch Protestants cashed in on the rest of the continent's paranoia and cornered the dope and sex markets.

From all over Europe people pour into A'dam to score or to visit the red-light area. During the Summer months American students, deprived of easy access to dope at home, fly across the Atlantic and arrive in Vondell Park, toking on a more-or-less legal joint or slaking their thirsts in the heads' mixed-media emporiums such as the Paradiso, Milky Way and Cosmos. Hash is so interwoven with business interests that the Hollanders would be cutting their own throats by putting any real pressure on the traffic. The American high-school kids spend rolls of dollars grooving about the city enjoying the goodies while their senses are extended by smoking hash. There's never enough hotels, boatels and sleep-ins to cater for the Summer multitudes, so Vondell Park operates as a mass open air crash-pad, lit up at night by a galaxy of glowing joints.

While they are picking up dope the visitors also pick up on the life-styles, *so we are dealing ways of living as much as drugs; trying to get rid of the sick or tatty imagery surrounding the dope scene,* coming on with plots and plans that are successful instead of goofy, and behind it all the means to excitement, travel and intensity – money.

International drug bartering in broken Spanish and bastard Italian. 'How much?' in pigeon German, ludicrous English, colloquial Norwegian, provencal French. Foreign phrases and dialects flutter through the conversations like coloured butterflies, conjuring images and exporting them to far away lands.

Our recent background of peace and goodwill left us ill-prepared for the heavies when we first arrived. Man's inhumanity to man shocked our cosmic complacency so that it still remained shocked even after violence had been accepted as an every day thing. The breadless are the nastiest and most primitive beings in the city. When money is short desperation meters are on max input, ' . . . an I'll tear ya fuckin face off if you don't let goa that bread!'

The Dutch run the hash and the brothels, the Chinese run the cafes and the smack, Double-Dutch dealing gets a shoot-out and no fucking about – blam blam fin. Then there's the assorted hustlers who lost their nationalities long ago – and some of them changed colour several times as well – those who are at heart dope fiends first and foremost and only incidentally the burglars, bandits and robbers of the fuzz files.

Chinatown. Little yellow men in dim lit cafes and gambling dens, slit-eyed skeletons with dead-pan fingers balancing the scales. Chinatown is the red-light area, or the red-light area is Chinatown, depending on whether you're looking for a fix or a fuck. The two zones overlap in a tangle of canals, bridges and crooked streets, so scoring has the glitter-flash of sex and glamour behind it. The choice of women runs up the spectrum of brown, yellow and pink races to big blonde Vikings and coal-black mammas with a spattering of extra-terrestrials and females from the centre of the Earth. The sweet lure of danger runs through it all like a Lou Reed number, a magic magnet pulling the blood across Damrak into the maze of capillaries straddling the red-light area.

The houses taken over by squatters are known as 'cracked houses', these 'Kraak' (meaning 'broken into' in Dutch) pads are the focal points for scoring. The most notorious of the squats, known throughout the continent as a never-ending source of supply, is a group of three houses, 65, 67 and 69 Kaisergracht.

In between 65 and 69 Kaisergracht, entered by way of 69, is a house that would be 67 if it were numbered. We moved into a hollow empty room on the ground floor, with a history of heroin pushers stretching back three occupants and ending in a sudden bust, and when the opportunity occurred changed into a huge room on the first floor – Room 13. We are nearer the light now overlooking a fairytale canal and Toytown barges through four large rectangular windows that open like double doors and allow us to scan the street for fuzz. No. 65, an old nunnery with chapel and stained-glass windows is a rabbit warren of numerous small cell-like rooms that zig-zag in Escherscapes up five floors of narrow stairways to a magnificent view over the hustlers in the street below. Sixty-nine and the mythical 67 were rich merchant's town houses, with wide stairways and cavernous rooms that shrink towards the top of the houses into random cubby holes, or expand into immense cavernous spaces that defy anyone to guess which building they belong to. The ultra-big pads have been divided by sheets of hardboard, making it possible for half-a-dozen people to keep their own scenes going, and completing the overall edifice of the three building complex as a four dimensional casbah.

There's Batman and Dr. Strange in the attic, Ogoth the Wasted living with the Austrian Hindus upstairs, Jerry Cornelius bitterly alone in the alcove, cowboys opposite and beatniks in the basement. There's Honeybunch Kominski at war with Elastoman, Flower Power arguing with Science Fiction, The Hulk preaching peace and love, the Furry Freaks pushing smack and Mr. Natural coming on as a Hell's Angel.

The Underground comics have really got the Tarot pack going here – cosmic jokers by the roomful – ever since I was a Fool I've known there was a giggle in everything, but not all the time, like you don't laugh in Nirvana, you might kinda half-smile like the Buddha, but anything more than that is positively coarse, so ya gotta have an elegant image as well, ain'tcha? It's illegal to have more than one image at a time, the passport I have says 'author' this year and 'artist' last, but passports are like leaves on a tree here and it's Autumn all year round.

The sign on the door said PUSH. When someone comes to score they step through the front door onto a wheel of chance that quite often drops them at Room 13. Got the wheel rigged of course, the cards marked and the dice loaded, but so's everyone else, so all in all it's about fair. But there's always one dude who wants to control the whole game, the Sheriff, and nearly always the Sheriff ain't got a chick.

The ganglia or electrical wiring, dangling through the halls and trailing up the stairs of the three Kaisergracht houses, are the tendrils of a weird, dangerous shock plant that throws the houses into total blackness whenever a smashed-out soul stumbles against it. Many a stoned acid freak has been flung out of the solar system for boogie-ing too close to the upstairs wall. Was the time 69's first floor toilet chain blasted you straight to Nirvana every flush. People sprang out with the Beatific vision streaming from their eyes, pants round their ankles and fingers still trembling from the touch of God. God leans forward and reaches out to touch the hand of Michelangelo's Adam; unseen by the artist a small, oblong packet changes hands.

There's a flippancy about money when you're pushing. Dutch banknotes look like R. Crumb drew them, none of the regal magnificence of the one pound sterling, or the heavy German Mark, or the all-American dollar, this money is for playing with, Franc and Mark as croupiers – dope roulette.

In between deals we read Marvel comix and Sci-Fi paperbacks, taking the occasional fix among hoards of bug-eyed quasi-beings, limboids and antagonistic semi-entities that plot ceaselessly to mismanage the galaxy. There's generally three or four deals going on simultaneously in different parts of the room with Liz or myself supervising and waiting irritably for them to make up their minds.

" . . . Twenty-four for Paki, twenty-six for Leb, nineteen for Ketama, got two K's Nep for thirty . . . "

" . . . did a year in Germania with this cat used to be a frogman in the Polish navy . . . "

" . . . microdots thirteen a thou, pyramids fifteen this week, windowpanes one thousand eight hundred . . . "

The characters are apt to come loose from the pages of the comic books and start arguing with us about the price of coke. Liz's close to Morbius the vampire at times, Red is Shuman the Human when he's at his best, so pretty soon it's Shuman reading about Barritt who's telling Liz how sweetly she's drawn when the Sewer Coolies of Coagular pour off the cover and burst in, ravening with chemical lust to score.

" . . . busted for ten keys of O by a warlord in Upper Thailand . . . "

" . . . doing three hundred years in the States . . . "

" . . . his chick left him for a quarter gram . . . "

"I won't beat about the bush, this is the best weed this side of Thailand, one blast on this and you're inspired, it was flown in by Jumbo jet, parachuted into the sea and picked up by frogmen – that's why it's a bit wet. I agree it does weigh more when it's damp but just think of the devotion that's gone into it at such a cheap price."

How to get it in, how to cross all those borders with the dope? Mostly it's smuggled in via invisible force-fields manipulated by telepathic monitor hooked to a computer in our pad, but we are working on a phase shifter that will manifest horse and hasheesh direct through a slit in the air. A time-tunnel is programmed to a stone in Liz's ring that sparkles before she speaks, she does the ordering while I check with a pocket calculator. Fu Manchu or Saladin get their bread via a Swiss bank or can buy time-shares or up to ten years in the Dutch Dope Industry.

Miniature submarines operate the canals and we use Neuroloids when doing business with the CIA or KGB. Recently the Kremlin has been co-operating with the Mafia to equip humanoids with psychologists' brains to act as double agents – little do they know it was the extra-terrestrials, working for us, who placed the idea in their heads to divert suspicion from the dudes carrying through the customs in packs.

The mushrooms come from Lapland brought down by reindeer sled, the coke comes from South America by Astral plane. We get the acid from various Stellar sources, that at this date it is not prudent to disclose, but I will say that XK90 is not unknown to the astro-police as a source of suspicious radiation.

Realities: deal for real, steal for real, feel for real and you might even heal for real. Right or wrong? On this level? . . . you *must* be kidding! 'Play ya for ya ethics – strip poker. Your deal acid or smack? Play ya for ya woman – stud poker. Play ya for ya after-life – seven card karma or faro.' Or you can always play Russian roulette with the fuzz. Only three laws in this gambling joint; bluff, brag and cheat.

There's something refreshing about cheating; when you know the guy you're doing business with will cheat at every opportunity, and he knows you will, it's kinda honest. A very astute and very rich art dealer once told me that honesty was only for amateurs, and he was one of the biggest crooks I've known. Sometimes by telling a lie hard enough you make it become true, tell somebody who's down that they look great and they might believe you and feel great. These are not black lies or even white lies (flattery) if they change a downer into an upper if they make someone glow in the dark, they're called fluorescent lies – and the instant they fluoresce they become truth.

"You tell me lies darlin' and I'll [illegible]d I'll . . . "

"What *will* ya do?"

"If they're big enough I'll believe you."

But if everyone cheated and told lies where would it all lead? Well we would be fanatically honest, that's for certain, and the rest would gradually follow until we had to turn dishonest again – evolution is provoked, ask any mutant. Where we are there's no opposites so we have to create them to get anything done at all, everything I write is bound to be biased if not a downright lie, 'The world is divided for love's sake,' said Aleister Crowley, so let's put the poles together. Genuine humour is the last step before paradox, wit is Zen, mini paradox stardust. By rubbing the poles together we start sparks flying and remember, only the glitter gets through. If words are fired from the spirit they shoot themselves into the future like projectiles and wait for your premonition to pick up on them; if you miss out they smooth you into the shape they want without you even knowing. Sixty-five, 67 and 69 Kaisergracht, trey of gambling clubs – jokers wild – Liz Elliot Queen of Hearts, Brian Barritt Knave of Diamonds, your deal.

THE GOLDEN DAWNING OF A NEW AGE

by
HARRY SHAPIRO

Inward expansion of human consciousness is never stronger than in times of outward rationalism when the artists, the romantics and the adventurers of society rebel against complacency, against mind-grinding boredom, against the current possibilities that stifle imagination. Such a crisis in the human psyche gained momentum during the 19th century against a background of crusading Darwinism and dour, brutalising industrialisation. Most were swept along by the carnival of burgeoning Western hegenomy, whether they wanted to be or not, but others, psychologically the same group of 'outsiders' as in earlier times, wanted to look beneath the surface in search of a more positive destiny for mankind, a spiritual rather than a scientific awakening. They eschewed the passive stance of orthodox religion (which paradoxically became any thing but passive in the hands of Victorian imperialists practising 'muscular Christianity' on the peoples of foreign lands), and some, often the most talented and inspired, embarked on the journey into inner space using psychoactive drugs as the signposts, the spirit guides to point the way. They plummeted deep inside themselves, instinctually ahead of, and then supported by psychoanalytic theory, to take a run up at the stars. Thus was born a new occult revival which has branched out along many different paths, but which has yet to run out of steam, if anything gaining in strength in these grim and uncertain times.

Around the middle of the last century there were simultaneous stirrings in Europe and America. For example, many of the French Romantics, such as Baudelaire, Gautier, de Nerval and later Rimbaud, belonged to Dr Moreau's Hashish Club which met in the Hotel Pimodan in Paris. They were interested in drugs like opium and laudanum from a scientific as well as an aesthetic viewpoint, but their first love was hashish, all the rage in the Paris salons of the 1840s. Arthur Rimbaud, in particular, was deeply emmersed in the occult from an early age His work was steeped in alchemical symbolism and he believed in the need to achieve oneness or unity with the absolute by self annihiliation, by destruction of the ego. In 1872, he wrote, 'I say that it is necessary to be a seer . . . to make oneself a seer. The poet makes himself a seer by a long, immense and reasoned unruliness of all his senses . . . he exhausts himself in every kind of poison, he becomes the unhealthy one, the great criminal, the great accursed and the supreme master – because he attains the unknown'. Well, as Baudelaire's spiritual heir to indulgence as well as genius, Rimbaud did all this and more, but crucified by the critics, he destroyed all his work and succumbed to an almost inevitable wanderlust, which in turn destroyed him physically and he died aged 37; with his ego went his health.

But what Rimbaud said of the poet, held true for the magician, as well (and often they were the same person): chaotic, inspired, neurotic, vilified – restless, wandering spirits who believed in the true essence of magic, that to aspire to the Gnosis, the Knowledge, you had to experience everything, be everywhere and be everybody. The magician has to be on the fringes – gods don't talk to chartered accountants and demons don't dance with dentists. Communing with the spirits demands that consciousness be displaced, shifted, that its instinctual and irrational areas are tapped; many prospected, few struck gold – one who did was Helena Petrovna Blavatsky.

1875 was a pretty important year for the modern occult revival; Aleister Crowley was born (making up for the discovery of America, so he said), so was Jung, Eliphas Levi the great French magus died and HPB as she was known to her friends, founded the Theosophical Society in New York – one of the most important occult groups next to the Golden Dawn. A woman of terrifying energies, Madam Blavatsky travelled to remote parts of the world, taught piano, joined a circus where a fall from a horse ruined her sex life, managed an artificial flower factory in Russia, assisted the famous medium D.D. Home and was herself a medium – spiritualism being one of the most widely publicised aspects of the occult revival. She was also a dedicated 'hashish eater' and hash played a significant role in her visions of Isis, forming the basis of her magnum opus 'Isis Unveiled', a majestic synthesis of religion, magic and mysticism covering everything from the Kabbalah to Taoism. It was published in New York in 1877 after two years incredibly intensive work. She wrote nearly all day, every day, smoking hash and strong cigarettes endlessly. As the Theosophical Society itself was dedicated to the 17th century Rosicrucian programme of building a bridge between science and religion through the powers latent in man, so 'Isis Unveiled' and later 'The Secret Doctrine' built a unique bridge between East and West, the first attempt to create such a fusion. The importance of this, as she realised, was that the philosophies of each by themselves were not enough – running off to India was no answer – all that was revealed in doing so was another view of imbalance. She wrote, 'I am solely occupied not with writing Isis, but with Isis herself. I live in a kind of permanent enchantment, a life of visions and sights'. With legal dope on tap and no hassles, small wonder she led a life of 'permanent enchantment' and her 'visions and sights' were enough for Aleister Crowley to praise her as an initiate of the highest grade, as he was himself through study of the rituals of one of the most influential occult groups of the modern day – the Hermetic Order of the Golden Dawn (GD).

It started in 1878 as a kind of Masonic/Rosicrucian hybrid of a distinctly English character, very secret with a well vetted membership in its earliest days and with credentials supposedly emanating from an ancient occult order in Germany. The GD quest for Rimbaud's absolute control eventually led to inflated egos and rapid decline, but in the process was created a blue print that many have followed.

Yet that blueprint, containing large elements of Kabbalistic, astrological and tarot-based teachings as well as Egyptian magic, was really the work of one man, Samuel McGregor Mathers, whose flamboyance and eccentricity were the hallmarks of his craft – totally unemploy-

She wrote nearly all day, every day, smoking hash and strong cigarettes endlessly.

Eliphas Levi

able in any ordinary job — occultist was all that was left! His genius was to tie together strands of a new way of thinking — that the gods on high, normally worshipped and occasionally invoked were actually within man himself. It was the difference between 'God is in me' and 'I am God'. Borrowing from previous expressions of the Godhead, Mathers wrote all the major rituals of the Golden

. . . by the age of 23, he had partaken of every drug he could lay his hands on . . .

Dawn and its higher grades singlehanded; Israel Regardie has detailed them exhaustively and many were indeed long and exhausting, but with a certain beauty of their own. What Mathers created was the first systematic exploration of inner space in the West and like Madam Blavatsky, the GD emphasised the psychological factors in magic as a technique of self development.

The aim of these rituals was supposed to be a contradiction of the go, becoming

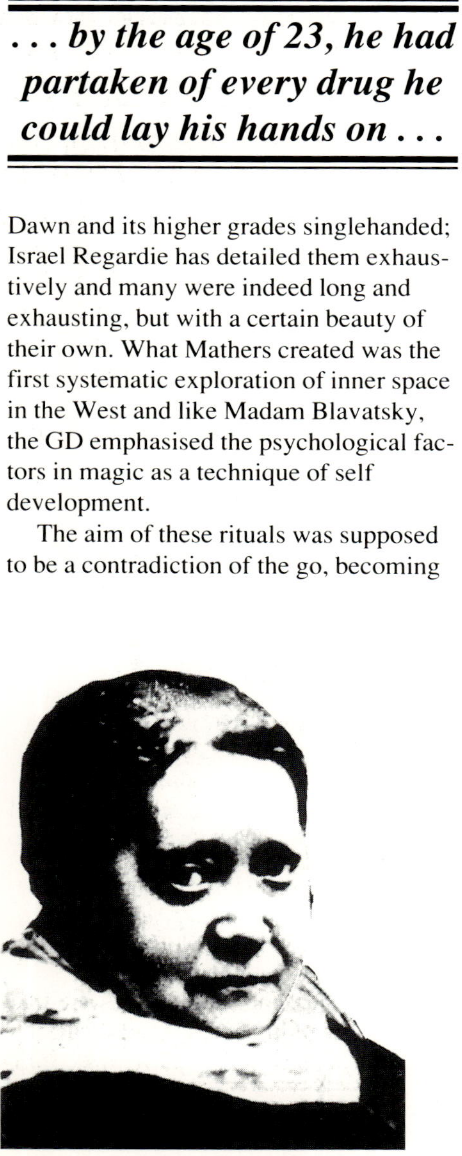

Madam Blavatsky

'non self'. However, what tended to happen was that egos became expanded — some GD members began to behave like Gods with a hotline to divine authority. Both the Theosophical Society and the GD were based (fictitiously) on the existence of Secret Chiefs who had selected certain individuals to lead these groups; belief in these supernatural beings seemed of great importance to the membership of both groups and it is unlikely that either group would have flourished without the promise of the revelation of knowledge hidden from the uninitiated. Inflated egos manifested themselves in the ridiculous mottoes that the initiates adopted. One of the founders of the GD, William Westcott, a humble London coroner, labelled himself 'non omnis moriar', 'I shall not altogether die', although Crowley's 'I shall endure', has proved to be a motto of more substance. Westcott typified the average middle class occultist, seeking no more than a cosy secret society where they served good claret. Later, when his professional standing as a coroner was in jeopardy through membership of the GD, he left. Such people were not the stuff of adepts, they were generally passive in their acceptance of Mathers, but when his dictatorial attitude became too much even for them, there was a palace revolution and various splinter groups rose from the ashes.

The rise and fall of the GD was a model of many occult groups. It attracted members of high intellectual and mystical calibre, but eventually suffered from internal dissensions, partly because it was based on the lie of divine revelation, but mainly because the instruction and development did not fundamentally change the nature of the members. The weaknesses and defects of some individuals were not eliminated and eventually the whole structure was weakened.

This is the tenor of the epitaph usually written by occult authors for the GD, but it is not entirely true; interesting things only come from interesting minds and those members of the highest calibre, those with the most vivid and far reaching imaginations were much affected by the occult rituals — among one of the most prominent members being W.B. Yeats, initiated into the GD in May 1887. He wrote, 'the mystical life is the centre of all that I do and all that I think and all that I write' . . . 'it was through him (Mathers) that I began studies and experiences that were to convince me that images well up before the mind's eye from a deeper source than the conscious or subconscious memory'. He moved from Theosophy to the GD, bringing Kabbalistic, Rosicrucian and astrological symbolism into his poetry. His work is impossible to fully comprehend unless his fascination with mysticism and the fact that his 'studies and experiences' included peyote are taken into account. He was introduced to the drug by Havelock Ellis, who published his own first-hand account of mescal use in 1898. 'Mescal: A New Artificial Paradise', precating Huxley's work by nearly a quarter of a century. Equally famous GD adepts were regular experimenters with consciousness-raising drugs; Allen Bennett presided over Crowley's earliest tastes of yet-to-be forbidden fruits both being GD members when they met. At the time Bennett was virtually a down and out; he stayed with Crowley, taught him much about ceremonial magic and in turn. Crowley provided the finances which set Bennett on the way to Indian and an Eastern way of life.

Crowley used drugs as he said, 'to give proof of a new order of consciousness' and he positioned himself at the centre of the drug taking literati and intellectual set — he was probably the greatest protagonist for drug use of all time even more than Leary. Crowley introduced Cole Porter to coke, Katherine Mansfield to opium, H. G. Wells to hash and it was in Crowley's company that Aldous Huxley first tried mescaline in Berlin.

However, the publicity given to Crowley and his circle tended to obscure the fact that there was an *anti-drug* lobby at work among the occult groups. Francis Barratt's ponderous but seminal tome 'The Magus', published in 1801 specifically described experiments using naturally working psychoactive drugs, but Crowley's mentor Eliphas Levi in his major works written later on in the century had virtually nothing to say on the subject. Such debate as there was seems to have invariably centred around the question of whether the drug-induced vision had any validity. However in addition, the 'medical model' drug addiction was fast gaining currency as an organised medical profession came of age and began flexing its muscles. It pushed successfully for therapeutic prescribing to be a medical prerogative while at the same time laying the foundation for legislative action against recreational drug use. Either the anti-drug occultists were won over by medical arguments or they just used them and the existence of laws against drug use to argue against a practice they disagreed with. In 'Psychic Self Defence' (1930), Dion Fortune, a former GD member wrote: —

'It is well known that there are various drugs which can be used to exalt consciousness and induce a temporary psychism. It may not be equally well known that most of these substances come under the regulations of the Dangerous Drugs Act and that to obtain them from irregular sources, or even to be found in possession of them save for a legitimate purpose, is to render oneself liable to prosecution and in this case too, the authorities are exceedingly alert and the magistrates exceedingly drastic.'

Quite obviously the main thrust of this argument against drugs (here meaning opium, cocaine and cannabis), is their illegality — nothing at all to do with their role in ceremonial magic. What is interesting is that the attitudes of occultists towards drugs changed in the same way as did that of the general public and many occultists knew as little about drugs as Joe Soap — third hand knowledge of Chinese opium dens and the activities of high society sensationalised in the press being the limit of what most people knew of the subject.

Ironically, those drugs most likely to cause most 'psychisms' however temporary, were not controlled nor hardly known except among the rarified atmospheres of the intelligentsia and certainly knowledge of such drug use by those ancient sages revered by many including those opposed to drug use in magic was in its infancy. However, given the Christian 'edge' to much occult ritual workings, perhaps this puritan attitude becomes less surprising. The Protestant work ethic would have been much averse to drugs which of course, like Access of Barclaycard take the waiting out of wanting! White magicians would also see a clear analogy between drug use and the practice of black magic pacts with the Devil — both supposedly offer immediate gains without immediate payment. Black Magic groups were and are feared as much for their licentious drug use and promiscuity as for more dubious activities.

None of this mattered Aleister Crowley, of course; by the age of 23,. he had partaken of every drug he could lay his hands on and all before there was any Dangerous Drugs legislation. He believed that the drug fiend was a superior man to ordinary mortals and that to master drugs you have to take them incessantly. Hence guests to his Sicilian abbey retreat found bowls heaped high with heroin and cocaine brought in from the Italian mainland. Crowley's drug use hinged around his dramatic reinterpretation of ritual magic which demanded that the magician meet with the Gods on the astral plane, rather than invoke them to Earth all the time — you had to get literally 'high'. Crowley restated the aims of magic in modern Freudian terms, the search for the true self, 'every man and woman is a star', a psychological basis for magic derived from Blavatsky's writings and from the teachings of the GD which made the connection between magic and human will.

So how *did* Crowley fit drugs into his magical schema? From the start Crowley ensured his basic philosophy would allow for indulgences of all kinds. He toured America, Mexico, India and the Far East until he found Egypt Around the turn of the century Egypt was a popular haunt of westerners eager to turn on to opium and 'find' themselves, serving much the same purpose as Afghanistan, India and hash did at the end of the hippy trail over 60 years later. While in Egypt, Crowley's Book of the Law was dictated to him by his spirit guide Aiwass who conveniently commanded Crowley that 'to worship me, take wine and strange drugs . . . Be strong O Man! Lust, Enjoy all!'

The magicians surrounds himself with various objects believed to have connections with the entities to be invoked — the magical link of correspondences. The veracity of these connections is neither her nor there — the magician's belief is all that's needed. In his essay on Kabbalistic taxonomy 777, Crowley used the principle of magical correspondences to classify various drugs in terms of the Tree of Life e.g. Mace and nutmeg — the second tarot trump (The Magus) — Mercury Peyote — Sefira Hod — also Mercury. The first correspondence is quite impressive given the relatively recent discoveries of the pharmacological links between mace and nutmeg and the second fits in with the ritual use of peyote in South America, because Mescalito was the guide and teacher bringing the word as symbolised by Mercury. In 1912, Crowley produced a visual representation of initiation, in the foreground of which are red and gold varieties of amanita muscaria.

The gathering together of objects linked by magical correspondence, rhythmic chanting of the names of power, an atmosphere pervaded by essences and perfumes sometimes hallucinogenic and a magician, usually a powerful magnetic personality, who has prepared for the ritual days in advance and who may now be under the influence of drugs, all builds up to a terrifying climax which can have a profound psychological impact on those present. This is the basis of many of the warnings against dabbling in the black arts'. At the climax of the ritual, the

Samuel MeGregor Mathers

fusion between man and god takes place all levels of consciousness merge — man *is* god.

Just as drugs are used to induce the trance essential for the performance of ceremonial magic, so they can be used to induce the trance for travel on the astral plane. Drugs possibly break down the barriers to the chaos of other worlds, and within this chaos lie great dangers, some of which are deliberately courted by the adept to strengthen the spirit.

. . . drugs . . . can be used to induce the trance for travel on the astral plane.

In Tibet, there is a dramatic and highly dangerous rite performed in a solitary place like a cemetery. The adept offers his astral body to the demons on the astral plane for them to devour, which they do, tearing the body to pieces. The adept physically feels all that is happening to him, but when it is all over, his astral body is reborn stronger than ever. Victor Neuburg, one of Crowley's most faithful disciples speaks of a similar rite in his magical diary — in this case, his astral body was hacked to pieces by a red giant.

W. B. Yeats

The hapless Neuburg suffered further horrors when under the influence of mescaline, he was leapt upon and half strangled by the demon Chronozon, thoughtfully conjured up by Crowley. Many of the visions described by occultists through the ages, voices, sounds, strange and alien landscapes are very similar to those described by those under the influence of hallucinogenic drugs.

In a sense, the magicians and philosophers *have* shown us a way using hallucinogens and in a sense too, these drugs have put modern man in touch with the shamans, enabling us to 'rediscover' one aspect of this awareness, a purity previouly lost through the prevalence of charlatanism in magic and the misrepresentation of witchcraft. The drug experiments of the early years of this century re-opened doors to the past precisely at a time when there was serious doubt about the revelation of civilisation caused by the immense psychological shock of the First World War, conceptualised in the art of the period, notably surrealism.

But there are dangers, there always were; the search for new horizons of the will, the inner being, cannot be undertaken in a vacuum, there needs to be a whole scaffolding of drama, conviction and purpose i.e. it needs symbolism. Break out of the magic circle and the demons of rationalism will devour you; break the barriers of constraint and you go mad – most magicians cannot face the world as we see it. And so it is with drugs; those in ancient cultures past and present for whom drugs played an important and *natural* role in the cosmology, did not have drug problems because drug use was part and parcel of ritual activities. But there is a world of difference between escaping from the 'one-self' into a wider cosmos and escaping from dullness and routine. Perhaps the 'rational' mind is not meant to see such visions – even the work of Leary and his friends had the hint of desperate intellectuals born into an industrial society and at the other end there was the hedonistic chaos of Charlie Manson.

It is worth noting that despite being such an extravagant apologist for drug use, Crowley emphasised the need for discipline and training in the meditative arts as a prelude to exploring inner space. Much more than Leary ever did, Crowley saw drugs for what they were, as mere tools, not substitutes.

'I have no use for hashish save as a preliminary demonstration that there

exists another world, attainable – somehow!.

Compare this with Frank Ferguson, one of Leary's former associates, who firmly believed that LSD could short cut the work of 20 years yogic meditation down to a few weeks. He had a point though – sitting around in our climate for 20 years would be no joke, okay in Bengal, but in Barnsley?

Crowley's antipathy towards taking the easy road has been echoed through the years by Jung writing in 1936 and by the Los Angeles poet Charles Bukowski in the LA Free Press in 1967. The two statements below are not only startling for their continuity of expression, but because of the cyclical nature of their relevance in different ages:–

'People will do anything, no matter how absurd, in order to avoid facing their own souls. They will practise Indian yoga and all its exercises, observe a strict regime of diet, learn theosophy by heart or mechanically repeat mystic texts from the literature of the whole world – all because they cannot get on with themselves and have not the slightest faith that anything useful could come out of their own souls'. Bukowski thought every drug should be available to everybody so they could make up their own minds, but what he objected to was that 'the LSD-craze-phase-blaze has been taken over by the hippies, the swing-kitties, the dull heads, as a kind of private stomping ground, as a substitute for the soul . . . Being unable to take the truth, being unable to face an honest mirror, they PLAY AT SOUL, at being IN . . . any damn thing to give them identity, to give them a facade or being to Cover the Horrible Hole'.

Those who we call visionaries or magicians or mystics were 'outsiders', not quite in the Colin Wilson sense, but generally not of our consciousness. Eccentric would be one of the kinder words used to describe them and there is no doubt that in trying to rid themselves of ego, such abandonment could lead to madness, a state sometimes deliberately sought. But this may be why our latter day 'intellectual shamans' have failed; great thoughts don't come about by deep thinking and reasoning – they come about by intuition and imagination, the spark of inspiration. Mathers and Crowley may have been 'head cases' by ordinary standards, but as Andrew Weil has pointed out, the psychotics are potential sages; they can change reality by changing the mind. The point is, that those who possess such talent and can harness the imagination and the will in such a way are a rare breed and must be recognised as such

Thus one might speculate that those who demonstrate such powers and others like ESP and psychokinesis which are now being seriously studied, are shadows of a new evolutionary development for mankind and perhaps the ability to handle drugs and benefit from the experience is also a question of evolution. After all, we are merely one end of an evolutionary branch, not necessarily the top of the tree – possibly we need to evolve away from our base instincts and emotions and develop a more mature, less primeval psychology. But these are the realms where only Richard Leakey and Carl Sagan dare tread – what is indisputable is that many societies on Earth *have* assimilated psychoactive drug use into their society through custom, ritual and education. In our society however, it is heresy to suggest that we should be educated in the use of drugs, that there is any kind of human right attached to the concept of an altered state of consciousness. Whatever its political beliefs, there is no modern body politic in the world that seems to be able to take some lessons from so-called 'primitive' societies, then perhaps we may get a tiny glimpse of the wizard's vision of the cosmos. Parallel realities are different and not necessarily better and what we do with such knowledge is another matter, but then that is what the occult is all about – that which is hidden behind closed doors . . . the doors of perception, the gates of distance.

'People will do anything, no matter how absurd, in order to avoid facing their own souls.

SMOKEY BEARS
8P.M.
CHESTER?
ANYBODY HOME?
LYDIA?
I'VE COME TO FEED YOU— YOU NEVER EAT PROPERLY ON YOUR OWN.
SEEN THE PAPERS?
NO...
WOW! "SEA DRAMA CANNABIS CHASE SHOCK!" "H.M.CUSTOMS FAILLED TO APPREHEND A FLEEING DRUG SMUGGLER TODAY. AN ESTIM-ATED TWO TONS OF "POT" WAS THROWN OVERBOARD DURING THE CHASE. POLICE ARE GUARDING BEACHES AT SOUTHTHORPE WHERE THE SEALED PACKAGES WILL BE WASHED ASHORE.
NEWS
DRAMA
EY UP!
JUST AS I THOUGHT! ACCORDING TO MY CAL-CULATIONS, THE CURRENT WILL DEPOSIT TH' STUFF AT GRIMSDALE POINT!
QUICK! PHONE ROCKY AN' TH' OTHERS!
WE'RE GOIN' T'TH' SEASIDE!
10P.M.
ZANG
GRIMSDALE 2 MILES
THIS IS IT, CHES!
DRIVE A LITTLE WAY DOWN TH' BEACH.
WITH ANY LUCK WE SHOULD HIT TH'...
...JACKPOT!
CRUMBS!
COME TO DADDY!
I SEE IT! BUT I DON'T BELIEVE IT!
YIP
YIP
11:30P.M.
THAT'S THE VAN LOADED UP!
PHEW! YEAH! —AN' THERE'S LOTS LEFT! YOU TAKE THAT LOAD BACK AND WE'LL STACK THE REST UP FOR WHEN YOU RETURN!
58

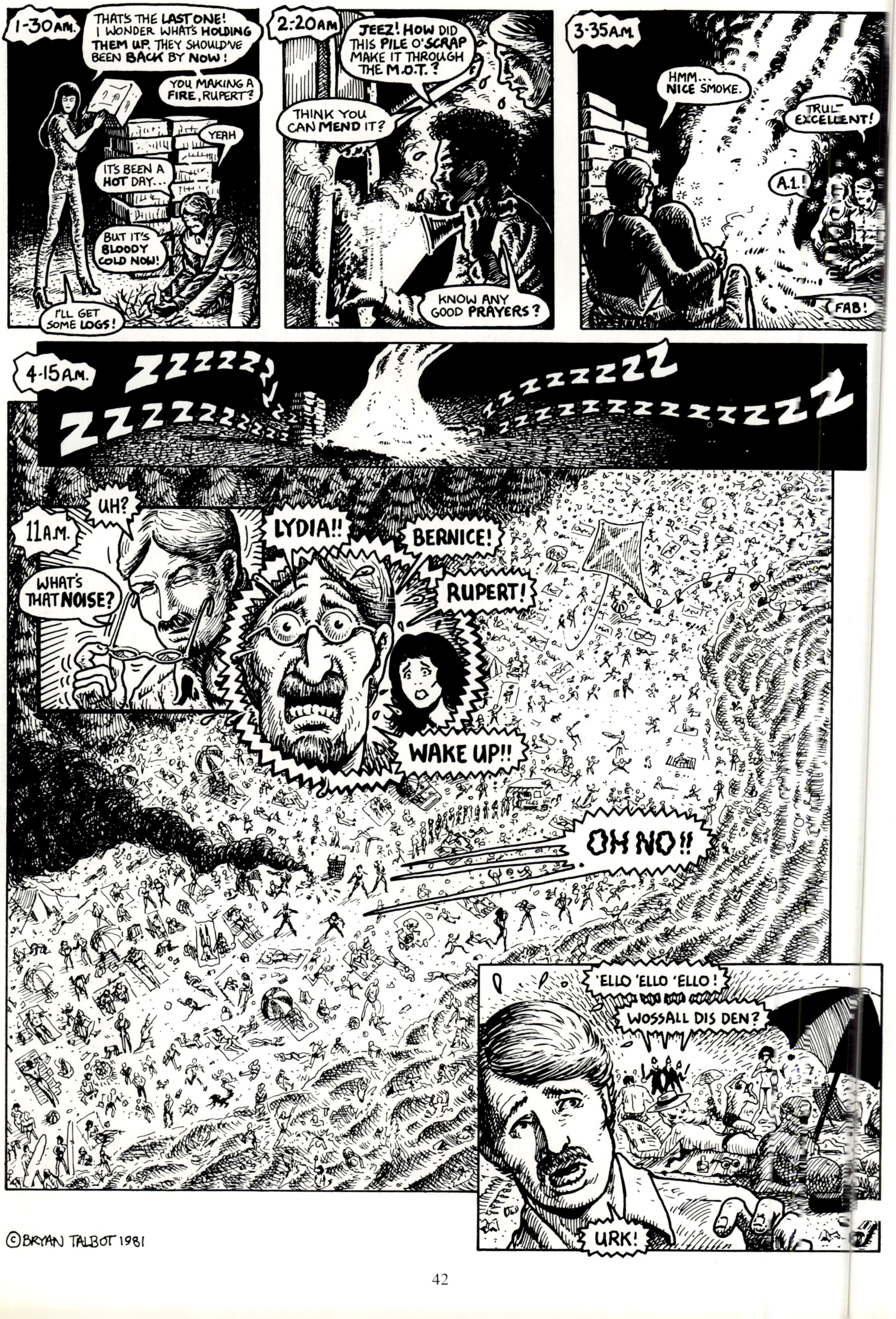

©BRYAN TALBOT 1981

BRAINSTORM STUDIOS

From 1949 to 1975 the CIA and the US military conducted a series of multi-million dollar programmes to develop ways of controlling human behaviour. In this first complete summary of the CIA experiments to appear in the British press, MICHAEL MARTEN reports on Operations Bluebird, Artichoke, MK–ULTRA, MK–DELTA, MK–NAOMI and Often-Chickwit: a tale of drug abuse on a massive and unprecedented scale.

With special thanks for source material to CHRISTOPHER EALAND in San Francisco, LEE TORREY in Cape Cod, and the American Embassy library in London.

How the Central Intelligence Agency Got Hooked on Drugs and Ran Amock

"Allen W. Dulles, then Director of Central Intelligence, ordered a crash programme. It was a normal reflex. People were always ordering crash programmes in those days. It didn't matter that they often ended in crashes."

— Russell Baker, in New York Times, 5.8.77

At the Nuremberg trials, in 1945, the victorious nations of World War II condemned the Nazi "medical" experiments on concentration camp prisoners and drew up a code of practice to prevent such atrocities occurring again. Experiments on human beings, they declared, should be for the good of mankind; they should not be carried out on unwilling or unwitting subjects, only volunteers; and prisoners and soldiers should be considered as volunteers only if offered no inducement or reward.

Four years later, in 1949, at the headquarters of the CIA in Langley, Virginia, Director Dulles authorised Operation Bluebird. It was the first in a series of programmes that would span a quarter of a century and subject thousands of Americans to unethical and illegal experimentation with drugs and other mind-altering techniques. In many cases drugs were administered with neither the consent nor the knowledge of the subjects. In other cases, "consent" was given for experiments never adequately explained. Soldier "volunteers" were rewarded with extra leave, a certificate of merit and a $45 per month bonus. Prisoner "volunteers" were offered remission of sentence and easier conditions; and drug addicts were paid, naturally, in drugs. Patients in mental hospitals were given no inducements: they were experimented upon as part of their "normal" treatment.

Operation Bluebird was renamed Operation Artichoke in 1950. Three years later the CIA's eager young deputy director of plans put forward a proposal for an improved and expanded programme, codenamed MK–ULTRA, whose purpose it would be "to research and develop chemical, biological and radiological materials capable of employment in clandestine operations to control human behaviour." This young man was Richard Helms, who would later become Director of the CIA under Richard Nixon.

MK–ULTRA in turn spawned other programmes: MK–DELTA, which tested drugs and other techniques in "operational situations"; MK–NAOMI, under which the CIA collaborated with the army to test LSD on soldiers; and Often-Chickwit, the last phase, which ran until 1973. Parallel with these efforts, the US Army conducted its own wideranging experiments; and the US Air Force got in on the act too.

The story is that the CIA first got involved in behaviour control to keep up with the Russians. "They had looked into the vacant eyes of Joseph Cardinal Mindszenty at his treason trial in Budapest in 1949," the New York Times explained recently, "and had been horrified." Agency officials were convinced the Cardinal's confession had been extracted under drugs, and that he stood in the dock in a post-hypnotic trance. Worse was to come. There were reports of massive Russian purchases of hallucinogens; two Soviet agents were arrested in Germany armed with hypodermics which, it was claimed, "would make the victim amenable to the will of his captors;" and in 1952, six US Air Force pilots captured by the Chinese publicly confessed to dropping germ warfare bombs on North Korea. The Free World would not be safe, the CIA brass argued, until the United States had taken the lead in the mind-control race.

When a military study group determined, in 1953, that events had not been what they seemed, that neither Russians nor Chinese had yet perfected means of making men into robots, and that there was little threat to "national security" the CIA paid little mind. Its defensive measures had become offensive. It was adrift on a sea of fantastic possibilities.

This, after all, was the era of Cold War, H-bombs and Berlin crises. The American public was drip-fed an intoxicating cocktail of McCarthy witchhunts, Korean "brainwashing" atrocities and Hollywood invasions of prairie hometowns by monstrous aliens. Every day was espionage day. Communism was not just a dangerous doctrine, it was a sophisticated and worldwide conspiracy to subvert and conquer the home of the brave and land of the free. Amongst the men of the CIA, anti-communism was a form of worship, an affirmation of their clean and crewcut young manhood.

Twitches, Jerks and Staggers

"All hands agreed ... that the Agency should purchase the LSD if possible and as soon as possible."

– CIA memorandum, 195[illegible].

Over the years the CIA experimented with marijuana, mescaline, psilocybin, LSD, sodium pentathol, sodium amytal, methedrine and benzedrine, barbiturates and tranquillisers, ether, ethyl alcohol, atropine and scopolamine, and nerve gases. They tested incapacitating agents, immobilising agents, "harassment" agents, and food poisons which tasted normal but, when eaten, created "confusion-anxiety-fear."

As well as drugs, they investigated the uses of hypnosis, electro-shock, sensory deprivation, conditioning techniques, brain surgery, and ultrasonics. They interviewed doctors and scientists around the world, studied the writings of Hitler's personal psychologist, and checked out "occult" techniques and "black psychiatry".

Amongst their more extraordinary ideas were schemes to dissolve the Berlin Wall, manufacture rubber from mushrooms, and locate enemy submarines by dowsing. They commissioned John Mulholland, a professional magician, to verify the claims of a "genuine psychic" who said he could transmit and receive messages anywhere in the world by telepathy. And they paid Mulholland $3000, in 1953, to write a sleight-of-hand manual to aid agents in surreptitiously administering drugs, whether in "solid, liquid, or gaseous" form. What Admiral Stansfield Turner, the current CIA Director, describes as "putting the mickey in the finn."

They were obsessed with pills. They wanted a "recruitment pill" to subvert enemy agents, a "knockout pill" to temporarily incapacitate a building full of people, an aphrodisiac pill to alter a person's sex patterns, a pill to make drunken agents sober and keep sober agents from getting drunk, and a pill to discredit prominent people by producing "aberrant behaviour" in public.

They arranged for the "collection, cultivation, propagation and testing of certain narcotic mushrooms by agencies, both governmental and private." They decided, in 1953, to purchase from Sandoz for $240,000, ten kilogrammes of LSD, enough for 100 million effective doses. And they spent $24,000, in 1956, to study the "feasibility of utilising aerosols as a delivery system" for LSD and other drugs. The study concluded that LSD spraycans would not make effective weapons.

One of their most pressing concerns was interrogation. Was there a "truth serum" which would make enemy agents talk? Were there other drugs which would enable their own agents to resist questioning, even physical torture? They conducted a variety of interrogation experiments using drugs, especially sodium pentathol and LSD, and other techniques. They established two "special interrogation teams" made up of a psychiatrist, a hypnotist and an interrogator to test "narcohypnotic" methods in the field. One team operated in Europe, the other in Asia. In 1952, the European team spent 11 days grilling three Iron Curtain CIA agents who were suspected of doubling for the KGB. The men were held in the basement of a suburban house and were guarded by armed military police in civilian clothes. They were injected with sodium pentathol and a stimulant, hypnotised, and engaged in "fantasies" by the interrogator and psychiatrist. One of the men experienced a "remarkable regression" and "actually relived certain past activities of his life, some dating back 15 years, while, in addition, he totally accepted Mr (name deleted) as an old and trusted and beloved personal friend whom the subject had known in years past in Georgia, USSR." The three men were cleared, and continued to be used operationally.

Because interrogation techniques could be used against them as well as by them, CIA officials were eager to find ways of producing "guaranteed amnesias". At one high-level Artichoke conference in early '53, "(name deleted) stated that some individuals in the Agency had to know tremendous amounts of information and if any way could be found to produce amnesias—for instance, after the individual had left the Agency—it would be a remarkable thing." The need for amnesias, another said, was particularly great in operational work: it would be extremely useful if an operative's memory of a clandestine mission, or even a murder, could be wiped out.

In addition to memory control, they worked on the "controlled production" of headaches and earaches, of twitches, jerks and staggers. They wanted to reduce a man to a bewildered, self-doubting mass so that they could "subvert his principles" and direct him in ways that "may vary from rationalising a disloyal act to the construction of a new person." They hoped to "crack the defences of enemy agents – to be able to programme both them and their own operatives to carry out any mission, even against their will and such fundamental laws as self-preservation."

Naive and bizarre though they often were, the CIA schemes cannot be lightly dismissed. This was a deliberate assault on the human psyche, sustained over many years. As MK–ULTRA progressed, its experiments and methods became more refined and purposeful. The intent, according to one CIA memo, was to reach a situation where "the basic knowledge of the effects of these drugs would permit specific hypotheses of a 'which drug which purpose' nature." Such hypotheses should then be "critically tested under field conditions: i.e. prisoners of war, if possible, federal prisoners, if possible, security officers, etc., under threat conditions beyond the scope of civilian experimentation."

DANGEROUS AND DEVIOUS

"They flashed their badges – they were employees of the Company."
– Dr Carl Pfeiffer, pharmacologist, describing his recruitment by the CIA.

The scope of the CIA experiments was massive. In its peak period, from 1953 to 1964, MK–ULTRA alone ran 149 separate projects at 154 institutions, including hospitals, insane asylums, private clinics, university departments, state and federal prisons, drug addiction centres, and

pharmaceutical companies. (Interestingly enough, while many of the academic facilities have been named, the drug companies all remain anonymous.) The CIA employed, directly or through front organisations, some 200 non-governmental researchers, including doctors, psychiatrists, neurologists and biochemists. Many knew they were working for the Agency, but others believed they were employed by respectable research foundations.

ULTRA was swathed in extreme secrecy, even by CIA standards. ULTRA officials pursued a policy of "minimum documentation" and relied largely on "oral communications". When the Agency's Inspector-General reviewed the programme in 1963, he found that "substantial portions of the MK–ULTRA record" resided solely in the memories of two senior CIA officials who applied the "need-to-know" doctrine to fellow Agency employees "to the maximum degree."

The men referred to were probably Richard Helms and Dr Sidney Gottlieb. Gottlieb was a biochemist who joined the Agency in 1951. A close associate of Helms, he rose to be director of the Technical Services Division (TSD) and the man in charge of ULTRA. It was Gottlieb who administered the LSD that led to Frank Olson's suicide, and Gottlieb who personally recruited many of the CIA's outside researchers, including Dr Pfeiffer. When Helms retired as CIA director in 1972, he ordered the ULTRA records destroyed, and Gottlieb personally shredded 152 separate files. Gottlieb himself retired the following year. At the congressional hearings on CIA drug tests in 1975, Gottlieb told the Senators that he "couldn't remember much about the project", though his name appeared on every ULTRA document. He was last heard of living abroad.

One of the most troubling aspects of both CIA and Army programmes is the apparent ease with which outside researchers – many of them top scientists in their fields – were enlisted to perform experiments which, even in those days, were highly dubious. The CIA was well aware of this. One memorandum states that "the professional reputations of outside researchers are in jeopardy since the objectives of such research are widely regarded as anti-ethical or illegal." Another memo declares that one candidate's "ethics might be such that he might not care to cooperate in certain more revolutionary phases of our project", whereas a second man's ethics "are such that he would be completely cooperative in any phase of our programme, regardless of how revolutionary it may be.

The CIA maintained an elaborate system to keep its sponsorship of experiments secret. Research was often conducted under a cover story. One series of LSD experiments, for example, was ostensibly seeking a substitute for codeine as a mild painkiller. Researchers reported back by devious means. In one instance a scientist despatched his results in double envelopes and signed himself with a pseudonym. Funding was invariably indirect, through other government departments or, more often, apparently respectable research foundations.

Three major conduits for CIA money were the Geschikter Foundation, a CIA front, the Society for the Investigation of Human Ecology (SIHE), another CIA front, and the Josiah Macy Jr Foundation, a genuine organisation. SIHE was set up in the early Fifties at the behest of the CIA by Dr Harold G. Wolfe, a Cornell University neurologist. Wolfe had become a close friend of Dulles' after treating his son for brain injuries received in Korea, and was also a leading authority on Chinese "brainwashing" of American POWs. Several researchers funded by SIHE and the foundations, according to former CIA officials, never knew they were working for the Agency. But what of those who did?

One lesson is that scientists were no more immune than anyone else to the paranoia of the times. Another is that science follows funding: if the bulk of the research money comes from the military, the corporations and the cloak-and-dagger merchants, the bulk of the research will be on weapons, corporate product and cloak-and-dagger techniques.

The Americans have no right to moralistically condemn Soviet psychiatrists who treat dissidents as mental cases when they themselves treated innocent people as guinea-pigs. In all the revelations about the CIA drug tests, there is only one instance of a scientist refusing to work for the Agency. Dr Robert Heath, the man who discovered the brain's "pleasure centres", was approached by a CIA doctor to work on the brain's "pain centres". He found the idea "abhorrent". "I took the stand," he said in 1975, "that if I were going to be a spy, I'd be a spy. I wanted to be a doctor and practise medicine."

THE EXPERIMENTS

"I will write you a quick letter as soon as I can get the stuff into a man or two."
– Dr Harris Isbell, in a letter to his CIA contact.

Only a handful of ULTRA's academic and medical experiments have been made public. They include:

* Experiments with LSD and other hallucinogens at the federal Addiction Research Center, Lexington, Kentucky, from 1952 to 1963. Addicts were "paid" in morphine and other drugs. LSD was administered in biscuits. Research director: Dr Harris Isbell. Funding: through Office for Naval Research. Isbell also purchased drugs for the CIA from European pharmaceutical companies who imagined they were supplying an American public health official.

* Experiments with LSD at the Boston Psychopathic Hospital, from 1952 to 1957. Subjects were staff members and students from nearby Harvard, MIT and Emerson College. Students were paid $[illegible] to drink a tall glass of water laced with acid and then take part in 10-12 hours of psychological tests. Research director: Dr Max Rinkle. Funding: SIHE.

* Experiments with LSD on about 100 prisoners at Atlanta federal penitentiary and Bordentown Reformatory, New Jersey, from 1955 to 1964. Research

director: Dr Carl Pfeiffer, who was paid $25,000 a year through the Geschikter Foundation. Pfeiffer has said all subjects gave "full informed consent"; said there were no after-effects except for some prisoners writing later to complain that the acid had "worsened their criminal careers".

* Various drug and brainwashing experiments at the Allen Memorial Institute of Psychiatry, McGill University, Montreal, from 1955 to 1960. One study involved "brainwashing patients instead of giving them drugs." In another, 30 nurses were subjected to sensory deprivation for half an hour. "One particular nurse thought there were snakes coming out from under her chair. She was listed a few months later as a schizophrenic and she had to go to the hospital." A third experiment studied the effects of thorazine and sernyl, two powerful tranquilisers. Sernyl has since been taken off the market and is now used only as an immobilising agent in animal studies. Research director: Dr Ewen Cameron. Funding: SIHE.

* In 1955, the CIA contributed $375,000 through the Geschikter Foundation to the building of a new wing at Georgetown University Medical School, Washington DC. The Agency was to get in return one-sixth of the floor space, where CIA biochemists planned to experiment with a "K" or knockout pill on terminal cancer patients. The medical school serves many of Washington's top people, and treated Edward Kennedy's son for cancer. Hospital officials have denied any knowledge of CIA involvement.

* Experiments with LSD and marijuana derivatives on 142 "sexual psychopaths" at Iona State Hospital, Michigan, from 1957 to 1960. The CIA believed that "sexual psychopaths have the kind of motivation for withholding certain information that is comparable to operational interrogation situations." Subjects were both drugged and hypnotised, then interrogated by teams of psychiatrists and psychologists. Sessions were tape-recorded, lie-detectors employed. Research director: Dr Alex Carty. Funding: SIHE. Many Iona inmates had been detained without trial under a Michigan law later ruled unconstitutional

As far as the men of the CIA were concerned, however, these academic experiments were mainly background research. "It is the firm doctrine in TSD," an Agency report said, "that testing of materials under accepted scientific procedures fails to disclose the full pattern of reactions and attributions that may occur in operational situations." The MK–ULTRA programme, indeed, specifically called for experiments with LSD and other drugs on unwitting individuals "at all social levels, high and low, native American and foreign".

The very first such test occurred in November 1953, and ended in death.

THE OLSON CASE

"Since 1953 we have struggled to understand Frank Olson's death as an inexplicable 'suicide'. Now, 22 years later, we learn that his death was the result of CIA negligence and illegality on a scale difficult to contemplate."
– Olson family statement, 1975.

Ten men attended the week-long technical meeting at a mountain resort in mid-November 1953. Four of the ten, including Dr Sidney Gottlieb, were members of the CIA. The other six were all from Fort Detrick, the US Army's top secret biological warfare research (CIA stockpiles at Detrick included anthrax, tuberculosis, food poisons, biological incapacitating agents, cobra venom, and shellfish toxin.) But Gottlieb also saw it as an ideal experimental situation. After dinner one evening, he and another Agency man, Dr Robert Lashbrook, slipped a quantity of LSD into a bottle of Cointreau. When the Detrick men had innocently drunk the liqueur, Gottlieb informed them that they had been given LSD and that their reactions would be observed.

Colonel Ruwet later described it as "the most frightening experinece I have ever had".

When Frank Olson returned home at the weekend, he was a changed man. His wife Alice has said that he "sat and brooded" and was "uncharacteristically withdrawn". Back at work he continued to show "signs of imbalance", and the following week, on November 24th, Colonel Ruwet escorted him to New York to consult psychiatrist Dr Harold Abramson.

Abramson was a former psychological consultant for the Army and one of the pioneers of LSD research in the US, much of it sponsored by the CIA. He would tell a scientific conference in 1959 that at the time of his early LSD work many of his colleagues had regarded him as "a sort of psychiatric Dracula."

Olson had two long sessions with Abramson, then returned to Washington with Ruwet on the morning of the 26th. But that same afternoon Olson returned to New York, this time accompanied by Lashbrook. They checked into Room 1018A at the Statler Hotel, and visited the psychiatrist the next morning. Abramson told Olson he was suffering from "severe psychosis and delusions" and should enter a sanitarium. Arrangements for this were made on the spot.

That evening, Olson and Lashbrook dined at the Statler's Cafe Rouge and retired to their room at 9.30 PM. They watched TV for an hour and went to bed. At about 3.20 AM Lashbrook was woken by "a crash of glass," switched on the light, saw that Olson was not in his bed, and realised that the window was broken.

That was what Lashbrook told the cops. He told Mrs Olson that he awoke to see her husband "going at a full run towards the window". He said he saw Olson "go through both the closed window and a drawn shade."

Cause of death, according to the Medical Examiner's Office, was "multiple fractures, shock and haemorrhages".

Lashbrook identified himself to the authorities as an employee of the Department of Defence. He did not tell them he worked for the CIA, nor that Olson had been suffering the effects of an involuntary acid trip, nor that Olson was under psychiatric care. The case was listed as a routine suicide.

The CIA's cover-up was rapid and efficient. Lashbrook was given temporary identification as an Army consultant. Federal employee compensation for the widow was approved six days before she filed the claim. And Lashbrook, in his Army guise, officially told her that Frank's death was "inexplicable". He did not mention the CIA.

The Olsons didn't learn the truth until 1975, following the Rockefeller Commission's report on CIA activities. They decided to sue the Agency, and issued a press statement which read in part: "We suddenly learn that for 22 years we were lied to, led to believe that Frank Olson had a fatal nervous breakdown. Thus, Frank Olson's children grew up under a double shadow, the shadow of their father's suicide and the shadowy inexplicability of that act". Son Nils told reporters that when asked about his father's death, he used to reply, "He died of concussion".

The government reacted promptly. In return for dropping their embarrassing lawsuit, Congress passed a law granting the family $750,000 compensation. And President Ford invited the Olsons to the White House and spoke to them for 12 minutes. He announced that Olson's death was "a horrible episode in American history"

MIDNIGHT CLIMAX

"Well, they'll stone you when you're trying to be so good,
"They'll stone you just like they said they would,
"They'll stone you when you're trying to go on home,
"They'll stone you when you're there all alone."
– Bob Dylan, Rainy Day Woman Nos. 12 & 35

Unphased by Olson's fate, Gottlieb and other ULTRA Officials pressed ahead with experiments on unwitting subjects. They wanted to be able to drug ordinary people in a more or less ordinary setting, so in 1955 they set up a "safehouse" in San Francisco, to which unsuspecting citizens were enticed by operatives planted in nearby bars. The subjects were entertained by prostitutes, surreptitiously administered "marijuana extract" or LSD, and observed through two-way mirrors by agents of the Bureau of Narcotics. A second "safehouse" was set up in New York City, at 103 West 13th Street, in 1961.

Both establishments consisted of adjoining studio apartments, the one for the subject's "entertainment", the other for observation. The bedroom in San Francisco was decorated with red curtains, Toulouse Lautrec posters, a painting of can-can dancers, a dressing-table trimmed with black velveteen, and elaborate concealed recording equipment. The operation was code-named Midnight Climax by an operative called Morgan Hall.

The two "safehouses" were run under an "informal arrangement" made in 1955 with "certain cleared and witting" members of the Bureau of Narcotics. This arrangement minimised the chances of CIA involvement leaking out. It was also advantageous to the narks, since some subjects were "informers or members of suspect criminal elements from whom the Bureau has obtained results of operational value". The CIA, however, worried that "Bureau agents are not qualified scientific observers". Indeed, the whole set-up was somewhat passive for Agency purposes, since subjects could only be observed, not manipulated or interrogated. Nonetheless, "the testing may be useful in perfecting delivery techniques, and in identifying surface characteristics of onset, reaction, attribution and side-effects".

It was the discovery of Gottlieb's top-secret Midnight Climax project that caused the Inspector-General's department in 1963 to investigate and review all ULTRA operations. The I-G recommended that tests on unwitting subjects should be halted – not because of any scruples about ethics or legality, simply because the risks of exposure were thought to be too great. The I-G found that "in a number of instances, the test subject has become ill for hours or days, including hospitalisation in at least one case".

The "safehouses" were shut down in late 1963, by which time hundreds, perhaps thousands, of individuals had been lured there and drugged. None of these "subjects" were physically or psychologically screened, either before or afterwards. None were ever told what had been done to them, and many must be worried to this day about the period of apparent "insanity" that followed their brief acquaintance with the friendly stranger in the bar.

CONCLUSION

"Possible sickness and attendant economic loss are inherent contingent effects of the testing."
– Inspector-General's report, 1963.

According to a recent editorial in the *Boston Globe* MK–ULTRA was "so exotic that it can best be explained as a psycho-historical fragment of the Cold War period". Press coverage has concentrated on the sensational or bizarre aspects of the CIA tests, and ignored its implications. We are even told that the hundreds of studies and millions of dollars produced, at the end of it all, zero results.

But even if many CIA projects *did* result in failure, they nevertheless acquired a vast mass of dangerous information. Scientific and technical knowledge progresses as much by finding out what doesn't work as by discovering what does.

The "Cold War aberration" theory is not a satisfactory explanation of the CIA tests. MK–ULTRA and the other programmes need to be seen in the context of a political and economic framework where individuals were (and are) regarded as expendable pawns in the global power game. The CIA's behaviour control experiments were a ruthless, sophisticated and sustained attempt to turn people into amenable tools of the State whenever the State deemed it expedient.

female plant grown in London: photographed Sept. 1978 by Chris Render

Greetings from California
AFRI #2
photos by Don Irving

EUROPE'S FIRST DOPE MAGAZINE
Home Grown

SINSEMILLA BUDS

by

Bud Reaper

BRYAN TALBOT 1981

OLD ENGLISH HERB BEER

OLLECTOR'S EDITION
Home grown
VOL.1 NO.1 45p
ADULTS ONLY
L.S.D. and the Mind Alchemyst
The Ganja of Love
Tim Leary's Declaration
Tokers Marijuana Annual Mixed
Plus Dope News and Views

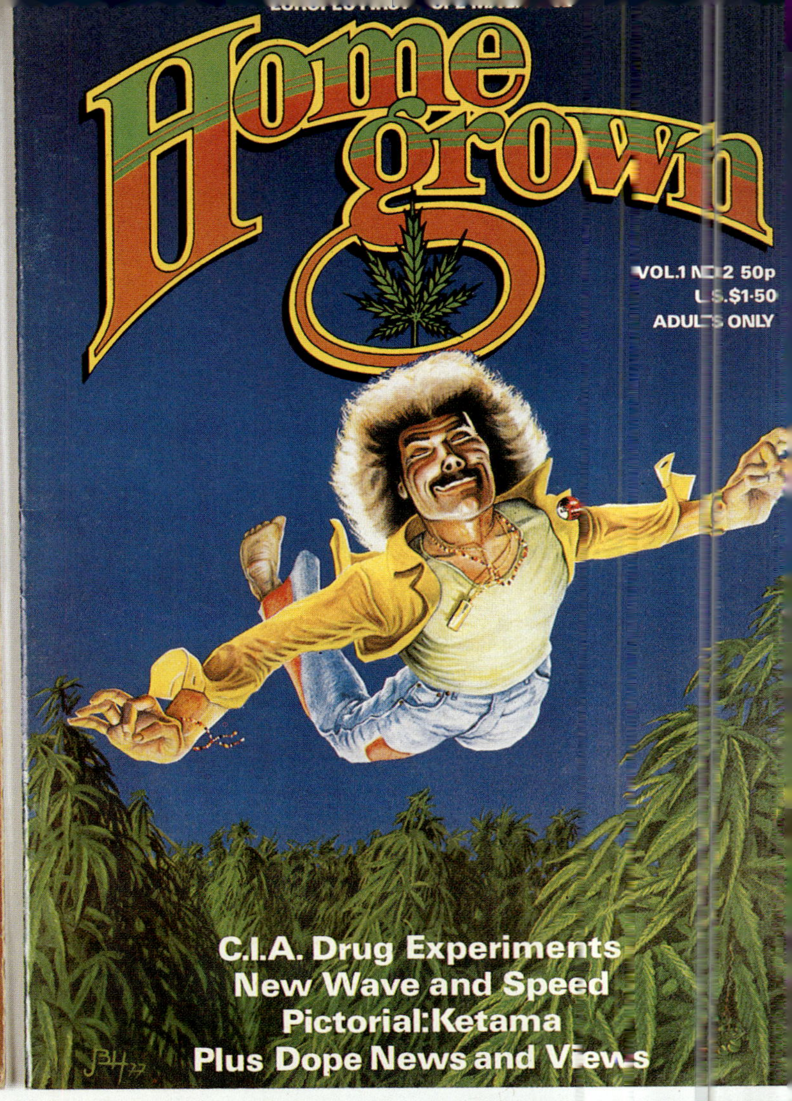
Home grown
VOL.1 NO.2 50p
U.S.$1·50
ADULTS ONLY
C.I.A. Drug Experiments
New Wave and Speed
Pictorial:Ketama
Plus Dope News and Views

EUROPE'S FIRST DOPE MAGAZINE
Home grown
VOL.1 NO.3 50p
U.S.$1·50
ADULTS ONLY

Vol.1 No.4 60p
U.S. $1·50
Home grown
ADULTS ONLY
grass roots issue
...AND FAT FREDDY'S CAT
MAMA COCA • PRISON LETTERS OF DANNY DE SOUZA
MICK FARREN'S COMPLETE HISTORY • SPIRIT OF ALBION
AMAZING CENTREFOLD • PLUS DOPE NEWS AND VIEWS

Underground comix are a modern art form with a large cult following. Like a hall of mirrors, they distort and exaggerate reality, turning the sublime into the ridiculous, the serious into absurdity, tickling the rib and poking an outrageous finger at social convention and humbug. The golden age of underground comix spawned artists like Gilbert Shelton and Robert Crumb, among others, with their unique and anarchic talents. Home Grown spoke to Gilbert Shelton, creator of Those Fabulous Furry Freak Brothers, when he was in London, and is proud to present him here, in his own words.

❛ I first smoked marijuana in Mexico in 1959, while I was going to the University of Texas. On weekends we'd drive down to Mexico, it's only 200 miles. It was just another form of entertainment. I remember we were so paranoiac at first. On the rare occasion when anyone would have marijuana to smoke we would all go into the bathroom and shut the door and put a towel under the crack in the door so that the smoke wouldn't escape and get out of the house and go down to the police station four miles away and cause the police to come and arrest us all. The laws have been changed since then, of course, and now Texas has a fairly liberal marijuana law, more liberal than California even. In those days though, you could get life imprisonment for possession of marijuana, third offence.

At the University of Texas, the Students' Association actually published a humour magazine which they paid the editor to edit, and in fact that was my education. I attended classes and got a degree, but actually my chief interest was working on the humour magazine. It was not a credit course, it was just for fun. The magazine was called The Texas Ranger. We would exchange magazines with other colleges, so the jokes and cartoons were published in more than one magazine. I did some Wonder Warthog comics, thats when I started it. There was a board of censors that had to approve of everything that went into the magazine. If the college magazines kind of mentioned dope, it would have to be a secret reference to get by the board of censors, who of course didn't know anything about marijuana. I remember it was quite a game trying to sneak things by the censors. In fact one entire editorial staff got fired all at once because they sneaked the word "fuck" by the censors by hiding it in an illustration, and after the magazine was printed and distributed to all the students, then the discovery was made. The dreaded word was printed in the magazine, so they were all dismissed.

When I was in the eighth grade, I presented a play at school that I adapted from a Donald Duck comic book, and memorised all the lines and had actors with duck costumes and beaks playing all the parts. That forced me to analyse that comic strip very closely. It was one written by Carl Barks, and it had Donald Duck, and it also had Donald's cousin, Gladstone Gander, the duck with the best luck in the world. We turned this into a fifteen-minute play. I was twelve years old at the time. After that I understood how to draw a comic strip because I had turned a comic strip into a play. I think it pointed out to me that what the comic strip could do I could not do live, and made me appreciate it. One of the things was to have an earthquake, that was part of the play. We simulated an earthquake by tossing the furniture around, that was the fun part of the play.

I always drew, I can't remember not drawing. I would copy comic strips out of the paper and draw things in my notebooks when I was supposed to be doing my homework, that sort of thing. When drawing marijuana helps a little bit because mainly it enabled me to sit still a little longer. It doesn't seem to act on that part of the brain that produces drawings, but it does produce patience, and concentration is the result. It takes hours and hours, a long time for me to finish a drawing. I'll put black ink down for awhile and then I'll cover up mistakes and changes with white paint, and then I'll go back and forth, back and forth with black ink and white paint. Maybe a real artist is somebody that can do it effortlessly, although that's the technique, I think. I don't think a good technique is necessary to make a good comic strip. It's the words and the story that are more important than the technique.

When I left college I didn't know what I was going to do. I went and looked up Harvey Kurtzman in New York City and he was very helpful. He printed my comic strips and paid me money. I was paid for the Texas Ranger job, that was a hundred dollars a month, enough to live on when I was a student. I earned as much later when I was working for Help magazine. They didn't publish as often. In fact Help finally went out of business forever in 1965. In New York I moved around a lot, you live off of other people, basically. One time in New York I lived in someone else's apartment in the living room on the sofa for three or four months. That was Terry Gilliam who is an American who now works with Monty Python. He was the assistant editor of Help magazine. He'd a humour magazine at his college too in Los Angeles, The Occidental College Fang.

In 1965 I went to California for the first time. At that time I went to Los Angeles, where I established to do the Wonder Warthog comics for Drag Cartoons. Then I moved back to Texas for two years, doing the Warthog comics and mailing them to Los Angeles. Finally that publisher went out of business in 1967, after publishing two issues of Wonder Warthog Quarterly. A sixty-four page comic book. That's what bankrupted him. Drag Cartoons had a tremendous circulation, I think it was around two-hundred thousand a month. They were very automotive oriented, most of it was done by the publisher himself, Pete Millar who is a cartoonist. I have an interest in cars and hot-rods that comes from growing up in Texas. I came to hate automobiles after I came to live in California for awhile.

Back in Texas in 1967, I and two of my friends, who happened to be working on Wonder Warthog Quarterly with me, opened up a headshop in Austin, Texas. It was the first one in all of Texas. It

I JUST GAVE THEM A LITTLE ACID!
ARRGGHH! YOU FAT
YOU'VE BEEN BURNED
"DADDY," GRUNTCAKES AND I NEED $400 SO WE CAN FLY HOME AND SEE MY DOCTOR AND MY SHRINK!
KNOCK KNOCK CRASH SLAM OPEN UP! THIS IS THE POLICE!!
CATS LOVE TO EAT KITTY KRUNCHIES!
HM.
MAYBE WE OUGHTA TRY SNAPPIER NUMBER...
I JUST LOVE THAT SHIT-KICKIN MUSIC!
FREAK
END.

was right across the street from the State Capitol building. It was first called Underground City Hall and then the name was changed to Oatwillies Campaign Headquarters. I left soon after the store opened. I couldn't stand the pressures of actually working in a headshop, even under the most favourable conditions in Texas. We put our earnings from Wonder Warthog Quarterly into that store, a cheque for a thousand dollars. We waited for months and months for that cheque. The shop is still open now, thirteen years later, due to the efforts of the current owners, the people who took it over after I left.

I suppose we were trying to imitate the Californian scene like everybody else was. We opened up a rock and roll dance hall, a big old delapidated building that had been a department store. We had remodelled and turned it into a concert hall, of sorts. I was the sign-painter. I painted a big sign for the outside front that said Vulcan Gas Company. Then I did a series of posters, each week we'd print up some nice posters, and put them up in various store windows all over town, on the model of the Avalon Ballroom and Fillmore West in San Francisco, who were having some really beautiful posters done by Victor Moscoso, Rick Griffin and Wes Wilson. Throughout '67 and '68 I was doing that. When I moved to California in '68, I seem to recall I was going to be a poster artist myself.

The Avalon Ballroom lost its licence to have concerts because of too much noise. I'd been doing posters for the Avalon Ballroom and invested in a printing press, we were printing the posters as well. When they quit giving the concerts, that's how the Rip Off Press got started. We were going to print rock and roll posters, however the reality of economics made us be in the comic book business. Besides me, there was the cartoonist Jack Jaxon and the guy who ran the printing press whose name was Dave Moriarty.

In early '68, back in Texas, I did a little ten-minute movie in black and white in 16mm called The Freak Brothers March on Capitol. Anyway, the only copy of that movie was lost. I did a comic strip to advertise the movie. In the comic strip the three Freak Brothers, Phineas, Fat Freddy and Freewheelin Franklin appear for the first time. It appeared on a single sheet of paper as a handbill. Now it's part of the Freak Brothers comic book, number one. It's the story about the giant magic marijuana seed, like Jack and the Beanstalk. People seemed to like the comic strip so much that I forgot about the movie and just kept doing the comic strips. I did it for magazines and comics. They were traded and exchanged around the underground press.

Fat Freddy's Cat first appeared when the Freak Brothers were in a weekly feature in the Los Angeles Free Press in 1970. It used to be on the back page every week with the Freak Brothers being most of the page and Fat Freddy's Cat would be a small strip down at the bottom. Which is like the old-fashioned, traditional form that the comics were in the American newspapers on Sunday. There would be a large strip and a related smaller strip. That Krazy Kat started as a small strip underneath a larger one. It was the cat that lived underneath the house that was occupied by the family. Later Krazy Kat became more important than the original large comic strip, taking up the whole page, and the original one was forgotten. I've been around cats a lot. Cats just get along better with stoned people. It certainly doesn't bother the cat if human beings just sit there and don't move, that's fine with the cat. Actually it was someone here in London who first published a separate edition of only the cat strips, a small edition but it sold fairly well. So we published our version of the same thing in San Francisco, from Rip Off Press.

I first became aware of Robert Crumb's cartoons in Help magazine. The first thing of Crumb's that I remember seeing was Robert Crumb Visits Harlem, it's kind of a spoof on a series that was in Playboy, called Shel Silverstein visits here and there. Robert Crumb's visit to Harlem wasn't funny like Silverstein's series, but instead it was a cartoony drawing of reality with all the real graffiti on the walls and everything. It was really fantastic and original stuff at the time.

Robert Crumb and his friends in San Francisco, did Zap Comix, that kind of started that side of the movement. There's a publisher in Berkeley called the Print Mint, it was doing first a comic newspaper, then a book called Yellow Dog. Then Rip Off Press started doing comix, and a third one called Last Gasp. Those three publishers started in the late sixties or early seventies. The word "comix" was probably Robert Crumb's doing with Zap Comix. For the lack of a better term, that's what it is, comix with an "x", or underground comix, but they're not, and never have been really underground.

The Fabulous Furry Freak Brothers, Number One, was printed by Rip Off Press in 1970. Up to date we've printed eight or nine hundred thousand, I should think. We keep reprinting them. I think the first print-run was 20,000. It's the famous Rip Off Press distribution system that uses the trickle technique, that is it keeps selling over a long period of time at a slow rate. That's how Rip Off Press got started, by groping around in the darkness, with the mailing list left over from the rock and roll poster business, that is the list of headhsops and record stores that sold rock and roll posters. I never had any capital, except the original 250 dollars it took to buy the printing press. I quickly refused to have anything to do with the printing press as it was too dirty to be a printer and an artist in the same lifetime. I had to do dark-room duty for awhile. Now, although I'm still an officer for Rip Off Press, I mainly do just drawing cartoons and a little public relations work, and the less I know about the business, the happier I am. That's the other department. There's Fred Todd, who's the fourth original owner, he's the president now. We are all from Texas.

I can't explain why the underground comix movement came to be centred in San Francisco, except that Robert Crumb lived there for awhile and started Zap Comix, which was the model for most of the succeeding comix. Rip Off Press just grew organically, kind of around the Freak Brothers comix. Being self-sufficient and independent was one of the most appealing things about the hippie ethic.

There's been a number of European translations of the Freak Brothers. I think Italy was the first country to translate the Freak Brothers back in '73, then France was next, then the English Fat Freddy's Cat book was done, and since then there has been various other translations, German, Danish, ten or twelve altogether. I've seen it in Finnish, Norwegian, but when I see it in Russian then I'll know it really translates.

In the summer of '79 Universal Studios in Los Angeles bought the movie rights to the Freak Brothers. I sold the rights first to Rip Off Press, and Rip Off Press in turn sold the movie rights to Universal. That's so I personally wouldn't have to be against fifty lawyers, Universal's law staff. It was a reasonable sum. The screenwriter and director is supposed to be Bill Norton. They're still working on the film or sitting on it or something, I don't really know, I'm not keeping in that close contact. The contact from my side is Dave Sheridan, who's supposed to be technical consultant, whatever that means. I trust Dave to see that it's right when they're doing it.

The Freak Brothers is being done now by Dave Sheridan and Paul Mavrides doing artwork and myself doing the writing, and I'm doing Fat Freddy's Cat by myself. That will appear in various places such as Knockabout Comix in London. I never know from one month to the next what I'll be working on. Rip Off Press, being a corporation is like a hungry live creature that is eating up everybody's lives now as it grows and grows, you know the way businesses are. I think it all started with The Whole Earth Catalogue, which had such a tremendous success ten years ago, and it led directly to other publishing and book distributing ventures which greatly strengthened the West Coast publishing thing. It strengthened what was just beginning to grow there. ❜

We would like to thank Gilbert Shelton for kind permission to reproduce excerpts from his work.

THE NEW VISION:

It was the summer of 1944, the place, New York City in war-time. A seminal sub-culture was emerging from the dark depths of the city's night haunts with its attendant mixture of hustlers, hoods, sailors, whores and jazz musicians. You could score anything around Times Square, it was a hustler's paradise. I came on the scene when I was eighteen and in the full flush of youth. I had been laid off a merchant ship having done a stint as a galley boy, and was naturally drawn to this scene, although I was a wild-eyed innocent adrift in a strange city. But I soon got the hang of it and learnt to hustle my way about. It was the beginning of my great voyage of self-discovery, my search in the big city for kicks and excitement, to experience to the depths of my being the instinctual urge of spontaneity. The Great American Dream had spewed a lot of us up, the under-privileged, the so-called spiritual and sexual cripples, who couldn't fit into their wholesome picture of what life was all about. We were the ones who didn't quite make it into their glorious war, but were affected by its consequences. There were plenty of us around and a great scene, if you were hip to it. Down in Harlem there was a new, cool and complicated jazz coming out of a club, which reflected the spirit of the times, hitting you in a strange speedy way. Man, you had to dig this new Bop, and the cats who were playing it were so cool and detached, with their berets, dark shades and goatee beards. Monday nights at Mintons young black musicians would drop in for a jam and the place would swing. There was the high-smiling Charlie 'Bird' Parker on saxophone, the mystic Thelonious Sphere Monk on piano, the great John 'Dizzy' Gillespie on trumpet and Kenny 'Klook' Clarke on drums, among others. The music was intense and powered with emotion, something quite different from Dixie and swing, and the music of that skinny crooner Frank Sinatra that you heard on the radio and nickel-odeon. This new Bebop was the music of the hipster who was evolving as an entity within the nightworld of the city, smoking reefers of grass, speeding the night away on Benzedrine, and sometimes being caught in the hazy grip of heroin or morphine. Everything was available, if you knew how to get it. If you were hip to it. Out of the psychological rubble of America, out of the bowels of this hustling, bustling city emerged the 'angel-headed hipster' ushering in, what Norman Mailer later called "the first wind of a second revolution in this century, moving not forward towards action and more rational equitable destribution, but backward toward being and the secrets of human energy'.

A SEASON IN HELL

BY AN ANGEL HEADED HIPSTER

THE BEAT GENERATION PART ONE

I had met up with a crowd who hung about at the West End Bar, mainly students at Columbia University, just across the street. They came from well-to-do homes on the whole. There was Lucien Carr, an amazingly beautiful young man with blond hair and slanted green eyes, with a lithe sensual swagger that turned men on as well as women. Although Lucien was only nineteen, he had a sophisticated, worldly outlook and a sharp, cynical wit that belied his tender youth. He was often accompanied by a tall red-bearded friend about ten years his senior, Dave Kammerer who you could see was madly in love with Lucien. And there was William Seward Burroughs, a strange kettle of fish, if ever I saw one. Somewhat cold and aloof, ordinary looking like a shy bank clerk, but well-groomed with steel-rimmed glasses, sandy hair and thin-lipped. Bill was about thirty, and was working as a bartender in the village, although he was living off a trust fund from money inherited from his family, part of the Burroughs business machine company. The three of them hailed from St. Louis. It was through them that I met this skinny Jewish lad from New Jersey with big ears and horn-rimmed glasses and burning dark eyes whose name was Allen Ginsberg. Allen, who was seventeen, had a room opposite Lucien's on the Columbia campus. I enjoyed listening to them talking about literature and books, as I had not bothered much with reading. Bill was the sort of big brother of the group putting us on to Spengler and Yeats and a host of others. There was a girl Edie Parker who used to sit there taking in all this intellectual claptrap. To me it was an awakening to new ideas which seemed strange and rather excited me.

Around June Edie Parker brought her boyfriend, who had just come back from a sea voyage, to meet the crowd at the West End. Jack Kerouac was his name, a dark-haired, athletic type who wore a sweat shirt and a black leather jacket. He was somewhat different from the others, coming from a mill town called Lowell in Massachusetts, he had won an athletic scholarship as a footballer to Columbia, and then had dropped out and got this seaman's job in the Merchant Marine. Jack, who was twenty-two, seemed to take to Lucien right away, attracted by his talk of Nietzsche and his dazzling good looks. Both of them wanted to be writers and together with Allen, who wasn't sure whether he wanted to be a social worker, labor union organiser or a poet, they would discuss the greats of literature. Allen had just finished reading Rimbaud's Season in Hell and quoted the line, "Now is the time of the hashishins". It was around that time that I first smoked grass. I had heard that it got you high, and I had a friend whom I had met at sea who knew a connection who could score some for us. The first time it didn't seem to have much effect and I was a little surprised. I had read all these articles in the newspapers about dope fiends and expected something weird and kind of depraved, instead I had this light creamy feeling, and was real hungry afterwards. I had taken Bennies before, as they were the craze, and was once up for three days and nights. I knew about morphine and heroin, through a few friends I had who'd acquired a junk habit. Most of them spent their time around Bickford's on Forty-second street, an all-nighter that attracted me with its endless comings and goings of hustlers and whores. Quite a few of the male hustlers on the street were doing it to support a habit, though you had to know a doctor to get hold of any. One night we were all at Edies's apartment on 118th street when Allen arrived with a twenty dollar box of grass and we all got high together. There was loads of laughter and a lot of crazy antics. Clever ideas were buzzing around and Bill Burroughs had us in stitches with his take-off of the laconic private dick, Sam Spade.

That summer New York was steamy hot. Jack and Lucien were making plans to go to sea, and Dave Kammerer could see that Lucien was slipping from his possessive grip. He was acting kind of strange of late, not saying much, just continually staring at Lucien who would naturally feel uneasy. Once at Bill's apartment at Bedford Street, they both grappled with a chunk of steak trying to tear it apart, another time Dave, who was becoming a pain in the ass, tried to strangle Jack's cat at Edie's place. I sensed that something could get out of hand, and it did, on the night of August the 13th. That night I saw Lucien and Dave having a drink at the West End. They hardly noticed me as they were engrossed in a heated rap. At closing time they took some beer with them and went up to Riverside Park nearby, ostensibly to get some cool air and continue their personal wrangle. Something happened between them that went out of control, and ended with Dave lying there stabbed to death with a pocket knife by Lucien. I heard that Dave tried to have sex with Lucien, but he didn't want to have no part of it. He was pawing all over him and Lucien was trying to push him off. He said he'd kill Lucien if he didn't fuck with him. Somehow Lucien stabbed him three times in the heart. Panting and sobbing he tied the hands and feet of the body with shoelaces, then tied rocks to it with pieces of his shirt, and pushed it over the side into the Hudson River. Afterwards he went over to Bill's apartment and told him what had happened. Bill listened coolly to Lucien, who was frightened out of his wits that he'd get the 'hot seat', the electric chair for what he'd just done, and advised him to get a lawyer through his parents who were well-off and give himself up to the cops. He could plead self-defence against rape, an honor slaying. Instead of doing what Bill told him, Lucien went over to Edie's place and woke up Jack to tell him what had happened. He was dry-eyed by then and ready to give himself up. Jack came out with him and kept watch while Lucien disposed of Dave's glasses and the murder weapon. His buddy was in trouble and he had to try and help him. They then went to have a last drink together, Lucien going over the incident repeatedly, telling how Dave lay there dying in his arms. Then, you wouldn't believe it, they took a cab to Lucien's psychiatrist, borrowed five dollars and went to see the movie The Four Feathers. They then wandered round Times Square, had a drink, visited the Museum of Modern Art, and then late that afternoon Lucien handed himself in to the cops.

SELF ULTIMACY:

The whole thing shook us all up, everyone was talking about it. Jack and Bill were booked as material witness to a homicide. Bill got bailed out by his family, and went back to St. Louis, but Jack couldn't raise the $ 5,000 bail bond. So he was carted off to the Bronx City Jail, known as the 'Opera House' because of the stool pigeons. He and his girl Edie devised a plan, and a week later, with special permission and under the watchful eye of a cop they got married at City Hall. A little later Edie's parents posted the bond and Jack was allowed out, and the couple left for Edie's parents' home in rich Grosse Pointe, Detroit. Only Allen was still around, but I didn't see much of him, as he was sick with hepatitis. In October, Lucien, having pleaded guilty to manslaughter was sentenced to one to twenty years in a reformatory, although he served just over two years before being paroled. By the end of the year Jack and Bill were back in town, but things weren't the same as before. The Lucien affair hung heavy over them, their talk was doom-laden and they were getting caught up in Benzedrine, removing the pads of soaked paper from the inhaler and swallowing it with cups of coffee. I bumped into Allen one night and went with him to the apartment on West 115th Street, where he was staying. It belonged to Joan Vollmer, a tall, attractive girl who was also into Bennies. She let her friends take rooms in the large apartment. Allen had just been expelled from Columbia over breaches of discipline, culminating in the Dean finding him in bed with Jack, a non-student. So they were now staying With Joan. It was in December that I saw Bill again in a bar along Eighth Avenue, he had a list with cryptic notes about gamblers' bars, fag bars, old queen bars and cheap liquor lounges, and we went to his apartment on Riverside Drive. Bill liked and respected me because I could hustle the street, I was a character of the underworld.

Bill, coming from an upper-class background and Harvard educated, was intrigued by the whole junkie, sex-hustler and thieving set that hung around some of the bars. He was a low-lifer by choice, seeking out the weird and wonderful in the gutters of life, but somehow seeming aloof from it, like an invisible intruder. Bill had got hold of some morphine syrettes and a sawn-off shotgun and wanted to get rid of them. I knew a guy who could arrange the deal, so I put Bill in touch with him. Later I went with Bill to this apartment on Henry Street. There were these two guys who had just come off a ship, and I could tell, had junk habits. The nervy little one, whose name was Herbie Huncke, thought Bill was the heat, he looked so straight and sort of out of place. The other one, Phil 'Sailor' White, looked him up and down and slowly said, "Maybe we can get a taste out of him.' We sat down at the kitchen table, someone went into the other room and brought back some grass, and rolled a few joints for us. Phil asked Bill how many syrettes he had. Several gross of them, was the answer. Some guy had ripped them off a drugstore. He then took a handful of syrettes from his pocket and flung them on the table. It brought a gleam to Sailor's eyes, who was just dying to shoot up. Bill gave them a taste, and as they cooked it, he decided that he'd also try some. It was his first time. I decided against taking a fix, and just went on smoking a joint. He took off his suit jacket and rolled up his sleeve, watching intently as Herbie and Sailor shot up. Now it was his turn, he was rather hygienic about it all, rubbing alcohol on his arm and cleaning the spike, watching them tying the tourniquet. Then he turned his head away as Herbie stuck in the spike, drew some blood and then took it out. The tourniquet was too tight so he loosened it and peered down as morphine shot into his arm. He closed his eyes and after awhile said, "Well, that's quite a sensation." He opened his eyes and nodded, "that's very interesting", as if he was appraising the situation scientifically. So that was Bill's first fix. The next day the deal was done with Sailor, and him and Herbie started seeing a lot of Bill. They had a common interest in the sweet taste of junk, the bright neon lights of Times Square, and the predators and prey of the city of night.

January 1945, out of the blue, Bill suddenly married Joan Vollmer, and moved into the apartment at 115th Street, although we all knew he preferred the young mavericks of the street. Edie had returned to join Jack, but they soon split up and she went back home. Allen was getting rather hung up on Jack, who didn't know if he should give in to his persistent demands. Jack was getting into a heavy Bennies thing, often sitting up all night scribbling in his little note book. Joan was speeding around the place trying to keep a semblance of order. I would drop in quite often. Sometimes Sailor and Herbie Huncke would be sitting around. Bill used to meet them at the Angler Bar, or hanging out at Whelan's Drugstore, on Seventh and 47th. Jack would tag along as they'd roam through the motley crowd of hoods, drag queens and other zombies of the night. I often saw them at the Greyhound Terminal, or in one sleazy bar or another. Sometimes Allen could be seen wandering about dreaming visions of the night. Here was life in the raw, spontaneous and vibrant with primitive animal energy. They were the seekers of souls, the street wanderers of the night, sensually exploring their emotions with an obsessive zeal, seeing in the rejects of this most abundant society. festering maggots that would bring the whole edifice crashing down. Herbie Huncke, the Professor Hip, led the way into this crazy twilight zone as if it were a triumphal processional, a holy place for saintly sinners. Bill had developed a devouring junk habit to match those of Sailor and Herbie. He was able to buy morphine scripts from a doctor on 102nd Street, but it was not enough. He and Sailor, who was an adept at picking pockets, 'worked the hole', rolling drunks down the subway. Jack had turned pale and gaunt from endless nights on Bennies, his wiry physique now resembled a bag of bones, with haunting eyes staring from his hollow face. Benzedrine intensified his awareness and made him feel clever. But it was a revelation into the self, a look into the dark corners of the mind, a struggle for identification in a world gone mad, the beginning of a new vision that would make them soar above the night, bursting with fresh imagery and apocalyptic flights of poetry.

"I saw the best minds of my generation
destroyed by madness, starving
hysterical naked.
dragging themselves through the negro
streets at dawn looking for an angry
fix,
Angelheaded hipsters burning for the
ancient heavenly connection to the
starry dynamo in the machinery of
night,
who poverty and tatters and hollow-eyed
and high sat up smoking in the super-
natural darkness of cold-water flats
floating across the tops of cities
contemplating jazz . . . .
who pass through universities with radiant
cool eyes hallucinating Arkansas and
Blake-light tragedy among the scholars
of war, . . .
who got busted in their pubic beards
returning through Laredo with a belt
of marijuana for New York,
who ate fire in paint hotels or drank
turpentine in Paradise Alley, death, or
purgatoried their torsos night after
night . . .
who chained themselves to subways for
the endless ride from Battery to holy
Bronx on benzedrine until the noise of
wheels and children brought them
down shuddering mouth-wracked and
battered bleak of brain all drained of
brilliance in the drear light of Zoo, .
Visions! omens! hallucinations! miracles
miracles! ecstasies! gone down the
American river!"

From Howl by Allen Ginsberg. Howl and Other Poems, City Lights Books, 1956.

JOURNEY TO THE END OF THE NIGHT

BY AN ANGEL HEADED HIPSTER
THE BEAT GENERATION PART TWO

The Winter of 1945 was icy cold and New York was a mean place for a hungry hustler. I was feeling weary and worn out by the incessant drift from one night haunt to another. After awhile, the scene sort of draws in on you and you feel trapped by your very own devices. Everybody looks mean and ugly after several nights up on Benzedrine, a nightmare of ragged characters all on edge. I was hooked on observing it all, lapping it up with compulsive zeal until I felt whacked and satiated. For some it was a time for whooping it up. The War was over in a great big Mushroom Cloud and it was the dawning of a new era of American progress and prosperity. The G. I.'s were back home, all rearing to go after the bitch-goddess that lures with dreams of money and success. But for me there was nothing but the daily grind of hustling to keep both body and soul together. Where did the good times go, the mad people that burn themselves out, those that are beat and gone? What happened to that close bunch of buddies that filled my days and nights with such gleeful joy? When you're feeling down, you look back and it all seems to glow, you get flashes and insights, fleeting glimpses that warm your soul. So much had happened this year, so many changes to ring out the old and usher in the new. We seemed to have just drifted apart, gone our separate ways due to chance or circumstance. By that Summer the communal apartment on 115th Street had broken up in a shambles. Things had just got out of hand. There is nothing like an impending bust to get everybody jumpy, and that's the way it was.

Old Bill Burroughs, caught in his junk trap, was starting to feel the heat catching him up. The world of junk is full of informers, and in no time they were on to Herbert Huncke, and then Bill. To get him out of trouble, Bill's parents had suggested that he move down to Texas. He found a smallholding near a little town called New Waverly, about fifty miles from Houston, and moved down there with Joan and her little daughter, Julie, with the intention of growing marijuana to sell on the New York market. Allen Ginsberg, who had worked in a shipyard and enrolled in the Maritime Service Training Station, shipped out as a messboy on a tanker heading South. And Jack Kerouac split back home to his parents' apartment in Ozone Park, where his father was dying of stomach cancer. The Benzedrine had been too much for Jack, and by December he had developed Thrombophlebitis in his legs, and was in the Veterans' Administration Hospital in Queens with his legs up on a pillow swathed in hot compresses. Looking back on it all in calm recollection, it was our journey to the end of the night.

In a way, we were all licking our wounds, lying low in fallow, for there is almost nothing time cannot heal. Winter is always followed by the Spring. I had heard by telegram that my father had died on the third of May 1946, and by some strange coincidence, Jack's father had died on the very same day. I didn't see much of Jack at that time, as he was staying at home writing a book incorporating some of his experiences. So it was time for me to leave New York for my father's funeral, and to comfort my mother and young brothers and sisters back home in Philadelphia, where I spent the rest of that year. At first it was great to be back home, the prodigal son returned to the fold. My mother was hoping I'd had enough of my "gutter-snipe days", as she called it, and that I'd meet a nice local girl, get a steady job and just settle down like all the rest of the people she knew. Sooner or later I knew the game was up and I'd have to return once more to Times Square, with its hustle and bustle, and all it entails. Having paid my filial dues to my family, I arrived back in New York fresh into the new year of January 1947, with a neat stash of dollars to see me by until I got a job as a soda-jerk or bartender. Those first few days I felt like a stranger as I wandered into the Angler Bar and Whelan's, looking for familiar faces. I soon bumped into Vicki Russel, a real character who was a seasoned hustler from way back, into the junk scene and doing tricks. She was a tall girl who managed somehow to retain her wide-eyed innocence and vulnerability, despite the active life she led. Through her old friend Herbert Huncke, we'd all met her and spent many crazy hours in her company. Once when Jack had become pale and thin from the Bennies, she'd applied pancake make-up to his face so that he wouldn't feel conspicuous while travelling on the subway. It was through her that I learned what had happened in my absence, who was still about and what they were doing. First of all, Lucien Carr had recently come out of prison on parole. On New Year's Eve, she and Lucien, Jack and a girl named Celine had gone to see the movie, Crime and Punishment, and then went on to some socialite parties getting crazy drunk. Allen had gone back to Columbia to study, but was still very much on the scene, experimenting with drug-induced poetics. And Herbie, who had taken a fall for possession of a five-dollar bag of heroin and done six months on Rikers Island, had gone to sea but was now back again. Of course, Bill was still in Texas, though Joan had turned up the previous fall, but too many Bennies had sent her to Bellevue Hospital Psychiatric Wing. It felt great to be back on Times Square.

It was around this time that a new character entered our lives, to lift us back into pulsating life and energise our rather beat existence. His name was Neal Cassady, fresh, vibrant, and bounding with animated excitement, and a sort of primitive sexual magnetism unrestrained by social convention. We had heard talk of Neal from Hal Chase, who stayed at the apartment on 115th Street and was also at Columbia. Hal had known Neal in Denver, his home town, before he had come up to Columbia to study philosophy, and on returning on vacation had told Neal about the mad gang in the big city, whetting his appetite for more thrills and kicks. It was at the West End Bar that I caught my first glimpse of Neal, sitting in a booth with Hal and this dishy young chick. I just nodded to Hal, and went to join my party in the next booth. I could hear this insane giggle of glee from the next table, and this torrent of words bubbling over excitedly as Neal got into his rap. Eventually, my curiosity got the better of me and I edged up on to the seat next to Hal, nonchalantly introducing myself to Neal and the honey of a blonde who was hanging on to him. I found out that she, Luanne, was his wife and turned out to be only fifteen. Bright-eyed and fresh-looking, with loose curls of hair, she sat starry-eyed taking Neal all in. Neal was two years younger than I, at twenty, and really enjoying the New York scene. Soon we were talking about pool, both Neal and I had a common hankering after seedy pool haunts. Neal had spent many an hour gracing the pool-tables of down-town Denver with his presence. He was mad about cars, and had acquired his learning experience at the age of fourteen when he engaged in a compulsive game of joy-riding. From then until he was eighteen, he had "borrowed", by his own count, some 500 cars, been arrested ten times, convicted six times, and spent fifteen months in reformatory. He was then working as a parking lot attendant at the Hotel New Yorker on 34th Street, moving cars around, swerving in and out of crammed spaces at a bouncy speed, and handling the wheel with magnificent ease. That was Neal, full of go, baring his adventures in a racy onslaught, randomly picking up crazy scenes from the past that gripped me with awed excitement. In the strange and lonely world of Times Square, I'd met the weird and wonderful, each with his or her own story to tell of a broken home, not being wanted and left to drift like garbage around the gutters. With Neal I felt a strong rapport. He called himself the "unnatural son of a few score beaten men", as at the age of six he'd gone to live in a bum skidrow hotel with his wino father, washing himself in the mornings in a common bathroom stinking with vomit and filth, surrounded by sad, old derelicts sprucing up for a day's begging. His experience and easy acceptance of situations, his open-faced candour and inate instinct for the beat of life, touched me quite deeply.

Hal had already brought Jack over to the cold-water flat in Spanish Harlem where Neal and Luanne were staying. It was an inopportune moment, as Neal opened the door to them stark naked, erection at half-cock, with Luanne jumping off the couch and out of view. Soon the seeds of a great friendship were sown. In Neal, Jack saw a brother-sufferer, a "wild yea-saying overburst of American joy" that made his heart pound faster. Neal was thirsty for intellectual knowledge, having read a few shelf-lots at reformatory, and admired Jack's knowledge and understanding of some of the great classics of literature, eagerly engaging him in great debate. Jack told Neal about the novel he was writing, *The Town and the City*, which figured different aspects of himself put into the sons of a family. As Neal and Jack became friends and went out, Luanne was left back at the flat more often. On one of these night-outs, I ran into Neal and Jack at the West End, and we had a drink. I was going to Vicki Russell's apartment in the East Eighties to smoke grass, or get high on some tea, as we called it. Neal had not smoked marijuana before and was eager to get high. They were to have picked up two coloured girls in a diner, but had been stood up, so we made our way up to Vicki's rather small studio apartment. She let us in with her dreamy eyes glassed up and shining, the sweet smell of tea

catching in our nostrils, and bop blowing from a horn on the radio. And who should be sitting on a stool, puffing on a water pipe, his large, dark eyes staring up at us? None other than Allen, whom I'd not seen since my return. Neal had met Allen briefly when Hal introduced them at the West End, but they'd not spoken much. Of course, they knew quite a lot about each other, through their mutual friendship with Hal. Allen lit up the water pipe, and we soon got nice and high. Neal and Allen just connected, and charged each other up. Neal was sitting there, his eyes gleaming in the half-light, his head bobbing up and down, exclaiming "yes, yes," and "that's right," as Allen opened up to him. Jack just sat back watching the two of them getting off on one another, ranting and raving on, getting higher and high-

er and more carried away. I could see Neal's features change, his face softening in moments of repose, and then he was off babbling away, a wicked, know-all glint in his eyes, arms flaying the air in bursts of hyper-manic exaltations. Jack likened them to "the holy con-man with the shining mind, and the sorrowful poetic con-man with the dark mind". The next morning we wandered off, still high and in exuberated spirits, Jack and I tagging behind the two of them.

During the following week Neal, who was working at the parking lot during the day, divided his time in the evenings between Luanne, three nights of love-making and fighting, Jack, two evenings in rapt intellectual conversation, and Allen, two nights staying up all night, seeing how far they could go before they bugged one another. Nobody but Neal with his abundant energy could have done it. Late one night Neal and Allen and some friends ended up at the tenement apartment I shared with a friend on 104th Street. As it was late, they stayed the night. There weren't enough beds, so Neal and Allen shared the same bed, and although Neal only seemed interested in making it with girls, he pulled Allen to him, and they became lovers for the first time. Though roughly the same age, Allen being nervous and self-conscious, was overwhelmed by Neal's lack of inhibition, and confident ease in sexual relationships. He fell in love with Neal, and they swore vows of love the following week. There was a great emotional bond between them, each filling a need in the other. As Allen got hooked on Neal, he in turn became more highly charged sexually to Jack but nothing came of it, and the three of them spent a lot of time together getting high on tea, drunk on beer, or speeding on Bennies. Meanwhile Luanne who had had enough, returned to Denver in a huff. Before she left she told Neal that the cops were looking for him because he was buying too much of that marijuana. A short while later, on the 4th of March, 1947, Neal Cassady left New York for Denver on a Greyhound bus headed west, wearing a dark-pinstriped business suit that he'd bought to impress the boys at the poolhall. Allen and Jack had both gone to see him off. They planned to meet together in Denver in the Summer, and who knows, they could go to Bill Burroughs' ranch-type place in Texas and introduce Neal to Bill. Then Neal was gone, and as I huddled up against that bitter March wind, New York seemed tight and cramped, lacking in life and lustre. I thought I kept hearing Neal's voice yelling my name from behind when the wind blew and howled, laughing madly in my ear, "He-he-hee-hee-hee", like the holy goof he was.

". . . The only people for me are the mad ones, the ones who are mad to live, mad to talk, mad to be saved, desirous of everything at the same time, the ones who never yawn or say a commonplace thing, but burn, burn, burn like fabulous yellow roman candles exploding like spiders across the stars and in the middle you see the blue centrelight pop and everybody goes 'Awww!' "

From *On The Road* by Jack Kerouac, Penguin Modern Classics.

THE DECLINE OF THE WEST

BY AN ANGEL HEADED HIPSTER

THE BEAT GENERATION. PART 3.

ILLUSTRATIONS-LAYOUT:- EDWARD BARKER

I often thought of Neal Cassady after he left New York for Denver in the spring of 1947 and knew deep down that it was only a matter of time before I'd see him again. I heard news of him though soon after he'd gone. He wrote Jack Kerouac a letter which he showed to Allen Ginsberg and I. Jack called it "the great sex letter", a drunken rambling story describing two hilarious and horny sexual encounters on the long bus journey home.

Neal's scrawling letters with their bad spelling and full of street-talk, had an ease and flow that Jack and Allen dug. Jack was doing quite a lot of writing himself, sitting at the kitchen table of his mother's apartment in Ozone Park, burning the midnight oil, trying to reach the halfway point in the novel he was working on, his literary knowledge inhibiting him from writing with Neal's spontaneous urgency. When he arrived in Denver I received a letter from Neal begging me to send him two overcoats in his size so that he could sell them and earn some bread. He knew of my penchant for gently removing coats off the stands at certain restaurants and cloakrooms. He needed them in a desperate hurry, putting this heavy obligation on to me. But he moved around quite a bit and I was never sure if they would get to him. I saw one of the many letters he wrote to Allen, who was profoundly moved by the love and need they expressed. Neal knew how to open himself up if he wanted to, displaying a gentle loving side that needed to be wanted and desired. To Allen he poured out in great flows of honesty the woes in his heart, his unsettled being fluctuating between the hassles of making ends meet, convincing Luanne to stay with her mother and trying to tie an emotional knot with Allen. Meanwhile Allen was preparing to join Neal that summer to cement their deepening friendship, and Jack was planning to meet up with them in Denver on his way to join an old school chum in San Francisco and become a seaman.

Before Allen left in June, we spent a night together roaming around our favourite haunts on Times Square, and spent the early hours of the morning at the Pokerino, watching the nightly drift of men who had nowhere to go and nothing but time on their hands. Allen had written a story in which he'd described the joint, and showed it to me. He sure had a way with words: ". . . beat, absolutely beat, characters . . . Teaheads from everywhere, hustlers with pimples, queens with pompadours, lushes with green faces, fat dicks with clubs, cherubs with sycophants, wolves with adenoids, faces with blotches, noses with holes, eyebrows with spangles, old men with the horrors, bums with the stumbles, and some squares with curiosity or just passing through to catch a bus . . ." We wondered what had happened to Herbert Huncke, now that he was away from the scene, staying with Bill and Joan Burroughs in Texas helping them grow marijuana and oriental poppies. We laughed as we recalled the time he'd blown marijuana smoke at the cockroaches so they wouldn't mess around with his bread and jam. Allen was looking forward to introducing Neal to Bill in Texas after they had spent some time together in Denver.

While Allen departed by Greyhound bus to Denver, Jack decided that he would hitchhike to San Francisco, spending a few days in Denver en route. One evening at the apartment in Ozone Park we sat poring over maps of the United States, and on a road-map was one long red line called Route 6 that led from the tip of Cape Cod clear to Ely, Nevada, and there dipped down to Los Angeles. Like the pioneer settlers one hundred years before him, he would blaze a trail of adventure as he crossed the country with the setting sun in his eyes heading west to California. After his mother had gone to bed, we sat in the kitchen high on Benzedrine rapping about all sorts of things. He let me read a few pages from the novel he was working on called The Town and the City, a sprawling tale about a family and their five sons. Jack had an amazing memory and in poetic images had captured the yearnings of a youth growing up in these times. He kept journal notes of odd incidences and events that he'd witnessed, and had put some of his friends into the novel like Lucien Carr, Allen, Bill, and Dave Kammerer, though he'd kept the stabbing out and romanticised it as a suicide. It was on this night that we realised that we shared a common sorrow, both our dads having died on the same day just over a year ago. Now at the age of twenty-five, having been a failure in his father's eyes for his lack of material achievement, he felt free to make his odyssey of self-discovery and in the process discover America. His mother, who was possessive and clinging, was resigned to the fact of his leaving, and in July he was gone. I could picture him walking across the land, strange and raggedly like a prophet.

It was not long before sporadic accounts of what was happening in Denver filtered their way back to me, sometimes from Neal himself in a jumbled note on Allen's typewriter. Allen described this period as "The Denver Doldrums", and no wonder. Even before he arrived, Neal had met up with a beautiful blonde who was studying at the University of Denver. Carolyn Robinson was her name, a Bennington graduate. Neal was quite stuck on her, and somehow she produced a sense of peace in him when they were together. He was still seeing Luanne on the quiet, as they had

. . . he would blaze a trail of adventure as he crossed the country with the setting sun in his eyes . . .

a strong sexual thing going between them, and there was Allen trying to resume their love affair in Neal's six dollar a week basement room. But Neal seemed to thrive on these endless emotional complications, rushing from one to the other and engrossing them with his marathon monologues as proof of how much he loved them. Allen felt dejected, as if he had been duped and manipulated by Neal. He was hurt and confused as he sat in the basement room trying to compose sad and heavy poems, waiting for Neal to turn up, often hours later than he promised. Then they would screw, take Bennies, and talk and write poems throughout the night. When Jack arrived, that was the situation he found. Allen took him round to the rooming house where Neal was banging Carolyn. He knocked on the door and Neal opened it stark naked and greeted him with genuine excitement, and later the three of them spent many hours together like old times in New York. But soon Jack ran out of money and after wiring his mother for more, set out on his journey to California in August, while Carolyn left to work in San Francisco and the divorce papers with Luanne were being sorted out. Neal and Allen decided that the time was right to go and pay old Bill a visit in Texas.

Well, I heard all about the Texas escapades from both Neal and Huncke when they came back to New York that autumn. Bill and Joan, who had given birth to a baby boy that July, had a cabin with some land in a sparsely populated area some fifty miles from Houston. It was beautiful bayou country and quite remote, as you can imagine. It beats me how they and Huncke made out during that period, hunting down supplies from all the drugstores in every town within a radius of fifty miles so many times that people were getting to wonder what was going on. Huncke and Bill were buying paregoric, sometimes in half gallons, and all the barbiturates they could get hold of, and a constant supply of Benzedrine inhalers for Joan, who went through them in no time. They also regularly copped marijuana from a coloured connection they had made in Houston, often smoking joints with the man and his old lady. Sometimes Huncke would score a young seaman and take him back to his hotel room to get stoned and then have sex. Bill had this jeep which meant that Houston was in easy reach. And sure as he said, Bill had this home-grown patch of marijuana plants that grew very tall by the late summer. Bill was thoroughly enjoying playing the country squire, practising his shooting with guns from a collection he was acquiring. In August Allen and Neal arrived and at first Bill didn't quite take to Neal as Allen would have liked, thinking him a conman. Then the sleeping arrangements were not to Allen's liking. He tried with Huncke's help to build a mutual bed out of two army cots for him and Neal to sleep together in, but it sagged in the middle and the whole thing was a miserable failure. Neal couldn't stand Allen touching him, and the more Allen tried, Neal found himself shutting off from him. Huncke would play his Billie Holliday records on the porch in the hot afternoons but Bill would request him to play Viennese waltzes on the tinny phonograph. After a week of rejection, feeling emotionally shattered by Neal's behaviour, Allen left to ship out to sea on a freighter carrying wheat to Dakar in Africa. The voyage took two months and the monotonous routine and isolation of the long sea trip made him feel introspective and brought about "The Dakar Doldrums".

That fall Bill, Huncke and Neal drove to New York with the jeep filled with mason jars of marijuana that they'd just harvested, ready to sell on the streets. Joan and the kids followed by train. In a matter of days I bumped into Neal and Huncke who were trying to fix up a connection to sell the tea. They'd tried a bellhop at one of the hotels but he wasn't interested because it was green and hadn't been cured. I took them to this chick's place in the Village and we tasted some, as Bill had given them a sample, and although it made me cough and splutter, it sure got me high. We all sat on the floor listening to records and blasting as Neal kept rolling them up. He was rapping to this girl who nodded in response, murmuring "that's cool" to everything Neal was saying. Later she gavc a whole pile of her records to him, as she saw that he really could get into the sounds. I had a headache which the smoke completely cleared, it was so good. A couple of days later I made a connection and Bill, Huncke and myself went up to do the deal while Neal stayed with the jeep and the jars of tea. After a bit of haggling we sold most of it to these four dagos for a hundred dollars. Of course the moment Bill hit town and had found a cheap hotel room, he made contact with an old junky friend who turned him on. He hadn't had any junk for about six weeks, except for the paregoric he'd melted down, and he got very spaced out. I took Joan out on Times Square late one night so she could get a can of milk for the baby, though I was a bit embarrassed by the straggly dress that she was wearing. Nobody else seemed to have minded in the cafetaria, and in fact, most of them dug her as she was so flipped out. Then Bill's parents came to see the baby, and they installed him into one of those exclusive beach clubs out on Atlantic beach. He lent Neal the jeep and we'd pick up junk and drive out there, about thirty miles, to get it to him. Soon Neal became restless and a bit

We all sat on the floor listening to records and blasting as Neal kept rolling them up.

tired of the running about, and managed to hustle fifty bucks off a friend of mine, promising to pay him back and all that, and left for San Francisco to join Carolyn, with the pile of records that girl had given him. Ironically, shortly after he left both Allen and Jack arrived back in New York from their respective trips.

As the winter of 1947 grew dark and cold, I felt a deep yearning to see my mother and brothers and sisters again, there were seven of us, and decided to put my pride in my pocket and go back home for awhile to rest my weary body from the frenzied pace of my Times Square existence. I'd had enough and felt that I was going round the bend. I needed to be back in the fold, cosetted and protected from a cruel and cold world, to feel the warmth and care of the mother I had left as soon as I was old enough. I stayed at home in Philadelphia that Christmas, bathing in the warmth of family togetherness, eating proper meals regularly for the first time in ages. I worked that winter as a warehouseman packing orders of kitchen utensils and crockery in a wholesale goods depot. By the spring of 1948, I was on the high seas again having shipped out on a cargo vessel bound for Marseille, working as a messman. I did that one trip and was glad to get back to New York once again to be part of the scene with renewed vigour and fresh energy. Huncke was the first one I ran into and we had a good time together spending my hard-earned money until it ran out. Bill and Joan and the children were now living in Algiers, a town just outside New Orleans in Louisiana. They had purchased a hundred acres of land in easy reach of New Orleans where Bill could obtain drugs in the seamy French Quarter with its beguiling mix of gamblers, drifters, seamen, tourists, whores and homosexuals, just like his New York habitat. Earlier in the year, when he was still hanging around Times Square, he had voluntarily committed himself to Lexington Narcotics Farm in Kentucky, and had undergone a cure, but left when the withdrawal symptoms had eased and stayed off junk for four months. Since Jack had come back from his cross-country trip, he had hardly been seen around, and by the summer had at last completed "The Town and the City". It was a thousand-page novel, written in a batch of student notebooks which he carried around in a shabby leather doctor's bag, so that he could show our crowd sections of it. I happened to have read some of it and was filled with admiration, wanting to read on and on. He seemed to be quietly pleased with himself and enjoyed the warm reaction of friends. He had been in correspondence with Neal who was living with Carolyn in San Francisco and working as a brakeman on the railroad. Neal was going to be a father in September, and Luanne was going through with the divorce, so that the baby could be born in wedlock. She was now also living there and had a fiance who was a seaman. Allen hadn't quite got over Neal since his return. That spring he was back at Columbia and living by himself in a dark and narrow cold-water flat in a slum tenement in Spanish Harlem. During the summer vacation he was working two hours a day as a file-clerk and spending his time aimlessly idling about or just brooding on things. To make things worse, his mother was going through one of her periodic bouts of madness and was in the Pilgrim State Hospital. I would visit him in that dingy apartment and we would end up seeing the utter futility of life, Allen feeling like "an eccentric dope in a world of mechanical supermen."

In July of that hot summer of 1948, Allen was lying on his bed reading the poems of William Blake having just masturbated for no love over Neal, his 'ultimate psycho-spiritual sexo-cock jewel fulfillment", when he had a visionary experience in which he heard Blake's illumined voice and felt that he had been chosen to experience a vast cosmic consciousness. Here he was, all of twenty two years old, becoming aware of a deeper, real universe, penetrating the surface of things, and perceiving the living hand that had placed it all in front of him. He understood Blake's dictum that the 'eye altering alters all". A sensation of light permeated his body and he awakened to experience what Blake saw, "Eternity in a grain of sand/Infinity in an hour". In his heightened state of awareness, with a sense of cosmic awe, he completely lost all sense of his body, normal time, and normal consciousness. When he looked out of the window at the old apartment buildings opposite, with an altered sense of perception, he became transfixed by the craftsmanship of the cornices of the tenement, the intelligence of the work-man who laid the bricks, the architect that had thought of it, the man who had smelted the piece of tin to make a cornucopia, the miner who had dug it out of the earth, the earth that had gone through eons of preparing it, the little molecules that had slumbered, and out of all of this he had a breakthrough from ordinary habitual consciousness into seeing heaven in the cornices of a building. For the next couple of weeks Allen was in an exalted state of mind and the visionary feeling came over him once again when he was reading a volume of Blake in the campus bookstore. He perceived that everybody was completely conscious, but that the fixed expressions that people have, the habitual expressions, the manners, the mode of talk, are all masks hiding this consciousness. But it

was difficult trying to explain all this to his friends, some of whom, thought he was going crazy. Why, who has visionary experiences in these modern times? He was seeing a Reichian analyst at the time, but was kicked out of therapy for smoking marijuana. Allen threw a party at the apartment one evening and a whole crowd of us came. I spoke to Jack, who was getting into the beer and having a ball. He was hoping that Neal would be able to make it to New York, or he would hitch-hike out to join him in California. The manuscript of his novel had been sent to a publisher, but had been turned down and was now at another publishing house. He was toying with ideas for a new book and finally decided to write about his trip across the country. It was going to be called, On The Road.

The late Forties were a strange time, a crazy time for us and America, which was in the grips of the Cold War that permeated an atmosphere akin to paranoia. We were the guardians of a free world fighting against the insidious menace of Soviet-dominated world Communism. Patriotism, that last refuge of the scoundrel, was rife with ardour, fuelled by the new technocrats, men who had too much money and controlled too many things. The ruthless power and looney fanaticism of the military mind held sway, bringing with it a stifling conformity in the name of God, the progress of technology, the family, and cleanliness and order. Mass Society emerged giving birth to One Dimensional Man who was encouraged only to consume, never to decide. Wht Allen Ginsberg called the Syndrome of Shut-down began, moving towards a closed society where all decisions would be secret, no final authority, rule by Nobody. This was the era that gave us that greatest of modern inventions, sliced bread in vacuum packs, along with the plethora of plastic products that would make us part of this planned obscolescence. It seemed as if the Second World War and the Atom Bomb that ended it, had so traumatised the post-war American psyche that only fear and loathing existed, soothed by mass conditioning through the media. Never has the desire for security been so strong, and never were people more insecure. To play against the system with its air of general anxiety about so much of no real avail, took a great deal of guts, for almost any action or aberration that was not considered common-place took a disproportion of courage to enact. It was in this climate that we experienced America, seeking the rebellious imperatives of the Self, a burning consciousness of the present through ecstatic states of being, be they madness, visions, sexual explorations, or just getting high on marijuana, benzedrine, booze or junk.

It was in this scenario of mayhem that I existed in the bowels of night city life, digging the free-flow beat of bop while high on tea, feeling the pulsating rhythms of New York in all its frenzy. I was an angel-headed hipster adrift in an eternal nightworld that seethed almost beyond the reach of the law. Being a seasoned hustler on those mean and moody streets taught me a lot about people that I couldn't have picked up elsewhere. I got to know so many of the characters that hung about, the whores who'd scored a john and were flash with their dollars around the bars, the cool black pimps in zoot-suits, who strutted about as if they owned the streets, the fly-merchant dope dealers that were here today and gone tomorrow, always out for a fast buck, the junkies in alleyways, endlessly waiting for the man to show up. Somehow we all seemed so inter-connected, part of a scene. If marijuana, or tea, wedded us together, the child was the language of Hip which gave expression to abstract states of feeling which we all shared at least all who were Hip. In the infinite variations of the new black jazz that stirred the soul and gave voice to our feelings of sensual pleasure, through the languid flow and spontaneity of bop, and the cool musicians who played it, we felt a deep affinity with the black man and the cultural dowry he brought with him, an ability to survive on the streets with a cool cunning and a consummate mental alertness so attuned to his surroundings that it must have derived from the art of the primitive. Here I was, in my early twenties, almost a deft hand at street survival, picking up the nuances and cadence of a scene that I felt irresistibly drawn to. I lived through these years, and recall the events that took place as part of this hip way of being, for a new breed of white urban adventurers drifted out at night looking for action with a black man's code to fit their facts.

Sacred and profane, holy herb and million dollar wealth spinner, healing of the nations and dope for guns, the ganja tree in Jamaica spreads wide its leaves. The symbolic power of that little tree of knowledge remains immense, raising dreams of freedom, peace and love, inner vision, revolution.

BIBLES IN THE GANJA FIELDS

by TIM MALYON

Photos by Tim Malyon

"A cultivation with about 5000 growing ganja trees and a nursery, containing about 2000 seedlings was found in the hills of Longville . . . and destroyed by a party of police . . . An open Bible, showing the 27th Psalm ('For in the time of trouble, the Lord shall hide me in his pavilion: in the secret of his tabernacle shall he hide me.') and held down by 2 stones, was found in the field on the ground. No arrest was made." (from The Jamaican Star)

"And if we should live up in the hills . . .' (Burning Spear)

The path climbed steeply, spiralling up towards higher heights, Blue Mountain Peak, at 7402ft the island's summit. Tiny terraced fields clung to the slope, irrigated by streams and intricate piping systems constructed from the ubiquitous bamboo pole. It felt good to be out, away from the oppressive heat of downtown Kingston, pacing the mountain in the morning light, breath and feet moving with one rhythm which held back tiredness. By the first wooden shack of the last village a young Rastaman stood and blew sweet smoke into the still air. As he saw me an inquisitive smile lit up his open, dignified face. I maintained pace, meditating on the stride, meeting smile with smile, returning his

frank gaze. Silently he fell in beside me, pace for pace, passing the spliff. Thus we trod easily up the village, burning herbs without a word.

"There's a natural mystic blowing through the air,
If you listen carefully now, you will hear." (Bob Marley)

Above the village we rested, squatting on the crest of the hill where I had gratefully dropped my pack. The sensation of throwing off a heavy pack after long trekking is one of joyous weightlessness, flying. On the opposite side of the crest to the village, far below us, lay a patchwork of fields and chaotic bush in a deep, bowl shaped valley. Raising eyes to the hills, the sun was setting behind Blue Mountain Peak. A small flat cloud hovered over the highest point, burning bright white. Against the darkening blue of the sky pencils of liquid gold, moving rays, arrowed out into infinity from behind the light of white — then slowly withdrew. With sunset mountain stillness deepened, and the soft blue shade of evening gloom darkened gradually into black.

My new companion was the local ganja farmer. Swiftly he disappeared, walking with that powerful bounce common to many Rastas, only to return with a 'whole heap o' herbs' wrapped up in brown paper. Tearing strips off the paper we each rolled cigar sized spliffs. Jamaicans do not generally pass spliffs, reserving that ceremony for the 'chalice,' the pipe of peace and communal meditation. Our recent stride through the village had been the exception, a spontaneous ceremony of sharing. Spliffs lit, our reasoning started, two people, sons of oppressor and oppressed, finding easy friendship at the day's end.

"We got the come together 'cause we are birds of a feather,
Got to realise we are one people
Or there will be no love at all.
Got to put aside them segregation,
Got to build our love on one foundation." (Peter Tosh)

Born in the country, Leon had moved, like many Jamaican youths, to Kingston. Ground down by poverty, unable, like one third of Jamaica's population, to find a job, he had returned. Now his income from ganja assisted him in building up his smallholding and achieving some measure of independence from the 'Babylonian shitstem' on which he was attempting to turn his back. His Rasta faith, stressing the need for pure food and movement back to the land had reinforced this. Another Rasta ganja farmer commented to anthropologist Dan Wight when asked what he did with the profit from his crop: "Not car, buy two goat." Whilst the majority of Rastas still remain living in the towns to which they or their families had migrated, unable or unwilling to escape. Dan Wight found that in the farming community where he lived for three months, those with the most positive attitude towards the country and farming, those who wished to stay on the land and had dropped western dominated big city aspirations were the Rastas. "As Jah say long time ago, man will come vile and der will be dread time, much fighting . . . war could happen any time . . . der will be killin' an' tiefing an' a whole heap of tings. Here in the hills is de best placed fe be . . . many peoples will hide in dem hills . . . Tings very poor in Kingston. Can't set up your own ting, man. Me want to live myself alone, have my own ground. Kingston very poor, very violent. Is calm here, can sleep peaceful in the country."

Fireflies glowed in the valley below. Against the deep black of the sky, stars shone brightly, white, orange, red, blue, colours visible in this clear high atmosphere. Gradually valley and sky became one, a kaleidoscope of lights sparkling in the void.

"There's a stalk of Sinsemilla blooming in my backyard . . ." (Black Uhuru)

It was morning, dew still glistening on the sticky bushes burning in the early rays. Unlike the mountain farm visited, where ganja was planted far out in the undisturbed bush, here cane, yam, peanuts and bananas hid the illicit crop. Three farmers were cultivating alongside one another, sharing duty watching the plants as harvest approached, sleeping in a hut hastily erected from wood and palm leaves. The oldest farmer grew traditional 'kali weed,' harvesting as soon as seed started to form on the female plants. His neighbours were growing 'sinsemilla,' pulling up males as soon as they could be distinguished, allowing the unfertilised females to keep on growing producing ever larger buds in their desire to attract male pollen. When I arrived, the younger growers were trying to persuade the elder man to pull up his males earlier so that their females would not be fertilised by them. The seedless trend has been set by California growers, and American buyers in Jamaica are persuading more and more farmers to make the change.

Whilst fearing discovery of their fields by police, they also felt threatened by a legal trade which might deflate prices and destroy the organic network of growers and dealers throughout the island who depend on the trade for their living. Clearly the size and traditions of the home market in Jamaica offers farmers some protection. In Colombia, for instance, the largest exporter of ganja to the US, domestic consumption is very small, thereby placing farmers at the mercy of exporters and export syndicates, usually western dominated, who pay farmers ridiculously low prices, 1% of final selling price according to a recent survey. The equivalent figure in Jamaica I would estimate around 10%. Whether Jamaica farmers could benefit from legalisation depends on many unpredictable factors, including the attitude of the Jamaican government, and governments and consumers in importing countries. Western nations have a long history which continues to the present day of grossly exploiting third world labour and agricultural markets. With this in mind the international Cannabis Alliance for Reform (ICAR), a union of legalisation groups around the world, is now committed to protecting the interests of farmers in developing, producer countries under any future legal system. Under the present illegal system, however, farmers are increasingly threatened by the power of major exporters who appear to be cornering export markets, paying off police, military and politicians and able to dictate terms to farmers and small traders with no recourse to legal protection. Such a development threatens local farmer and small, 'righteous' western dealers alike.

Babylonian Shitstem

Jamaica's cannabis exports, with Bauxite and the tourist industry, are increasingly relied upon to bring in vital foreign exchange. One estimate published in the *Financial Times* last year quotes income from ganja money to Jamaica at around $200 million per annum, roughly the island's annual balance of payments deficit. The US *Washington Post* pushed the stakes higher. "By many estimates, including those of US officials, the island's marijuana business is worth $1.1 billion a year, almost equal to the government's entire foreign debt and greater than all other exports combined." Whichever guesstimate is chosen, it is hardly surprising that following last year's election one of the first speeches made by the new conservative Prime Minister, Edward Seaga, was directed towards Jamaica's bankers, acknowledging the crucial role played by ganja money in keeping the island afloat, and requesting banks "to take foreign money from clients without asking too many questions." (*Jamaica Weekly Gleaner*, 19th Nov. 1980). In a separate interview during his US visit last year, in which he reputedly hit it off famously with Ron Reagan, Seaga concluded: "Regardless of whether we want it or not, the (marijuana) industry is here to stay."

. . . the legality of sacred ganja use is now being hotly debated . . .

Given the size of the trade, it is common knowledge that army, police and politicians are involved. I myself, during my visit to the island, was mistaken for an exporter whilst photographing an airstrip used by ganja planes and was informed by the army officer who made this mistake that to land and take off an aircraft would cost me $5000 Jamaican, or £1000. Babylon can be terribly blinded by the glare of bright coins. Commenting on this aspect of the trade, Seaga again recently stated: "Medical reports seem to suggest that there's no conclusive evidence that ganja is harmful, and therefore the extent to which it can be considered a moral problem in that respect is not clear-cut. But there is a moral problem of a different type, and that is the bribery that runs with illicit traffic. And in at least two cases, we know of gun trafficking that has been associated with it." According to the *Chicago Defender*, Peter Whittingham, a former deputy leader of his own party, the Jamaican Labour Party, was serving time in Miami on ganja trafficking charges when Seaga made this statement. Furthermore, during the run-up to the 1976 elections, and ten days after Michael Manley's at that time ruling People's National Party had declared an official State of Emergency (increasing political gun violence had claimed over 100 lives during the last 6 months),the same Peter Whittingham was arrested in Jamaica. Security forces allegedly found handwritten documents in his briefcase describing the operations of a secret paramilitary group called "Werewolf". The documents listed personnel and weapons, including 100 submachine guns and 200 rifles, available to the group, which was described in the seized papers as a "militant underground movement . . . willing to take up arms against the communist regime and purge them from our shores."

Sacred Profanity?

Last September a twin engined Beechcraft landed on an air strip owned by the Ethiopian Zion Coptic Church. Police seized the machine and impounded it, but arrested nobody found no papers in it, and had no idea from whence it came. Three armed officers guarded it for the next one and a half weeks, until early one Sunday morning shots rang out from the surrounding bush. Simultaneously a light aircraft appeared overhead and strafed the runway with machine gun fire. The police fled, the attacking plane landed, a pilot jumped out, took over the controls of the impounded Beechcraft, and both machines disappeared into the blue. Following this incident, the government, police and army expressed grave concern about the large number of airstrips on the island and the frequent illegal landings of foreign aircraft in Jamaica.

Whilst no evidence exists to connect the airstrip owners with the Beechcraft incident, nine members of the Ethiopian Zion Coptic Church have recently been convicted in Miami on 45 different counts involving the importation of some 105 tons of ganja into the United States. The defendants are appealing against conviction, but Church members face further charges arising out of another bust in Maine last year involving some 20 tons of herb. Two years ago Jamaican police ripped up five acres of prime plants on Coptic property but charges were dropped for lack of evidence directly connecting Coptics with the patch.

The Ethiopian Zion Coptic Church, not to be confused with the Ethiopian Orthodox Church, is a fascinating example of herb power, profane and sacred united in one highly efficient operation, or, as some would contend, a white dominated attempt to draw off power from Rasta. Mainly because both Rasta and Coptic fight publicly to free up the herb, many Jamaicans with whom I spoke, in particular country people, confused the two, thinking them to be the same. The Coptics grew up in the thirties, like Rasta, in response to the teachings of radical black pride prophet Marcus Garvey. They believe in sacred herb, Africa for Africans, that the Jews were the chosen black people, descendants of the great kingdom of David and Solomon, that their church has inherited that lineage, and that the established white churches of the west, in particular the Roman Catholic Church, are Babylon incarnate, the devil come to rob black people of their most crucial spiritual heritage and aspirations. Coptics do not believe in the divinity of Haile Selassie, a great bonus when attracting white people to the sect, nor do its members grow licks, insultingly referring to the Rastas as 'ropeheads'.

The Coptics are fantastically rich, operating the largest container transport business on the island handling both government and private contracts between Jamaica and the US, a furniture business, a large car importation and spares business which is a leading dealer, according to their advertising, for British Leyland, Toyota, Datsun, GMC and Volkswagen, and a large food supermarket. The latter is stocked with produce from their farms, covering at least 4000 acres on the island. Stateside, they also own a Florida farm, in concealed tunnels underneath of which 10 tons of herb were seized in 1977. In the same year they paid $270,000 cash for a large mansion on fashionable Star Island in Miami. They employ over 1000 people in Jamaica, and are naturally popular with local politicians, enjoying a reputation for paying good wages and bringing wealth to poor areas. Visiting their Jamaican farm is akin to walking onto a different island, an island of shiny rich cars, new buildings, prosperous economic activity. During my visit, however, a large number of small tenant farmers were protesting at being turned off land by the Coptics with inadequate compensation and nowhere to go, land which they had farmed from hand to mouth for many years. The Coptics had just bought the large estate to which these plots were attached. As a further indicator of Coptic wealth, in March 1978 US Internal Revenue revoked their tax exempt status and handed them a bill, estimated on visible possessions, for $2.3 million in back taxes. Customs are also claiming duties of $15.5 million for one 20 ton ganja seizure alone!

The Coptics are fighting in a extremely well organised and uncompromising fashion for herb liberation. Part of their defence against the importation charges, and one ground upon which they will be appealing conviction, is the clear statement that the whole prosecution is unconstitutional because the herb is a sacrament of their church, and to deny access is to deny freedom of worship as guaranteed by the constitution. Former US Attorney General Ramsey Clark pleaded this case for the Coptics at their trial, so whilst their chances of success may be small, their legal representatives are the best, and the argument is not to be immediately dismissed. In Jamaica itself the legality of sacred ganja use is now being hotly debated in legal circles, a debate fired to some extent by Rita Marley's placement of a ganja stick in Bob's coffin.

The Coptics are proposing one further constitutional ground for appeal, that the ganja laws are illogical and arbitrary, therefore unconstitutional. As evidence they are drawing on current research, such as the Ganja in Jamaica study which finds no

'. . . some people can smoke marijuana in high doses for 16 hours daily for up to 50 years, without apparent psychological or physical harm".

significant health differences between user and non-user groups, as well as wide-ranging medical tests on ganja using church members who, as I can testify, smoke almost incessantly. They were found to be a remarkably healthy group of people. As one of the medical reports concludes: 'even though the numbers we examined were relatively small, I think it is extremely important to make the observation that some people, at least, can smoke marijuana in high doses for 16 hours daily for up to 50 years, without apparent psychological or physical harm."

Unlike Rasta, whose organisation is somewhat anarchic with a very loose leadership structure and many followers belonging to no organisation, the Ethiopian Zion Coptic Church runs a very tight show, a highly centralised organisation led by Keith Gordon, a Jamaican whom I would describe, after one brief encounter, as

Photos by Tim Malyon

being 'worldly wise'. The people in key organisational posts handling money, both in Jamaica and the US headquarters in Miami, were white. Despite tracing their existence as a church back to the 1930's, the Coptics' immense wealth would seem to date from the early seventies when Keith Gordon took over leadership and white people first joined and assumed important positions. Having visited the Coptics myself, both in Miami and Jamaica, I am sceptical about the organisation despite their courageous defence of the herb and the fanatical vehemence with which they pushed their religious beliefs. Indeed, it was perhaps this vehemence, including an obsessive denunciation of 'abnormal' sex, which first worried me, reminding me uncannily of moonie rantings which I once had the misfortune of experiencing. It also concerned me that Coptic should level classic 'gutter press' accusations such as violence against Rasta. Certainly many Jamaican Rastas whom I met, including Rita Marley, are deeply suspicious of Coptic motives.

For there is an important political dimension to this strange cross-roads at which ganja finds itself in Jamaica. Whilst remaining aloof from party politics, the Coptics are virulently opposed to socialism and communism. Rasta remains similarly aloof, but through the immense attraction which it undoubtedly holds for the youth, and through its music, reggae, it has played a leading role in the movement of black people to assert their culture and throw off their chains. Rastas played an important part, for instance, in the recent Grenadan revolution. As Jabulani Tafari, a leading 'Twelve Tribes of Israel' member told me: "Ancient African civilisation was communal and socialist in nature ... Rasta history has always been in the forefront of the anti-colonialist, anti-class struggle."

We've been trodding on the
Winepress much too long
Rebel, Rebel.
(Bob Marley)

You drink white rum, you tumble down.
You smoke kali weed, you succeed.

Herb Power

"They try to make me white. But from I start to smoke herb now, I start to read between the lines. Is like wool was removed from before my eyes. That is when my rebirth start, my reincarnation, when I start to smoke herb. The government knows from a man start smoke herb he be aware of some things. That is when he start to come off the brainwash, when he start to smoke herb. That's why them is against the herb so much." (Jimmy, a Rastafarian. From Dread *by Joseph Owens)*

"And the truth is, that the reality of ganja is related to its rebelliousness, its restiveness among the native populations of colonised countries, the fact that people use this and will disobey the ruling dictates of the time." (Dr Freddy Hickling, Senior Medical Officer, Bellevue Psychiatric Hospital, Kingston, Jamaica.)

"Dagga (ganja) breeds courage and clarity of purpose. Why do you think the whites decided to prohibit use? They knew it was the only way of taming us so that they can walk all over us, and we would be afraid to rise in protest." (Mr Gaza, South African ganja smoker, from Cannabis in Africa *by Brian Du Toit.)*

"Undoubtedly one of the highest rates of marijuana use for any population in the western world," is how *Ganja In Jamaica*, a US government commissioned study described cannabis use in Jamaica in 1972, estimating that "some 60-70 per cent of the lower section of the rural population, men, women and children, inhale, ingest or use ganja in some form." In 1980, Dr Freddy Hickling estimated that "perhaps 80 per cent of the population use it, middle and working class." Referring to an unpublished survey which he had conducted at the University of the West Indies, Dr Hickling noted that the ganja smokers "were all showing a shift from middle class religions into other types of religions which were more working class, notably the religion of Rastafari." The actual and symbolic associations in Jamaica between race, class and ganja smoking are very clear. The island enjoys one of the lowest rates of alcohol induced mental illness in the western world, but the heaviest drinking occurs amongst British residents and other members of the white and middle class black population.

The alcohol/ganja split is not simply due to economic factors. "Smokers unequivocally maintained that ganja is superior to alcohol." *(Ganja In Jamaica)*. One popular rhyme I heard repeated runs:

You drink white rum, you tumble down.
You smoke kali weed, you succeed.

The alcohol/ganja split, and its connotations of rising against oppression date from slavery days, where in one of history's greatest crimes, the 'glorious' British Empire traded a race and almost obliterated a culture, to work the island's sugar plantations and produce the 'national' drink, rum. To this day, some Rastas will not work the sugar plantations, so powerful is the association between them and slavery.

Ganja is smoked in Jamaica to aid relaxation, meditation and spiritual contemplation, and to assist in hard manual labour, on the sugar plantations for instance. Ironically, it was plantation owners and the white established church, enslavers of body and enslavers of spirit, which led moves to outlaw ganja, resulting in possession of ganja involving a mandatory, unavoidable one-year prison term between 1941-1972, and harsh police repression under the pretext of ganja control.

In 1940, one of the most influential of Rastafari's early preachers, Leonard Howell, purchased a large estate in the hills outside Spanish Town named Pinnacle. An estimated 600 Rastafarians moved there, determining to live a life independent of 'Babylonian society'. In 1941 huge numbers of police raided the community, arresting 70 people, 28 of whom were imprisoned on violence and ganja charges. Howell himself was incarcerated for two years. On his release, he re-established the community, which functioned in almost total independence, growing its own food and ganja, until 1954. In that year Pinnacle was once again heavily raided, and broken up. 163 brethren were arrested, the rest being forced to move to Kingston, from which time the most brutal harassment of Rastafarians dates, including police beatings, shaving of locks, and frequent prison sentences. Such harassment, using ganja possession and cultivation as a pretext, reinforced the plant's symbolic connotations of revolt and maintenance of black cultural identity against white oppression and ruling, white dominated, bourgeois morality. Such harassment continues to this day, from the streets of Kingston, Jamaica, to Brixton, London, or St Pauls, Bristol, where black and white youth, dissenters from imposed values, are stopped and searched, humiliated, their houses and clubs 'trashed', in the name of stamping out that little weed.

Herbal Roots

Between 1494, when Columbus 'discovered' Jamaica, and 1655, when the British took over occupation from the Spanish, the island's original population of some 60,000 Arawak Indians were wiped out by disease and brutality. Nobody on Jamaica now has roots there. When the British arrived, they first imported African slaves, then later after slavery was abolished, Indian indentured labourers to work for them. Africans now form 90 per cent of Jamaica's population, Indians 3 per cent, and are the island's two largest ethnic groups. Some 1 per cent of the population are of European origin.

Ganja is smoked in Jamaica to aid relaxation, meditation and spiritual contemplation.

Ganja has occupied a central role in this barbaric history of transportation. If the hemp plant is allowed to grow and reproduce itself in northern climes, it develops into a hemp fibre producing plant. It was this fibre which provided ropes and sails to power the slave ships and the Navy which protected them. Indeed, in the early 19th century Britain experimented with growing cannabis for fibre in Jamaica, but failed. The fibre was apparently too fine for rough cordage. Indians and Africans, however, carried on their ancient traditions of cannabis use for sacred and medicinal purposes.

A young dreadlock approached me as I stood by the roadside. We talked, then he asked me to take his picture. His Indian ancestry shone through his features, it was important to him that this union, Africa and India, be recognised. As he spoke, this Rastaman of India, he evoked powerful memories of Indian Saddhus, holy men who follow an age-old tradition of cannabis use to help their meditation and break-through to enlightenment. This Indian tradition stretches beyond 2000-1400BC when the Atharva Veda was written, the sacred text which calls ganja "the sacred grass". It leaves its clearest mark in Jamaica in the vocabulary, 'ganja', 'chillum', 'kali weed', Indian words with the possible exception of 'kali' which is Hindi for 'bud', Swahili for 'strong or sharp'.

Some researchers believe that cannabis did not arrive in Jamaica before 1845, with the first Indians, and that West Africa, from whence most Africans taken in slavery to Jamaica originated, did not see herb use until during and after the second world war. Whatever may be the truth of this, the African tradition in contemporary Jamaican ganja use is stressed the most strongly, and ganja use in Africa is age-old. The oldest hunter/gatherer tribe known to humanity, the 'Bushmen' of the Kalahari desert, have traditionally used the herb. Cannabis fibre 3500 years old has been found in Egypt, and more recently two 13th century ceramic water-pipe bowls were dug up near Lake Tana, in Ethiopia, both bearing traces of cannabis. In the original Hebrew and Aramaic versions of the Bible cannabis was an essential ingredient of Moses' holy anointing oil. (In Sanskrit, *cana* means *reed, bosm* means *sweet*).

"The cigarette of our forefathers," was how African ganja, or dagga users in Natal evoked the power of herbal tradition. (From *Cannabis In Africa* by Brian Du Toit.) "Cannabis was the smoke of the ancestors. It was smoked by all the great men who were fierce fighters and wise in deliberation. And since it is the smoke of our fathers, it is said, we must smoke it too." The Zulus are one of the many African tribes that use ganja, and have used it over generations. The following is an old praise chant for their holy herb:

Burn machine of the mind
Burn shadow of the fowls
You remind me of the other side of the mountains
Where heroes have assembled.

"Rasta Is Calling For A Spiritual, Internal Revolution. We See Herb Now As A Part Of That Process."

Streams of figures converge on the bank of a dry river bed, an isolated spot outside Kingston, enclosed by fence of wood. The atmosphere is Biblical, mountains glowing blue in the distant haze, dust, a determined, dignified assembly united in one purpose. Nowhere was this meeting publicly advertised, it happens by the power of that most irrepressible of telegraph systems, the voice of the people, an old network of friends, family and neighbours who pass the word.

Inside the enclosure, some thousand red, gold and green 'tams', the blood, wealth and verdant pastures of ancient Ethiopia and Africa, shine in the evening light. Whole families are present for this meeting, this 'grounation', this coming together of members of one Rastafarian movement, the 'Twelve Tribes of Israel'. As the only white person present, I feel in no way threatened by the curious, yet friendly gaze of people who notice me, although it was clear to most that I had come in the company of a Rastaman, Jabulani Tafari, who spoke the words above.

Above the attentive crowd, the strong smell of ganja hangs sweet in the air, the ancient herb of meditation, of dream and vision, the little plant which has woken many a dormant mind. Sacred and profane, we must deal with you wisely.

The 'groundation' starts, a moving blend of religious service and practical meeting, discussions, prayers, chanting, how to raise money for the 'Twelve Tribes' PA system, news from other areas of the world to which Rasta has spread. A sister from Birmingham, a brother from Vancouver recount their experiences. Whilst orderly and well organised, the meeting gives space for anyone to contribute.

Mind surrenders to the measured and dignified cadences of the voices, the meditations of many flowing together into one powerful river of thought. This is no unity created by leaders and mass media, but a communal will to reassert the rights, culture and spirit of Africa, of the roots of humanity, of *Logos*, the word at the beginning. Let me be clear. I am not a Rasta. I do not believe in the divinity of Haile Selassie. I find it impossible to reconcile my beliefs on equality of the sexes with those of Rasta. Yet here, on this night, I could feel the unity of the message, the striving towards t he seed at the heart of humanity, the root beneath all and each of us. Look below the words to the images, mistake not the finger pointing to the stars for the stars themselves.

Haile Selassie is Jah incarnate, claimed descendant of ancient royal lineage, of David and Solomon, historical figures, kings of Israel who lived around the 10th century BC, and of the Queen of Sheba, the union with Africa. Lineage is roots, spiritual roots, blood roots. The vision goes back further, to Ethiopia as the cradle of civilisation. "The Ethiopians call themselves the first of all men and cite proofs they consider evident. It is generally agreed that born in a country and not having come from elsewhere, they must judged indigenous. For it is likely that located directly under the course of the sun, combining with the humidity of the soil, produces life, those sites nearest the equator must have produced living beings earlier than any others.
The Ethiopians also say that they instituted the cults of the Gods, festivals, solemn assemblies, sacrifice, in short all the practices by which we honour the gods." (Historian Diodorus of Sicily, writing in the 1st century BC). Some archaeologists now believe Kenya and Ethiopia to be one of humanity's birthplaces, where homo sapiens started to develop. Myth, history and image intermingle.

Rasta looks back with longing to a past age when humanity was more in touch with itself and surroundings, with sun, moon, stars and nature. Awareness brought a certain kind of knowledge, a blend of spiritual and scientific. Echoes of that knowledge are to be found in the Pyramids, or Stonehenge or the intricate system of ley lines that many believe criss-cross this island. As selfish desire, the will to possess and oppress took over, that unity of knowledge was lost, and more materialistic civilisations arose, church joining with state to chain body and spirit. destroying all memory, cutting off all search for our divine inheritance. "The transparent myth of the recent origin of true civilisation is . . . destroyed by the evidence for the survival into recent times of the same tradition as that which inspired the builders of the Pyramids at the very start of our era and which they preserved from the ruins of a stricken world."
(John Michell, *The View Over Atlantis)*

Rasta looks forward also, to armageddon, that time when we possess the ultimate in material power, the ability to obliterate ourselves from this earth, and to redemption. Babylon will fall, the Jews will escape out of Egypt, Noah's sons will survive the flood, destruction and redemption, myth and fact, history repeats itself, time is a 'recurring decimal'. The crucial symbol of Rastafari, a meditation image, is the lion, symbol of Haile Selassie, the manifestation of visible divinity, yet also God in Man, Man in God'. Every Rasta is a lion or lioness. Rasta youth are 'young lions'. We have only to realise this power and dignity in us all and direct it towards beneficial aims to be saved. We hold the key.

Thus when material power reigns supreme, the seed of spiritual 'overstanding' sprouts once more, tapping our lineage, be it Stonehenge or the Pyramids, Glastonbury or Ethiopia, returning old heavens latent in all of us to reality. "The music of our heart is roots music, music which recalls history, because without the knowledge of your history, you cannot determine your destiny; music about the present, because if you are not conscious of the present, you are like a cabbage in this society; music which tells about the future and the judgement to come."

A DAY IN THE LIFE of a CALIFORNIA GROWER

by Bud Reaper

Once upon a time a light aircraft swerved from its steady trajectory and swooped down to encircle the remote homestead of Green Acres. Jake was nervous of small planes, close to harvest, and he sensed that his time had come: he was being buzzed! He fumbled for binoculars and peered up at the little wasp on its spy mission to seek out plants. It made a second bank around the South-facing spur of his property and he had no doubt that his gorgeous ladies had been spotted.

Shit. If it's not the Sinsemilla Task Force then it's the Mafia and he was going to be cleaned out next morning.

On the side of the plane he just managed to make out an identification number: B/740/13/Y. He dropped his watering can and galloped back to the log cabin where his wife Matilda was practising her therapeutic belly dancing. He grabbed a pencil and paper to write down the number. The heat was on. The terrible moment they had feared was upon them.

Jake raced out of the house past the hot tub and the chicken coop and jumped into his ageing Chevy slant-6 pick-up. He started the motor and roared off down the eight miles of dust track which lead to the highway. Green Acres was very far-out having no electricity or telephone – and he had to get to a telephone, quick! Twenty minutes later he screetched to a halt at the payphone in the one-bar-town of Smithville and dropping seventy-five cents into the machine was in seconds talking to his friend Rocky who was a mechanic at Ureka airport. B/740/13/Y he blurted. Less than two minutes later Rocky came back with the bad news which Jake had anticipated: B/740/13/Y had been leased that day to the Humboldt County Police Department. The Sinsemilla Task Force were onto him!

It was already late in the afternoon and unlikely that the bust would happen that day. But first thing tomorrow morning and he would get it! So Jake headed back upto Green Acres to take care of his ladies.

As Jake drove along the highway, images of his youth flashed before him: the bronzed surfer boy growing up in Long Beach; his first acid trip when he'd nearly drowned; the move upto San Francisco with morning glory flowers in his hair; hanging out and dealing on Haight Street; going straight and selling pretzels on Telegraph Avenue; playing a trombone dressed in a gorilla suit on Fisherman's Wharf; Krishna Consciousness and bio-energy and bottles of ginseng; concussion in People's Park during a student riot; the biker phase; the mime artist; the years on a commune in Mendocino; the trip to Oaxaca when he got busted by the Federalis and spent six months in a Mexican jail; the day he met Matilda at the Redding pop festival; the mellow home delivery of their beautiful baby . . . He had done so much and he reflected that life was sweet.

The Sinsemilla Task Force were known to make their raids early in the morning.

When Jake pulled-up at the cabin his hands were trembling. First thing he did was have a stiff glass of Jack Daniels, then with Matilda carrying their son Shanti-Om on her back, rushed down to the lower secret garden on the South facing spur. There they were: his lovely, precious ladies swaying gently in the evening breeze catching the last rays of a warm September day. What a shame! Seventy-five of them, just three weeks from maturity, their buds already swollen and sticky but not quite ready and perfect. Timing was so important in this business. All those months of preparation: the digging of massive holes, the humping of sacks of earth-worm castings, fish emulsion, manure and loam, the careful balancing of nutrients to create the ideal pH, the endless watering by hand, the meticulous elimination of any plant declaring male gender, and then the sheer love, good vibes and daily meditation directed at his crop . . . all for nothing? No way, baby! Seventy-five plants were seventy-five plants and though these ladies were a touch pubescent they were not going to end up in a Smokey's incinerator if he could help it. And neither did he intend ending up broke after a hard season or even behind bars. This was a tough game and he was going to play strictly to the rules.

He kissed the first lady goodbye and with his bow saw cut smoothly through her 1½ inch stem and let her drop. Matilda did the same, then Jake chopped another, and another. Seven feet tall. Nine feet. Twelve feet, some of them. One by one the lovely ladies hit the dust until they were all down. All that remained were seventy-five stumps – and for stumps you could not be busted. Ungraciously the plants were stuffed into sixteen sacks and dragged upto the Chevy. A tarpaulin was pulled over them.

It was already dark and Jake and Matilda knew they were safe at least for the night. The chances of a night time raid were very slim. The Sinsemilla Task Force were known to make their raids early in the morning. Jake relaxed for fifteen minutes to smoke a joint with Matilda and have another glass of Jack Daniels. They agreed that Matilda would search the house for stashes and juicy old roaches for burial in the garden. Meanwhile Jake would drive off with the plants to deposit in a friend's barn.

Jake gave Matilda a big hug and a kiss and gazed meaningfully into her eyes. It'll be OK honey, we're cool — and he set off on the most dangerous part of the mission. As he drove down the dusty track he told himself there would be no problem. Nothing suspicious about a pick-up truck in Humboldt County unless the police stopped him for a driving violation and sniffed his cargo. He started mumbling his mantra to steady his frayed nerves and told himself that it was all Maya anyway.

Forty-five minutes of driving along the remote stretch of State Highway and not a single incident. Gleefully he hung a left onto a dust track which led to his friend's property tucked away four miles from the highway. Roy and Nancy were old friends and though they grew a few plants for their own consumption they were not relatively big-time like Jake. After all, they did not have an $85,000 loan to pay off. If you grew just a few plants, then nobody would bother you. Fifty was said to be the unofficial limit for personal use, and often people stuck to twenty-five to be on the safe side. (Though twenty-five female Indica giants grown by a wizard could fetch as much as $50,000 in a good year). Roy and Nancy had seven spindly specimens, ludicrously within the safe limit. Not even a high school kid would bother to rip *them* off.

Jake pulled up at the wooden house which Roy and Nancy had built themselves, noting that no strange cars were parked. He burst into the house to find Roy and Nancy tripping on mushrooms — it was the season, after all — and Roy was sitting in a G-string playing his sitar in the corner while Nancy was going through the kicking section of the Tai Chi Chuan. A single candle provided the only illumination.

Jake! Far fucking out! Hey man, I am receiving you! Wow! Is this real? Too much! Wanna drink some tea man? It's a 'special' brew. Ha ha!

Jale was not exactly in the mood. He reached for the bourbon and slumped down in an armchair beside the candle. Nancy continued her slow-motion kicks in time to the wavering raga. Well, there was no hurry. He had not been followed. Jake picked up a copy of the local paper, the Humboldt Grapevine, and flicked through. The headline had caught his attention: 'Grand Theft — Marijuana'. It recounted the story of a local man who had been robbed of his twenty plants by teenagers. Such rip-offs were not uncommon, especially since the local high school had started a flying club. Dammit! That was the worst thing that could have happened to Humboldt County giving redneck teenagers the chance to overfly remote plantations. But in this case the police – not altogether unenlightened — had acted without precedent by catching the thieves and charging them with Grand Theft, Marijuana. The stolen plants had been returned to their rightful owner against whom no charges were made! Only in California . . . ! At the back of the newspaper Jake spotted a rather striking advertisement put in by a local automobile dealer: 'Congratulations to all the successful growers', it read, 'come up to Datsun with a 4-wheel drive pick-up to get to those hard-to-reach out-of-the-way places'!! And a local attorney's Ad simply read: 'Busted?' and gave a name and phone number. That was not a particularly counter-culture newspaper but it clearly showed that the times were a 'changing. Last year, marijuana sales in Humboldt were so high that they were a close second to the massive lumber industry, the County's first. It was a big, big business which brought a lot of bucks into an economically depressed area. There were mellow growers in those hills who were raking it in and the local traders were the last to complain. Even some enterprising freaks had started their own businesses to cater for the well harvested Sinsimilla farmer. There were whole department stores — kind of Alternative Sears Roebuck — which sold everything from 'Bloom, the miracle fertilizer low in nitrogen to really push those buds for their last month of glory' to head shop paraphernalia. They had every kind of alternative technology from expensive solar-voltaic panels to air-tight stoves to make life more comfortable in out-of-the-way places. For its sheer capitalist potential, marijuana cultivation had become Establishment and socially acceptable — though it was still illegal. The inland revenue could not tax it, for one thing, and though the authorities were lenient with the small grower, they come down heavily on large scale producers like Jake.

Roy and Nancy had been just peaking when Jake entered, and the last thing he wanted to do was bring them down prematurely. He let a few inches of bourbon and a couple of hours go by before presenting his problem.

Seventy-five plants! Roy gasped. Far fucking out! Jees! Well, why not? Let's go hang the beauties up in the barn, Godammit!

Jake was very relieved at how coolly they took it and hoped they would feel the same way in the morning. They spent about two hours lugging sacks down to the barn and stringing up the seventy-five ladies to dry. Jake promised them a generous cut of the proceeds and headed back to Green Acres around three in the morning.

Jake and Matilda could have split for the anticipated raid, but they preferred to ride the storm in person and not have any cops nosing around the property in their absence. Jake arrived home and slipped into bed with Matilda and Shanti-Om. He slept for about two hours and then, sure as clockwork, Apocalypse Now hit them. Promptly at six a.m. they woke to the whorring of a helicopter overhead. Jake got up to perk coffee and glancing through the window saw a convoy of three pick-up trucks led by a police car all enshrouded in a great cloud of dust. Seconds later the Smithville sheriff, his deputy and three burly men wearing jeans and T-shirts emblazoned 'Sinsemilla Task Force' entered after a perfunctory knock. Matilda who was sitting on the bed breast-feeding Shanti-Om gave a sheepish smile and Jake offered them coffee. The sheriff declined and flashed a search warrant at Jake. Jake nodded and the sheriff led the way down past the solar water panel and the bio-gas generator, past the goat compound and along the edge of the plum orchard to the South facing spur. The Sinsemilla Task Force specials carried sacks, secateurs and a small chain saw.

The policemen knew exactly where they were headed and when they arrived at the innocent secret garden the sheriff gave out an intense groan. Jake grinned and invited the cops to take their time but be careful not to trample the comfrey. He repeated the offer of coffee for when they were finished.

The men spent about three hours searching the forty-acre property and then went through the house from top to bottom. Of course, not a bud nor a seed nor the slightest roach were found and to Jake's surprise the cops did not turn heavy but became quite amicable. There was nothing they could get him for, at least not this year, and they would never go to the trouble of tailing him for months all over the county in the hope that he would lead them to the missing plants.

The cops became so friendly that they congratulated Jake on his efficiency and then they all sat to coffee and fresh cream waffles prepared by Matilda before driving off in a cloud of dust.

The sticky young buds seasoned peacefully in Roy and Nancy's barn and were later sold and smoked with great pleasure throughout the Bay Area, while Jake and Matilda and Shanti-Om lived happily ever after.

BUSTED

BY MERVYN HARRIS. DESIGN BY EDWARD.

"Wake up. Wake up."

The voices filtered through to my subconscious from far off, like echoes in the caverns of my mind, until suddenly they were next to me. I opened my eyes and struggled to raise myself on one elbow out of the cobwebs of sleep.

Beside my bed knelt a slim man and behind him stood a big, burly man. The man who was kneeling, stretched out a hand and sifted through the grass on the table.

"We're police," he said.

Still a little drowsy, I stared at them with a blank and uncomprehending expression, trying to fathom out what was happening. I saw the man sift through the grass on the bedside table and wondered whether some of Jake's friends were playing a joke on us. I listened to find out whether anybody was in Jake's room. Sunlight pierced through the window above my bed, shedding light, but not much warmth.

"He's still drugged out," the burly man said.

This stirred me into action. I flung aside the blankets, saying: "I'm getting up."

The burly cop went out of the room. While I was putting on my trousers, the other one pottered about the room and asked: "Have you got any more stuff hidden over here?"

"No." I felt calm and fully alert. From the door of my room I could see into Jake's room. The sideboard cupboard had been moved away from the wall and everything that had been inside was sprawled on the floor. A man on his knees was rolling up the carpet. Kevin was leaning against the far wall, puffing a cigarette.

Stepping into the corridor, I had a clearer view of things. The flat was choking with policemen. There must have been at least eight of them, all in plain clothes. The full meaning of the fuzz scurrying about, searching and looking under the beds and in cupboards, dawned on me like a thud in the chest, momentarily taking my breath away. The flat was being raided.

Jake came out of the other room. His face looked strained. "He is not involved in this," Jake said of me to the burly cop who was standing with his hands in his pockets, his ruffled shirt masking a growing paunch.

"We found some stuff in his room," he said.

"We gave him that for his own use," Jake said. "He wasn't in on the deal."

I now knew that they had found the stuff. We had been busted. Now that the lid had been blown off, I felt some of the tension ooze out of me. There was nothing further to do or plan, but to play along with events as they unfolded.

"Mind if I make some coffee?" I asked one of the cops.

"Sure," he said. "Go ahead." Seeing that Jake was co-operating with them and none of us was offering any resistance, the fuzz had themselves turned friendly. They went about their tasks, but there was no overt hostility. Nevertheless, a policeman followed me into the kitchen while I put on the kettle and watched me as I made three cups of coffee. He also followed me into the toilet when I went to have a piss.

"Too many of you to make coffee for everyone," I said, handing Jake and Kevin a cup each.

Kevin was looking downcast and sullen. We were now all in Jake's room and a policeman came and took our names, writing them down in a notebook. It was only after I had drunk some of the coffee that I felt a queasy feeling. After the first couple of puffs on a cigarette, my throat was parched. I noticed that it was just after 6.30. They must have started on the raid at the crack of dawn.

It was only a little while later, when we were leaving the flat, that I was struck by the full implications of what was happening. As we went down the stairs to the street, a policeman walked on each side of me and one of them put his hand on me. It was an uncomfortable feeling which brought home to me the fact that I was being arrested for a criminal offence. Although I still hardly knew anyone in the neighbourhood, I was glad that it was early morning and few people were up and about. A man walking on the other side of the pavement took little notice as the police van was opened and we were trundled into the back. Two of the policemen got into the back with us.

On the way to the police station, Jake and Kevin exchanged a joke and some remarks with the fuzz, but I did not follow what they were saying. A cold sweat had broken out on my forehead and I could feel that my shirt was sticking to my back. We could not see outside and the van seemed to twist and turn innumerable times. After what seemed a long ride, it jerked to a halt.

The back door was opened and we stepped out into the yard of a police station. A hand was again touching my arm as we went into the station. Do they think I am going to run off, I found myself thinking.

We were led through a passage and into a large room. There were some policemen in uniform and a few other people, probably also brought in that morning. They had a listless, blank look on them. I saw that just being on the wrong side of the police benches gave one a shabby, decrepit look. I instinctively straightened my shoulders, but found them sagging shortly afterwards. A sergeant behind a desk took some details from each of us. A short biography. Date of birth, education, jobs. I found myself slowly reeling out the schools and universities I had been to and the degrees I had obtained. Then we were ushered into a cell on the side of the room.

It was the first time we had all been together on our own that morning. Jake let out a groan and Kevin slumped onto a chair. I reached for my cigarettes, but the packet was empty. We had been smoking almost non-stop without noticing. Kevin handed me a cigarette.

"I can sure do with a joint right now," he said.

I smiled wanly. "What happens now?"

Speaking in muted whispers, we exchanged information. It turned out that both Jake and Kevin had a previous conviction for being in possession of cannabis as well as

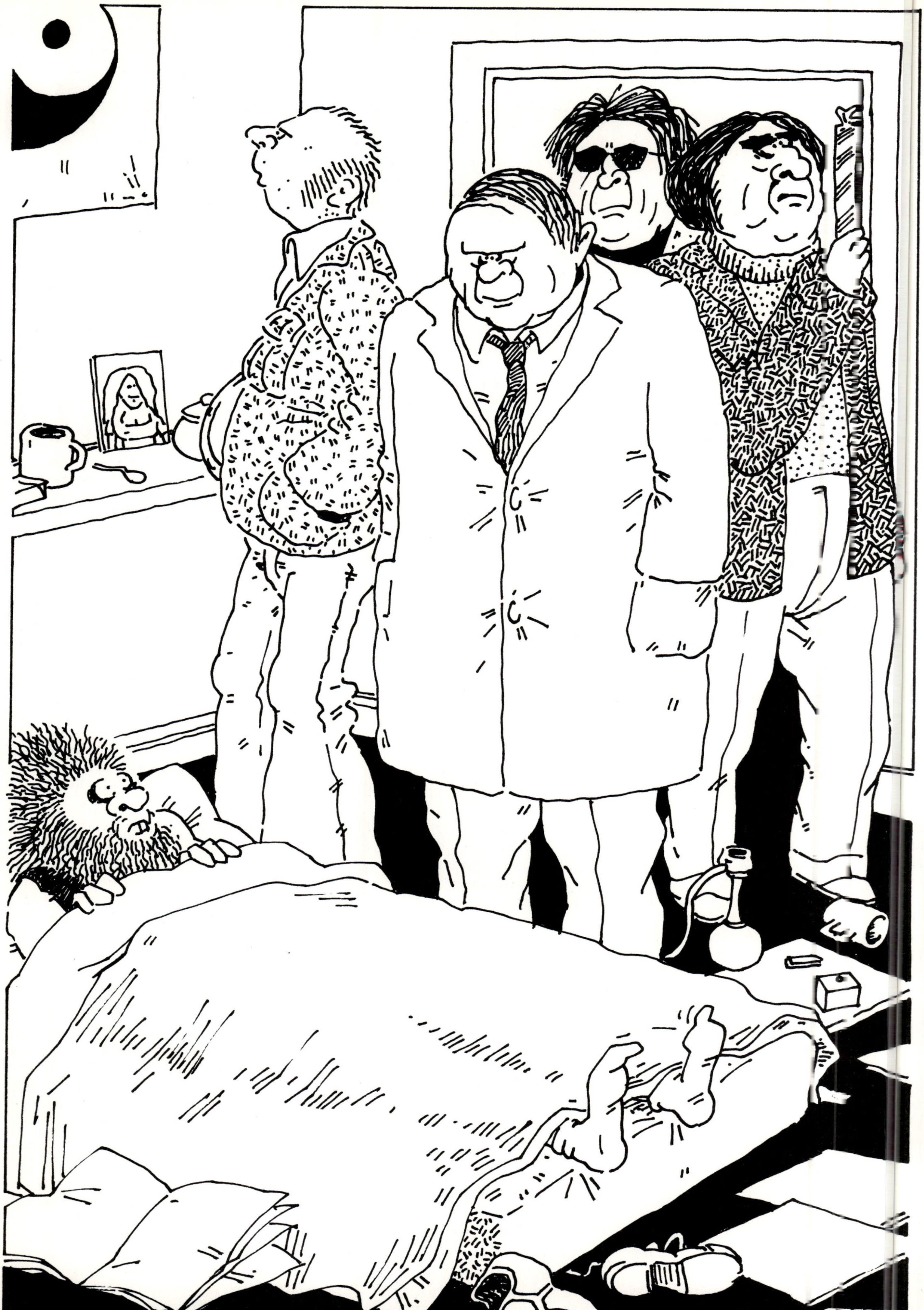
ELWARD

Kevin having a conviction for attempting to steal goods from persons unknown, this so-called offence dating back to the time he had hung around Piccadilly Circus.

I felt a pang of regret that my clean record would vanish. As if to rub this dismal prospect into my flesh, the door of the cell opened and we were each taken out to have our fingerprints taken. I was now a marked man with my imprint in the police files. Disconsolate and depressed, I was accompanied back to the cell.

Jake and Kevin were discussing who we should get to stand bail for us. My mind raced through a few alternatives, but each was swiftly rejected. My sister would be too alarmed and even panic-stricken were she to suddenly receive a call that I had been arrested. My previous acquaintances were all so conventional that I found the thought of approaching them distasteful. My comrades in the socialist movement would be appalled at the decadent level to which I had sunk. Betraying the revolution. I could telephone Karin, but that would me under obligation and renew a bond I wanted to dissolve. Fortunately, in the course of the next couple of hours this was all arranged.

Jeremy, a friend of Jake's who lived in the ground floor flat, had seen us go out of the building and realised what was happening. He had alerted another friend and found out to which police station we had been taken. With his help, it was sorted out who would stand bail for each of us and surety of a few hundred pounds. It took a little arranging as some of the friends already had convictions and therefore could not stand bail.

We were let out the cell and stood hanging around a desk while all these arrangements and formalities were carried out. A young cop, who had participated in the raid and who had later taken down particulars of my curriculum vitae, came up to me. He circled slowly round the desk on which I was leaning, scratched and faced me with a quizzical expression as if he were trying to formulate his thoughts.

"Tell me," he said, "why do you think this country's going to the dogs?" Before I could even consider a reply, he continued: "I mean just look at the economy, strikes, inflation, violence." He waved his hand as if to encompass many other woes.

I looked at him and wondered whether, like Queen Victoria, he wanted the whole truth in one word. "It all depends on the way you look at things," I ventured to say.

"The old standards are crumbling. Not," he hastened to add, "that that is necessarily a bad thing. The right kind of new ideas can do the country a lot of good. But some of the things happening here ...' He left off as if it was not necessary for him to enunciate the things that were happening.

I was getting a little irritated by the implications of what he was saying. It was not really my opinion he was interested in, but was indirectly accusing me and my attitudes of having something to do with the decline of the country. However, I did not want to get involved in a discussion with him, especially at this venue, and so just muttered vaguely.

"If you don't like something, it's no good destroying it unless you have something constructive to put in its place," he was saying.

We had been at the police station for more than two hours and Detective Haynes, the big, burly cop, seemed as keen as us to get out. He had become quite genial, joking with Jake and Kevin. He had a successful morning's work behind him and could go home and enjoy the weekend. I could not bring myself to participate in his good humour and was glad when the formalities were completed and we could leave the station. We were remanded on bail to appear in court on the following Monday.

Outside the station, we chatted for a few minutes with those who had come to stand bail for us. We were going to have coffee at a local cafe, but as it was Saturday and Portobello Road would soon be crammed with people, we decided to go back to the flat instead. On the way back in Jeremy's car, Jake told us how he had been woken up by a knock on the door early that morning.

"Usually I ask who it is before opening the door. Still being half asleep, I opened the door slightly and saw this chap outside. 'We're police,' he said. 'Open up. We've got a warrant'. For an instant I didn't know what to do. Then I opened the door to let them in. I couldn't very well have slammed it shut in their face."

"If you could have shouted or signalled to me in some way," Kevin said, "I might have had time to get rid of the stuff. Throw it out of the window or something..."

"And you think they would have waited patiently outside the door," Jake said irritably. "It's easy to talk about it afterwards."

"One of the fuzz kicked the mattress and says, 'O.K., get up mate'. I nearly grabbed his foot," Kevin remarked angrily.

"Let me finish," Jake insisted. "Well, when they came in, I just showed them where the stuff was. It was better than having them tear up the place. Besides, I think they quite liked us for our attitudes and I don't think they'll put the squeeze on us."

Jeremy brought up some cannabis to roll a joint. I made coffee while Jake got a few things ready for the stall. We were also able to have a joint of grass, for as one of the fuzz remarked as we were all leaving the flat that morning, "We've left you some crumbs for you to have a smoke when you get back." We were all still a bit on edge, sometimes all talking at once, filling in the gaps of each other's stories and incidents that had occurred. It was a way of letting off steam and a way of easing the tension.

"Did you find out how come they raided your pad?" asked John who, having heard of the raid, had just come in.

"Detective Haynes told me," said Jake. "It seems the pad used to belong to a dealer. They were keeping a watch on it and were just on a routine raid."

News of the raid was quickly circulating among friends and acquaintances. The telephone was ringing and some people were coming round to hear for themselves and reminisce about their experiences when being busted. It seemed that most people who smoked pot in the area had had an experience of being raided, a brush with the fuzz or even a conviction or spell behind bars.

During the course of the rest of the morning and at lunch-time when Kevin and I went to have a drink at the pub, a constant flow of people came up to ask about the raid. I often felt as if I was being congratulated on some achievement. This did not exactly please me as I did not think the morning's events warranted any special praise. It was as if I had suffered a wound in battle and was beginning to think of the repercussions. To those who came up to me, it seemed more like an initiation I had passed. Despite my relatively short hair and straight appearance, I was now accepted as one of them.

SEX, DRUGS &

Ian Dury's instant classic really came as something of a surprise. The surprise wasn't that he did it, but that nobody had thought of doing it before.

Since the beginning sex and drugs have been inextricably bound up with rock and roll music. In fact, those eminent psychiatrists, frenzied Bible Belters and rabid conservative moralists who prophesied in print and pulpit that rock and roll was a "communicable disease", that it led to drug addiction, promiscuity, juvenile delinquency and the probable downfall of Christian values and civilisation as they knew it were absolutely right. They may have got the reasons pretty ass backwards, but in substance they were right. Wasn't that, after all, why we liked the music?

There can be no doubt that rock and roll has always needed high octane fuel. Anybody who tells you different is a damn liar, and about as trustworthy as that godforsaken individual who passes up a joint or a mirror or whatever with a superior smile and the statement, "I don't use the stuff, I'm naturally high."

If you don't believe that rock and roll ran, right from the start, on one kind of scheduled drug or another, go ask Screaming Jay Hawkins, or Little Richard, or Johnny Cash or even Elvis (although that would admittedly prove difficult without the services of a high priced medium). Best of all, ask Jerry Lee Lewis.

Jerry Lee Lewis has to be the archetype and the ultimate survivor of that time when rock and roll was getting born in the back of a station wagon on some back road of the South, en route to a one night stand in a high school gym or Legion hall.

At the start of the sixties Lewis and his band, the Memphis Beats, were busted at a motel in Grand Prairie, Texas, and charged with possesion of 700 amphetamine capsules. This was in the days when being busted for speed meant a traffic offence, not a narcotics beef.

Before it had even begun, rock and roll was in the grip of its very first amphetamine cycle. It never had a chance to do anything but run the distance. The pattern was, after all, set up in front. At the start of the fifties, Hank Williams had dropped dead in the back of his limousine from too much speed. It was the drug of Dixie, the trucker's friend, the LA

turnround in all shapes and colours. Too many good old boys had come back from World War II with a taste for the big bags of benzedrine that the US Army and Air Force were prone to hand out to combat troops.

Alan Freed may have tried to shuck the world into believing that rock and roll was good, clean, youthful high spirits. The truth was Jerry Lee playing with a machine gun in his hotel, Gene Vincent and the Blue Caps crazy and crawling in some redneck town they couldn't even remember the name of, washing down pills with Wild Turkey or Rebel Yell Confederate bourbon and trying to persuade a waitress or high school cheer leader to come back to the motel and see if the South could rise again. Then having to split town early in the morning before daddy/husband/brother/boyfriend came after them with a pump shotgun or length of primary chain off a Harley Davidson because Peggy Sue was back home sobbing she'd been raped.

Of course, that speed cycle like all other speed cycles had to end, if nothing else, to let another one start up again after a few months of lying low.

In London art schools and the coffee houses of New York and San Francisco something new was going on. Smoke from a hand-rolled kept under the hand, made from the contents of a foil package bought with the thrill of fear from a romantic blackman, was filling the air.

A new generation of white kids had discovered dope, and were working their way through passages of their minds that mom, dad and teacher hadn't let on existed, if, in fact, they'd even known about them in the first place.

Like all new generations of white kids who discover dope, they got to thinking. One of the first realisations was that Cliff and the Shadows or Bobby Vee were simply not easy on the ear. You just couldn't loll back and listen to a Dansette portable scratching on about some damn rubber ball going bouncey-bouncey, bouncey-bouncey. It could rot your brain and make you physically ill. It's easy enough to get sick and ill without having music that does it to you.

ing out of the radio or the TV. You couldn't find it in the High Street Record Rendez-

ROCK'n'ROLL

vous. It had to be sought after in back alley specialist shops and word of mouth contact. Finding Chess R&B, Prestige jazz, Jimmy Smith, Chuck Berry, Howling Wolf or Charlie Mingus could be as much trouble and as much adventure as actually copping the reefer.

With a wind of change blowing through the Dansette's 7 inch speaker, the decks were cleared for action. The new generation of white kids who'd discovered dope said to themselves, "Why can't we play music like Jimmy Smith, Chuck Berry et al.?" Of course they couldn't, but they could play something.

Change was in the air. It was a new frontier, the white heat of technology; the planet was attempting to drag itself kicking and screaming into the second half of the twentieth century and cheap, red, electric guitars were in the window of the local record store. It was time to move and get down with the change.

Then JFK was iced on Dealey Plaza, and as the joint went round a lot of people in a lot of basements realised that the faceless men who really run things weren't messing around.

With an attitude of stoned, aggressive, paranoid optimism, a thousand Brian Joneses picked up their Futurama guitars and a thousand Johnnies started mixing up the medicine. Once again, rock and roll had to move back onto high octane fuel. Yes, you guessed it. A new speed cycle had started up.

Mod: a new five ply mohair suit and purple hearts at a tanner, Georgie Fame and the Blue Flames and going to a go-go. You were part of the now. Know what I mean, John? How many rock and roll empires were founded on flogging pills to the kids queuing up outside the Marquee to see the Who on a Tuesday night (maximum R&B)?

Blocked was the expression of the time. Stumbling, glazed, stammering, incoherent and young, all style and aggres-

sion, but no brains. Go straight at it, the freak shall inherit the earth. Mods and rockers made the headlines in their actions of evolution, Cro-Magnon v. Neanderthal. Blue nylon against black leather. That was something that they could quite easily grasp at the *Daily Sketch*. What the media missed was the movement that was formlessly growing in basements and attics all over the western world.

Even before the hippies hit the streets, rock and roll was pushing at its outer limits, both in terms of lyric and musical structure. It wouldn't be any exaggeration that psychotropics had a major hand in the perception that brought about all this new ground breaking.

Speed may have been the fuel for the live show, but marijuana was the great aid to the recording studio. A heightened perception coupled with a rapidly expanding technology and increasingly sophisticated recording techniques enabled rock and roll to go in every direction but down. The Beatles and Rolling Stones took the simple R&B structures that were the base of rock, and moulded them in elaborate and increasingly baroque directions. Dylan was writing lyrics that would have been scarcely believable to anyone in the fifties. Brian Wilson layered harmony upon harmony, bringing an unprecedented lushness to a simple

vocal workout, while Jeff Beck Eric Clapton and, a little later, Jimi Hendrix produced sounds from the electric guitar that were undreamed of by Duane

Eddy or Hank B. Marvin.

All this experimentation alone would have constituted both a major achievement and a giant stride in the development of rock and roll. There was something about the sixties, however, that just wouldn't allow things to stand still. Only a couple of short years after the rock generation had first grappled with the new visions and perspectives revealed by marijuana, LSD-25 hit the street market and quickly grabbed half the youth of the west by the synapses.

The effect of acid on rock and roll was immeasurable. The idea of actually translating the mind wrenching revelations of the new wonder drugs was an elusive prize that numerous rock and roll bands grasped out for. Only a very few managed to come close to reproducing even a single facet of the psychedelic experience.

Jim Morrison of the

Doors freely admitted that he "gobbled down acid like candy" during his days as a Venice, California, beach bum, when he conceived and wrote the major percentage of his songs. Morrison delved deep into the subconscious and used the images and fears that he found there to create a nightmarish, sinisterly erotic fantasy world where mystic killers roamed dreamlike highways, virginal princesses sacrificed themselves to black leather monsters, cities burned, violence was always lurking just below the surface and reptiles abounded. Morrison presided over his strange creation in the role of his lizard king character.

The Pink Floyd took an almost diametrically opposed position. Half hidden by the

swirls and blobs of one of the first lightshows, and motivated by the brilliant but far from stable Syd Barrett, they produced a cold, aloof form of music that evoked images of both the glittering icy void of deep space and the chill isolated corners of the paranoid mind.

On a gut level, Jimi Hendrix, another self avowed psychedelic stunt pilot, came close to the jangle, the loop and the curve experienced by the acid saturated brain. Hendrix, more than all the other guitar gods of the late sixties, had such a physical rapport with his instrument and equipment that he seemed almost capable of weaving dreams out of the magnetic fields of his banks of Marshall amps and communicating them directly to the audience. This, coupled with Hendrix's overt sexuality, made him able to strike all manner of responses from his listeners.

Acid, however, like marijuana, wasn't the ideal drug for a coherent live show. Maybe the Grateful Dead could tank up on psychedelics and play a five or six hour show of erratic brilliance, but they were definitely the exception. More often than not, a bunch of acid before a show could lead to scattered impromptu outbursts of the kind that Jim Morrison was famous for, or else total confusion and breakdown of even the

slimmest musical continuity. A typical case was Eric Burdon who, at a legendary San Francisco concert, spent more than an hour on stage, unable to do anything but wander, awestruck, around the stage gazing at the lightshow and murmuring "Gosh, wow" periodically into the microphone.

Again, amphetamines became the favoured fuel for the live show. The useful familiar pills did their rounds, but in addition to the well known Dexedrines, spansules, Drinamyl and the rest, a new super-upper appeared on the streets. Methedrine quickly proved to be the big brother of all the other forms of speed. Either in clinical ampoules, bootleg pills, capsules or powder, it was more powerful than anything that had previously gone the illicit distribution route.

The major medical use for methedrine was only emergency injection to revive victims from a state of technical death due to heart stop. In other words, it was for waking up corpses. The speedfreaks didn't see it that way. If taken in sufficient quantity, methedrine could produce a manic, hallucinatory state that might be a whole lot of fun at the time, but could be so physically and mentally depleting that the various hippie ghettos of the western world had suddenly to get used to an entirely new breed of damage cases.

At its most terminal, methedrine could produce extreme and often violent paranoia and hallucinations as scary as alcoholic DTs. From a [illegible]d-

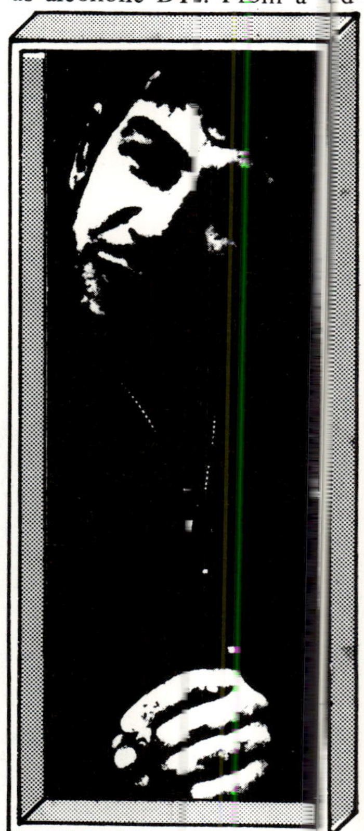

dering, stammering mess the whacko speedfreak now had the potential to turn himself into a full blown, wild eyed psychotic.

Surprisingly, methedrine claimed only a limited number of rock and roll victims. Most of them came from the lower echelons of touring bands. Even before meth mania had reached its peak, the big stars had moved on to the smoother, less instantly damaging and infinitely more expensive joys of cocaine.

The meth ethos did, however, produce a crop of suitably demented songs. Favourites among the San Francisco speedfreaks were an outfit called the Blue Cheer. Almost a prototype of today's heavy metal bands, the Blue Cheer relied on sheer volume to punch across their point, boasting anything up to two thousand watts of guitar amplification. Legend has it that at one concert a dog who happened to walk on the stage dropped dead of a brain haemorrhage. Their music scarcely translated onto record, and even the semi-hit "Summertime Blues" lacked the awesome weight of the Blue Cheer's live sound.

Worldwide, the speedfreaks' favourite recording had to be the Velvet Underground's notorious cut "Sister Ray". Nobody could deny that it fitted the mood exactly. In its twenty minute duration the song screeched its way through a high velocity ribbon of the most disquieting jangle the world had ever heard. All across the planet, a grungy basement, four amps of meth and an autochange set to repeat "Sister Ray" over and over again. Of course, nobody listened to the music too much, not even the almost inaudible, but oft repeated, lyric line "I'm searching for my mainline". The freaks were too busy babbling into space. The record wasn't there for aural gratification, more to heighten the illusion of jagged, high power madness.

By very definition, the meth craze had to wear itself out in short order. The rock and roll narcotic top ten ground round until it was pointing in the diametrically opposite direction. Heroin became the number one fashion turn on.

got too intense. Heroin was simpler, easier, more to the point and, in the long run, much more deadly. Certainly smack does hold the pressures at bay and gives the user not only mental space but cocoons him in a psychological capsule that pain is unable to enter as long as he keeps taking the medicine.

The one thing that heroin doesn't protect against is death. The long roll call of dead rock stars can only attest to the vulnerability of the junkie, whatever his or her income or status.

Possibly one of the main problems of the seventies was that no new dug appeared on the streets to jerk both the consciousness and the music of rock and roll. For over half the decade, both music and the drug consumption seemed to stabilise and turn in on itself.

Experimentation was constricted to flirtations with the trappings of glittering homosexuality, right wing politics and other chemicals like animal tranquilliser or angel dust. For the most part the successful consumed cocaine, the unhappy used heroin, the struggling took speed and downers and just about

The downer temptation has always been strong in rock and roll. In a world that is always overcrowded with people jostling in search of the magic point that is exactly where it's at, liable to go crazy without warning and attempting to run twenty four hours a day, sleep, and a certain measure of psychological space, become premium needs.

In the days of Marilyn Monroe, Seconal provided the answer to those needs, but the late sixties, the more sensual down of Mandrax or Quaaludes replaced the cruder barbiturates. A handful of downers after the show made the hotel room party easier to handle and the few hours sleep before the car, truck or plane a lot less elusive.

Unfortunately, downers have two major drawbacks. The first is that they just won't allow themselves to be confined to one portion of the user's life. They have this tendency to spread out and take over. The second is that downers come closely followed by tolerance. The combination of the two cause too many fine musicians to turn themselves into stumbling, vomiting avocados. Some managed to ease themselves out of this less than attractive mess. Others, like Paul Kossoff, didn't.

There was another alternative when the daily pill intake

everyone used as much booze and marijuana as they could get their hands on.

Just as it began to look as if the seventies weren't going to produce anything of value, the new wave broke. A new generation of feisty young kids marched into the picture with new ideas, new fashions and a more raw energy than had been seen since the mid sixties. The music, which had previously been moving through an unadventurous and inward looking phase, became stripped down, energetic and quite prepared to kick out at old or redundant ideas. Once again rock and roll seemed ready to face the strain.

The new wave also brought back the need for fuel. Failing to find any exciting chemical innovations, the punks, just like their spiritual fathers before them, turned back to the tried and trusted standby. A new amphetamine cycle started, proving that the direction of rock and roll is probably more circular than linear.

"Wait a minute," you say, "didn't the title of this piece say something about sex?"

True, it did, but this is, after all, a family magazine.

CANNABIS A COMFORT IN YOUR OLD AGE?

BY MAX ARBESFELD PHD. ILLUSTRATION BY CAROL GREGORY

In western countries the garden for old people is, as Simone de Beauvoir has passionately demonstrated, a pathetic kindergarten. Unless one is fortunate enough to be a politician, an Emeritus professor or a patriarch, old age is a time of endless frustration and agitation. No-one expects anything from you except nagging dependency. You are either in an institution, alone, or somehow tolerated by a reluctant family. Often poor, cold and miserable, you have continuous ill health aggravated by anxiety produced by an impossible social position.

It is also evident that there is at present no suitable medication that can make life more pleasant for the aged. Antidepressants are given which do not really lift depression but leave it hanging in the background. Antianxiety drugs, of the valium type, do not remove anxiety at all but deaden the ability to feel it, along with pleasure and a few other things. Stimulants have side effects and cannot be given for long periods. Other psychoactive drugs which are commonly given to old people are the cerebral vasolidators, drugs which increase the circulation of blood in the brain and help keep the tired old brain cells well supplied. However these can only be given in severe cases.

What about cannabis for the aged? It has special antidepressant effects, often experienced as an euphoric "high". Indeed the first known written record of cannabis use, notes by the Greek writer Herodotus in the fifth century B.C., explains with astonishment how the Scythians (warlike people of Asia Minor) employ a strange

Health problems which may be associated with long term cannabis use would not necessarily apply to the aged, and with them fall one of the main pillars on which the anti-legislation argument rests.

rite at funerals. They secrete themselves under a felt blanket in company with an incense burner upon which they burn cannabis as well as frankincense, myrrh and other aromatic substances. Soon "howls of glee" can be heard issuing from under the blankets.

Cannabis is a psychotropic drug which may tend to produce mild disorientation, introspection, inner peacefulness, self-acceptance and creative insight leading sometimes to explosive uncontrolled laughter, especially with those unfamiliar with the drug and with Scythians. Would not some of the elderly appreciate a state of mind that may allow forgetfulness of a world of miserly pensions, the bureaucracy of distant paternalism and the National Health? Could it not be helpful to those attempting to adjust from a respected and useful life to a life of joy, despite membership of the social rubbish dump?

The opponents of marijuana legislation have often associated it with "escapism" to a fringe world of unconcern for society and its problems. But the old are already in a pointless fringe world, and it is society which has placed them there. Should we not give them every assistance to turn their lack of social responsibility from a curse into a blessing? Advanced age can be the time of release. When duties are done and a family raised there is nothing more to do than give oneself to the world of the spirit. The four stages of life, as recommended by the Vedas, end with a time to leave home and devote oneself to contemplation, to achieve inner liberation and prepare for death. There is little sign of this sensible practice in the West. On the contrary the old are often more trapped by a miasma of petty interference than at any other time, for they are dependent on handouts and more worried about breaking out of the protection of social welfare. It is perhaps under these conditions that cannabis might be of profound value. It might be the catalyst which would lift old people out of bored dependency and show them another way.

Health problems which may be associated with long term cannabis use would not necessarily apply to the aged, and with them fall one of the main pillars on which the anti-legislation argument rests.

For example, there is the possibility of lung and throat infections and lung damage as a result of heavy smoking, and this could be a problem for old people. Yet hashish can always be eaten, and this may avoid another possible adverse effect of hashish smoking – a reduced resistance to disease as a result of immune depression. In any event ganja is smoked in India, by boys as well as hoary old Saddhus without, as the Chopra Commission remarked, any apparent ill effect.

In fact there may be strong arguments for using cannabis in old age on health grounds alone. The active constituent, THC, has been found to lower blood pressure in animals and man. It works by encouraging messages from the brain to the blood vessels to relax, causing them to expand and allow the easier passage of blood. Arteriosclerosis, the blockage of blood vessels, is the single major killing and disabling disease of the aged of the Western world. Cannabis or THC could contribute to the control of the disease in some people particularly by reducing the tension, anxiety and undischarged stress where these are the causes of arteriosclerosis and other diseases.

It is easy to forget that cannabis was used medicinally for thousands of years, and it was a minor drug in the United States Pharmacopoiae until 1937. Tincture of cannabis was available on prescription in Great Britain in the 60's for anxiety, anorexia (self-starvation), restlessness, insomnia and other nervous conditions, and these conditions are a particularly great nuisance to the elderly. Barbiturates may be used to assist sleep but they are far more poisonous than cannabis. Compared to the thousands of people that commit suicide by swallowing barbiturates, the medical literature records only one attempted suicide using cannabis. A French soldier smoked nearly 4 ounces of hashish at one sitting for that purpose. He spent four days in a coma after which he awoke cheerful and in possession of all his faculties.

Marijuana is now being seriously studied as a way of relieving migraine headaches and asthma. Dr Mikuriya recently suggested at a meeting of the California Medical Association that research should be directed towards testing the possible value of marijuana or THC in the management of pain, chronic disorders of the nervous system, convulsions (e.g. epilepsy), migraine, anorexia, mental illness and surprisingly, bacterial infections. It has already been used with

A French soldier smoked nearly 4 ounces of hashish at one sitting for that purpose. He spent four days in a coma after which he awoke cheerful and in possession of all his faculties.

some success in the treatment of convulsions and migraine, and as a general antidepressant.

A curious and little known fact about cannabis constituents is that they are able to quickly lower body temperature. Indeed they have been used for the instant treatment of sunstroke. Professor Roy Walford of the Department of Pathology at University of California has been promoting the idea that cannabis could be used to lower body temperature for long periods with the possible result of extending the lifespan. However preliminary trials with laboratory animals did not give grounds for hope.

Perhaps the most telling message of the possible value of cannabis to the old and infirm is a recently published study where cannabis was given to advanced cancer patients. The despondency, loss of appetite, and pain of cancer victims is part of the horror of the disease, but it is also, to a much lesser extent, part of the experience of the aged, and in both cases there are no current medicines of any long term usefulness. In this study cannabis was given for a week, and the patients examined before during and after this period. There was no reduction in the amount of pain or sickness. However the patients appeared to be less depressed, more for-hright, less tense, more tranquil, more stable and more self reliant (not so clinging and hypersensitive). They were less concerned with their inner urgencies and more with the outside world. They gave the impression of relaxed withdrawal. Astonishingly they gained an average of 1¼ lbs in weight during the week when they were given cannabis compared to an expected *loss* of 21¼ lbs without the drug.

The body is wonderfully resistant to external abuse and vulnerable to internal abuse. Tough living conditions, mild

Astonishingly they gained an average of 1¼ lbs in weight during the week when they were given cannabis compared to an expected loss of 21¼ lbs without the drug.

diseases, hard work and little food are often the very conditions encouraging longevity, while anxiety, tension, frustration and dissatisfaction are as powerful a cause of early death, as a recent study reported, as any amount of cigarette smoking or poor diet There will always be older people for whom cannabis will not work. But for those who achieve a more peaceful relaxed inner state with cannabis, it will do more for general health than anything else in the medicine cabinet. If that state is attainable without any drug, so much the better.

One should not need to justify cannabis use on medical grounds, in the same way that one does not need to defend listening to music because it lowers the blood pressure. Yet at a time when there is so much hostility to plant medicines in general and cannabis in particular it may be necessary to demonstrate that there are special advantages in this form of quiet enjoyment. There is a time to laugh and a time to cry, and old age need not be a time to cry. The struggle for survival has been fought and won. Duties and responsibilities should slip away leaving a residue of experience to supply a reflective fantasy. It is a time for serenity.

Max Arbesfeld, Ph.D. is the nom de plume of a scientist and author with a special interest in gerontology.

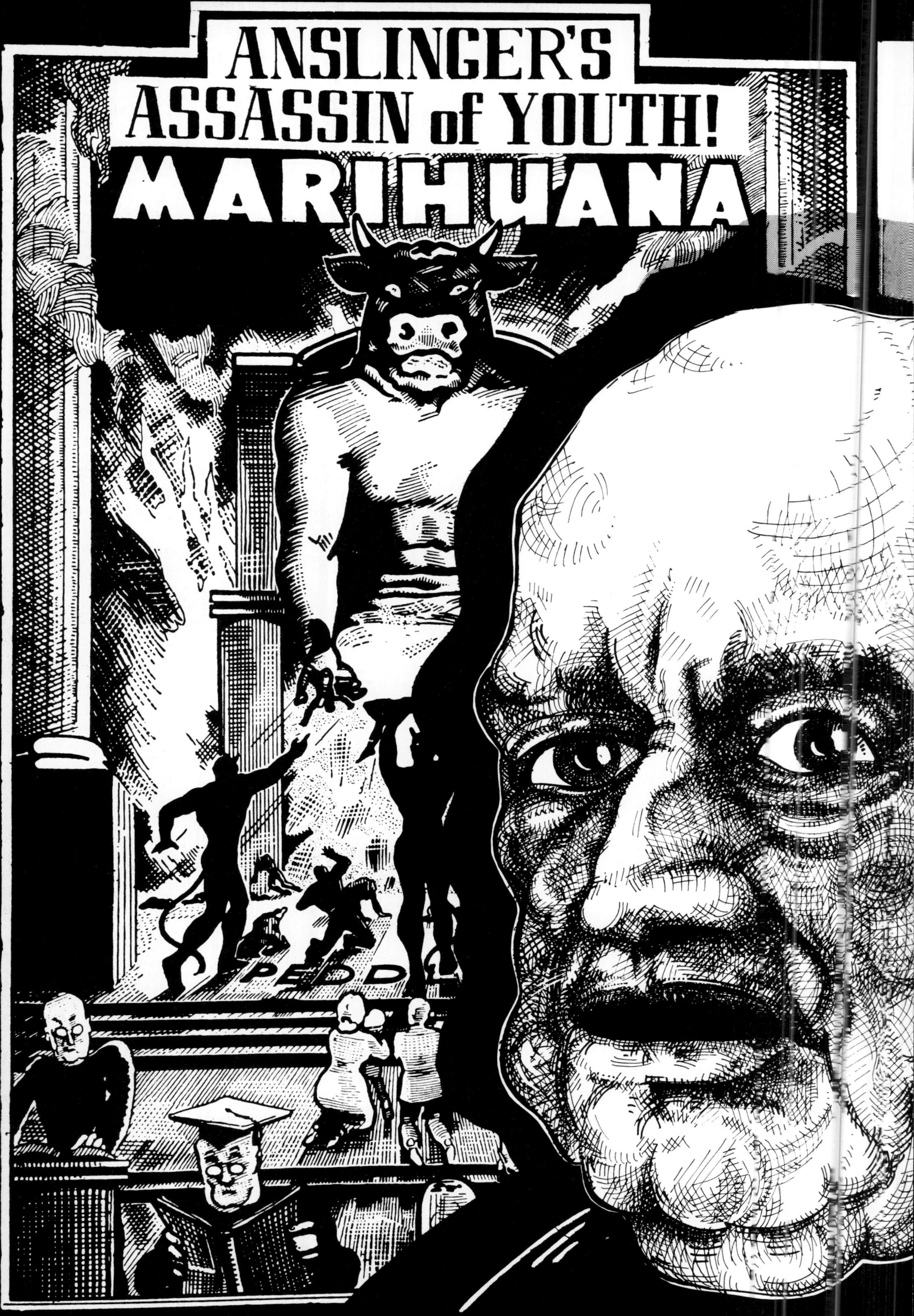
ANSLINGER'S ASSASSIN of YOUTH!
MARIHUANA
PEDD

"HERE WE HAVE A DRUG THAT IS NOT LIKE OPIUM. OPIUM HAS ALL THE GOOD OF DR. JEKYLL AND ALL THE EVIL OF MR. HYDE. THIS DRUG IS ENTIRELY THE MONSTER HYDE, THE HARMFUL EFFECT OF WHICH CANNOT BE MEASURED ...."

HARRY J. ANSLINGER, THE MARIJUANA TAX ACT HEARINGS OF 1937.

by LEE HARRIS

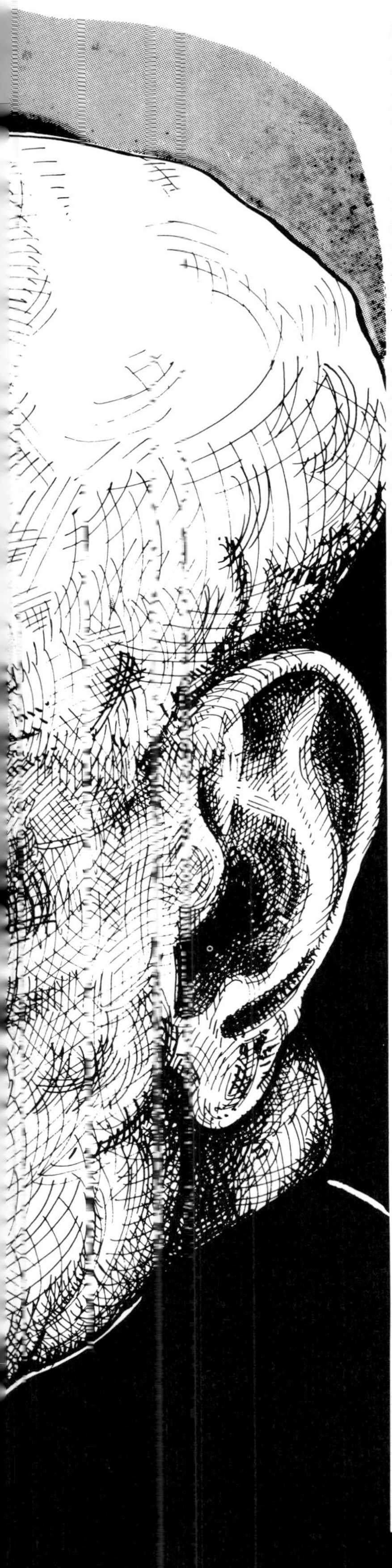

The history of marijuana in America is a fascinating one. It is the story of repression of minority groups by the zealous efforts of one man, the late Harry J. Anslinger, Commissioner of the Federal Bureau of Narcotics for 32 years, who wielded a cunning power throughout the years over the lives of countless Mexican immigrants, blacks, jazz musicians, beats and hippies. He was the man who invented the myth of Marijuana, the Assasin of Youth.

In a new book out **"Reefer Madness"** (The Bobbs-Merrill Company Inc. Indianapolis, New York. S12.95) the author, Larry Sloman, charts the efforts of Anslinger and his Bureau in their crusade to discredit the weed and all who used her. At the age of 38, Anslinger assumed control of the newly-formed Bureau of Narcotics in 1930, at a time when concern over marijuana was just beginning to have a national impact. Born of Pennsylvania-Dutch Calvinist stock, he was a bureaucrat whose career included a spell as a consul with the Diplomatic Service, assigned to The Hague, Hamburg, Venezuela and the Bahamas. Before taking up his new job he had worked briefly for the Treasury Department, trying to enforce the prohibition of America's favourite drug: alcohol.

If history is the juxtaposition of people and events, then the stage was set. Here was a man who had a traumatic experience as a boy of twelve, that would affect his judgements in later life. He had heard a neighbour's wife, who was a morphine addict, screaming in terrible pain. Then her husband asked the boy to go and fetch a packet from the drug store. When he returned the woman was given her dosage and her screams subsided. Anslinger was never to forget those screams, nor the fact that the morphine she required was sold to a twelve year-old boy. This incident would later give way to a morbid interest in lurid and violent case histories as exemplified in the pulp, war-against-crime fiction of those times. It was an interest that would be given full vent in the course of time.

The smoking of marijuana in the United States first became defined as a social problem in the early part of this century. It was used by Mexican "wetbacks" who came to work in the beet fields of the Southwest. Among the first Americans to adopt its use were the blacks of the South. The first cities to perceive it as a problem were border towns like El Paso and New Orleans, who attributed its use to "prostitutes, pimps and a criminal class of whites." Although state after state enacted some form of marijuana prohibition, it was still perceived as a local problem until the early thirties when sensational accounts of its use began to appear in newspapers in many parts of the country and pressure mounted on the Bureau to act.

THE VIPERS

This was the era of depression, the lean years and as the hysteria grew the small deviant reefer-culture of sailors, jazzmen, circus people, entertainers, gangsters, the odd cowboy, along with the blacks and Mexicans, formed a native mythology around the weed. It was known as gage, shuzzit, muta, loco weed, Mary Warner, tea, muggles and reefer, by the "vipers" who smoked it. Out of the depth of Harlem night life, fusing with the unique vocal scatting style of Louis Armstrong and "Mezz" Mezzrow, the vipers came to being with a mode that encompassed jazz, language, dress and choice of intoxicant. "Light up and be somebody" was the slogan of their day. By the early 1930's more and more whites were sojourning uptown to the Harlem scene to pick up on good music, the fine dancing, and the righteous bush. Part of the scene's charm and power came from its exclusivity. It was through a secret inner city code that the "tea pads" and "rent parties" could be found. Contrary to popular myth, there was no real attempt to proselytize the virtues of the weed outside their immediate circles. If marijuana was anything, it was a psychic equaliser that would confer status and dignity on an outsider while at the same time provide a sensual treat that could allay the heaviest of depressions.

THE GORE FILE

Meanwhile back to Harry Anslinger, who was poised to launch his campaign against this weed that grew wild in many of the states. With a strong following which included many highly placed pharmaceutical executives, right-wing newspaper editors, and some influential congressmen, he devised a strategy to arouse public opinion on the marijuana issue. He would link it with crimes of violence, rape and murder. His agents would collect cases that he could use in his gore file, however tenuous the link with marijuana use. Usually there were racist overtones, and a fair share of sexual depravity. Anslinger was gearing up for the Marijuana Tax Act of 1937.

Here are some tit-bits of horror from the gore file:

Two negroes took a girl fourteen years of age and kept her for two days in a hut under the influence of marijuana. Upon recovery she was found to be suffering from syphilis.

Coloured students at the University of Minnesota

Atlanta Georgian. Feb. 27, 1935

partying with female students (white) smoking and getting their sympathy with stories of racial persecution. Result pregnancy.

In Texas an oilworker, good character, smoked a cigarette, raped his six-year-old daughter. When his wife returned home in the evening, she found him lying across the bed in a stupor, and the little child torn and bleeding. He couldn't remember. Was sentenced to death.

In New Jersey in 1936, a particularly brutal murder took place, in which case one young man killed another, literally smashing his head and face to a pulp. One of the defences was that the defendant's intellect was so prostrated from his smoking marijuana cigarettes that he did not know what he was doing. The fury of the murder was apparent. Not content with killing his friend, he tore out his tongue, his eyes, and so mutilated him that even the hardened coroner had to turn his eyes away from the gruesome sight.

And this from a man who had never smoked a joint in his life. Anslinger had found his theme and a slick, gutter style of presentation. He knew what excited the mass media and aroused public emotions.

But there was one case, that of Victor Licata, which became Anslinger's favourite and a cause celebre that was widely reported in the popular press of the time. Anslinger's files would later sum up the case:

A twenty-one-year-old boy in Florida killed his parents, two brothers and a sister with an axe while under the influence of a marijuana "dream" which he later described to law enforcement officials.

When the slaying occurred in 1933, over three years before Anslinger became aware of it, the local paper reporting the story first mentions marijuana a good few paragraphs from the beginning. In the same paper, the police chief vowed: *"Maybe the weed only had a small indirect part in the alleged insanity of the youth, but I am declaring now for all time that the increasing use of this narcotic must stop and will be stopped".*

The consequences of the growing stream of hysterical propaganda about the crime-causing properties of the weed, was that any and every two-bit hoodlum began pleading insanity due to the ravages of those "mutas" that they had smoked before committing the crimes. It was in this paranoic era that the "dope fiend" emerged, smoking his "devil weed" and corrupting innocent high school kids.

Anslinger was able to protect his concept of marijuana from any scientific assault until 1944, when the long-delayed "La Guardia Report" was finally published. It was a bombshell, exploding the myths so earnestly perpetuated by the Bureau. This prestigious report stated that the use of marijuana did not lead to physical, mental, or moral degeneration and that no permanent deleterious effects from its continued use were observed. The Bureau with its stalwarts of women's clubs, religious groups and the right-wing press railed against the findings, and a new strategy against the weed was devised.

THE COLD WAR

By the late forties another, more sinister drug emerged on the scene — heroin. Some soldiers had come back from the war and had caught the habit, and it was spreading. America was in the grip of the Cold War, and what better excuse than to blame the whole heroin epidemic onto the much-maligned marijuana plant. A new myth was about to engulf the nation, that smoking marijuana leads directly to heroin addiction. It would serve Commissioner Anslinger well for the next twenty-odd years of his

New Orleans, Times-Picayune, June 5, 1930

crusade. But it was in the fifties that the Draconian penalties associated with the drug laws were enacted amid an atmosphere of controlled hysteria. McCarthyism and rabid anticommunism was the order of the day, and drugs were sinisterly linked with the Red Menace. Anslinger had succeeded in convincing the American public that there was a grave new narcotic problem which could be contained only by a strong punitive approach.

However, by the end of the forties a new group of young white intellectually inclined jazz devotees began experimenting with the weed. They would later become known as the beat generation, and through the writings of Burroughs, Ginsberg and Kerouac, they would throw light on the experience of marijuana as a catalyst in re-examining other social attitudes. Even up until 1960 most of the users of marijuana were still non-white, and invariably those at the bottom rung of the social ladder. The turbulent sixties would see all that changed as Mary Warner left the ghetto.

COUNTER-CULTURE

The early sixties saw changes in many directions, and chinks began to appear in the Bureau's armour. The Single Convention Treaty regulating narcotic drugs throughout the world, was passed in 1961, and although Anslinger was a prime-mover behind the convention, a last minute move to dilute the strength of some of the prohibitions meant that the United States did not become a signatory to the Treaty at that time. In 1962, President Kennedy used the mandatory retirement clause to get rid of the Commissioner, who had reached the age of seventy. But the Old Man was far from powerless, still representing his country on all its international United Nations dealings, a vantage point from which he would be able to gain his last move against the burgeoning marijuana movement that was gathering pace. In May 1967, the Single Convention Treaty was passed by the Senate after a one day hearing

As the sixties progressed marijuana would become a vital armament in a counter-culture that sprang up, manifesting itself as a full frontal attack on the social and economical institutions of America. Pot was politicized, its powers embellished, its myth enlarged, and its use further ritualized. As early as 1964, Allen Ginsberg and some friends formed the first pro-pot lobby called "LEMAR" (Legalize Marijuana). Its use spread among the white middle class youth on the college campuses, and it became linked to the anti-Vietnam war lobby of the New Left and together with LSD, was the great rallying point of the hippies and "flower power".

In 1975, at the age of 83, Harry Jacob Anslinger died and an era was at an end. Marijuana was to be decriminalized in state after state as more than 20 million ordinary Americans were smoking it on a regular basis. Dope busts rose to a phenomenon half a million a year, the majority being young citizens for simple possession. The Drug Enforecement Agency super-seded the old Bureau of Narcotics and the number of agents employed in the battle against drugs increased from 400 when Anslinger left the Bureau, to some 10,000 agents scattered throughout the world.

All this and more is told in Larry Sloman's informative book, "Reefer Madness". The other two sections of the book comprise a racy, stoned account of the middle-class marijuanists of today and the new politics of pot, ending in the bunker with the last straight in America.

SMOKEY BEARS
FREE THE WEED
Featuring
CHESTER P. HACKENBUSH
The Psychedelic Alchemist
I GOT THIS 'SPECIALLY FOR YOU, CHESTER —FROM A FRIEND WHO'S JUST RETURNED FROM THE MIDDLE EAST . . .
HE GOT IT FROM AN ARAB MYSTIC.
IT'S SUPPOSED TO HAVE BEEN MADE BY HASSAN-I-SABBAH HIMSELF IN THE TWELFTH CENTURY IN HIS FORTRESS AT ALAMUT!
GO ON.
...STILL AS FRESH AND POTENT AS THE DAY IT WAS PRESSED!
THAT'S WHY IT'S SO EXPENSIVE, RIGHT?
HEH HEH HEH! WHAT A SALESMAN! HE SHOULD BE SELLIN' LIFE INSURANCE! HE COULD GO INTO ADVERTISING...
...IF THE WEIGHTS AND MEASURES SQUAD DON'T GET HIM FIRST! HEH HEH!
NOW TO SAMPLE TH' MERCHAND..
WOOOF!
SPLUT!
AARGH!
I AM THE GENIE OF THE DOPE!
DO NOT BE ALARMED, O MASTER!
DIG THIS: I HAVE THE POWER TO GRANT YOU ONE WISH!
DEFINITELY NO! PEACE ON EARTH IS A BIT HEAVY FOR ME!
THEN WHAT ABOUT.. ..PSST..PSST..PSST..
5 MINUTES LATER...
O.K. I SHOULD BE ABLE TO MANAGE THAT.
...WHEN THE UNEMPLOYMENT FIGURES SOARED PAST THE THREE MILLION MARK THIS WEEK. STILL UNEXPLAINED IS THE MYSTERIOUS RAIN OF MARIJUANA CIGARETTES OVER ENGLAND EARLIER TODAY. POLICE EXPERTS FAILED TO ASCERTAIN THE CAUSE OF THE...
FINIS
BRAINSTORM STUDIOS
©B.TALBOT 1980

ROBERT JACOB GOLDBERG ALIAS *PLEASURE*

Born New York City – February 11th, 1943. First arrest December 25th, 1960 – jumped bail. Arrested Flensburg, Denmark – December 17th, 1971 in possession of 40 kilos hashish. Sentenced twenty-eight months imprisonment. Released September 17th, 1973 for repatriation. Escaped custody Copenhagen Airport. Flew Geneva on American passport issued in name of George Katz. Traced Ibiza, Spain, September 28th, on Canadian passport in name of Gerald Arthur Cohen. Evaded arrest. Seen Paris October 6th. Now believed heading East....

THE 100 KILO CLUB

BY SIMON GANDOLFI

They parked the bus in the shadows off the road. Abdul led them down a lane and into a small tea-house. Lit by a paraffin lamp, it was one room no more than three by four metres. Half a dozen Afghani men squatted barefoot on the carpet-covered platforms which ran round all but the entrance wall. By the door a small boy boiled water for tea on a charcoal brazier set on a stone. Underneath the platforms ran a shelf for shoes.

Other than a brief nod of greeting, the Afghanis ignored their entrance. Shedding their sandals, they clambered up on to the carpet. Abdul had chosen a corner. Looking at the American, he raised his eyes to the ceiling. Pleasure glanced up to see a wooden trap-door with a crack of light showing between the planks. Abdul winked, then called to the boy for tea.

The pot came served with a dish of sweet pink candies. There was no sugar. Pleasure explained to the two Canadians the Afghani trick of holding a sweet on the tongue then sucking the hot tea over it. The candies left a flavour in the mouth of mint and cheap scent.

Two men came in. Throwing their cows back with a flick of their heads, they nodded to Abdul. Pleasure noticed they kept the open doorway covered with their bodies. Standing up, Abdul knocked twice on the trap door. It opened. Down came a wooden ladder.

'Quick!' Abdul ordered.

Up they climbed. Four of the Afghanis followed. There were already six men in the room which was the same size as the one below but lower ceilinged. The only light came from a charcoal fire laid on a clay trough set in the centre of the floor. At the head of the ladder a tall figure greeted them quickly, then passed them back to the end of the room. The light was so dim they could only see shapes at first; no details. The scent of the room was hashish. The walls, once whitewashed, were now smoked brown: the ceiling black. Backs against the walls, the Afghanis squatted, waiting and watching the foreigners. With their beaked noses and their shoulders hunched up over their knees, they resembled perched vultures. Their leader who had greeted them at the trap-door now sat between Pleasure and the two Canadians.

'Suleman', he introduced himself.

He held out his hand. Pleasure took it. Hands firmly clasped, they inspected each other. Beardless, the Afghani looked to be in his early thirties. His face was both harder and more open than the usual Kandahar hustler. He could be cop or robber, Pleasure considered – but not an in-between type Judas.

'You have pollen?' he asked.

Suleman nodded. 'First quality.'

'Yes?'

A large plastic bag materialized out of the shadows. Suleman opened it. Dug in his hand. Palm extended, he offered a small heap of golden brown powder for inspection.

The American took a pinch between thumb and first finger. Sniffed it. Spread it lightly to feel for stalk or earth.

then kneaded it hard to test for the tackiness of resin. The scent was fresh and strong. He could feel no impurities and the resin count was high. Satisfied, he passed what was now a crumbly ball to Jesse.

'It's good,' he told the Canadians.

Jesse rolled the ball a couple of times between his fingers, sniffed it, then passed it to Uri.

'How much?' Pleasure asked.

'Powder?'

'Pressed.'

He had a feeling that it had been LSD that had brought the big-money concept into the business. It took capital to set up an acid laboratory, capital to buy the chemicals and pay the chemists. The profits had been enormous. All the greedy beady-eyed fraternity had come flocking in like vultures to the kill. Then, when the bottom had fallen out of the acid market, they'd moved on into the hashish business. Long-haired gangsters with guns playing at being spiritually enlightened. At least the Brotherhood had never sold bad acid, which was more than could be said for most of the other organizations.

Palm extended, he offered a small heap of golden brown powder for inspection.

Suleman shrugged. 'First we smoke,' he told them.

He flung the bag down the room to the old man squatting closest to the fire. This was Hassan, the factory's chief presser. He took a tablespoon of pollen in the palm of his left hand. Spat into it. Then he started to knead, using the heel of his right hand. He worked the powder into a flat fish shape then dropped it on to the charcoal for the resin to melt. Retrieving the piece, he added more pollen and more spit. Again he kneaded it with the heel of his right hand but also now he alternated this style with a squeezing movement in which he sandwiched the fish between the heel of his left hand and the first two fingers of his right, then clamped his left hand tightly closed.

More heat. More pollen. More spit.

He worked the fish each time till all the pollen and spit were absorbed into the whole. The rest of the men watched in silence. The atmosphere of the room was almost religious in its intensity. They watched a master at work.

Sitting exposed downstairs. Pleasure had felt a slight paranoia. Here, in the almost dark, that feeling had gone. Like the Afghanis, he squatted with his back resting against the wall. He was at home. This had been his life for ten years. Watching Hassan press, he felt nor remorse – only a quiet sadness that his time was running out.

Perhaps he should have made enough to retire on when the game had still been easy. He could have, he knew, but he'd never tried to make big money. Had never done more than enjoy what he was doing while earning enough to support his own way of life; a way of life which had never been opulent or ostentatious. based as it was on his studio apartment in Ibiza at forty dollars a month. No Ferrari, no Cadillacs, no night-clubs, no fancy restaurants – his only real conceit had been the kilo jars of pure Rosemary honey he'd stored on top of the ice box in the dairy; honey to eat with his breakfast yoghurt . . . and his Bultaco with the bored-out engine.

Mini Mafias, Pleasure thought bitterly. If the acid came out bad from the test tube then don't waste it – add a little speed – a little strychnine; anything to give it a kick, and screw the casualties.

He was brought out of this reverie by Suleman nudging his side. He looked round. The factory owner held extended an open tobacco tin of red powder. The American thanked him. Taking the tin he spooned a small quantity on to the lid and flicked it into his mouth where he held it under his tongue. Then he passed the can to Jesse, who looked at him questioningly.

'Green tobacco ground with red chilli and hash pollen,' he told the Canadian. 'It's hot,' he warned. 'And don't swallow or you'll lose your dinner.'

Jesse looked slightly sick. 'Do I have to?' he asked.

'Depends on whether you mind hurting their feelings.'

Jesse looked sicker.

'Take a little,' Pleasure told him. 'Smile and pass it on.'

Looking down the room he saw Hassan was finally satisfied with the press he's achieved. Shuffling back against the wall, the old man passed the fish to the Afghani on his right who sniffed it appreciatively, flicked at it with his index finger a couple of times to hear its ring, then bent it backwards and forwards.

'The bending's to check the resin is properly worked,' Pleasure explained. 'A bad press will break or crumble. So will hash with a low resin content.'

The fish went round the room. In turn each man made the same critical inspection. Again there was a feeling of taking part in a religious ritual. Finally Suleman handed the fish to the American.

Weighing around thirty grams, the piece was warm, smooth and flexible. He held it up to his ear. Flicked it. A dead sound would have indicated an incomplete press. This rang hard. Its scent was thick. Its colour was burnt honey. He handed it to Jesse.

More heat. More pollen. More spit.

Smuggling had been a game – now it was a profession. If he'd wanted a profession he could have stayed home with his father in New York. And there wasn't much to choose between his father and half the young kids now in the dope business – despite their long hair. The kids were merely capable of greater self-delusion or hypocrisy. Both sides wanted to end up millionaires. At least his father admitted this. The heads pretended to be anti-materialistic revolutionaries, while they bought themselves ranches in Hawaii or Laguna Beach – the Brotherhood.

'Feel it,' he told him. 'It's good shit, well pressed and strong enough to pin your ears back.'

Which was true, as he soon found out.

Suleman prepared the water pipe himself. The water container was a one-foot high, blue-and-white glazed pottery vase. Into this fitted the clay bowl with its stem wrapped in damp cloth to seal the joint. The mouthpiece was a long bamboo which stuck up nearly vertically from the side of the vase. The bottom of the pipe bowl was protected by fine copper mesh.

On to this Suleman placed half a dozen glowing shards of charcoal from the fire. Then he broke the fish into fragments which he laid over the coals.

As reward for his pressing, Hassan was given the honour of lighting the pipe. His two neighbours held flaming matches over the hashish. Standing up to the mouthpiece, Hassan took two deep breaths of air, then, emptying his lungs completely, he put his lips to the bamboo. He drew the smoke in short drags, held it for a moment, then exhaled in a burst of rapid-fire coughs which were deliberate – intended to force smoke and oxygen up into the brain.

Long-haired gangsters with guns playing at being spiritually enlightened.

The pipe travelled to the right. As each man smoked the room became more totally fume-bound. The solemn silence was over. Hassan broke into a long rambling story. Pleasure caught only a few words but these were enough to get the gist. It was a peasant farmer's tale of how good the crops had been long, long ago. Here the crop was hashish, in Ibiza it would have been almonds or algaroba beans. Grapes in Provence, corn in the Midwest; the story was always the same: it was the springboard to old men's memories.

The pipe came to Suleman. Silence. His left-hand neighbour lifted the bowl free of the vase to allow the factory owner to clear the stale smoke from the water vessel. He stood with his left foot raised on the fire-brick. He blew three clear trumpet notes through the bamboo. Every face was turned to him. He nodded. His neighbour clamped the bowl down tight. His shoulders came back square to open his lungs. Then he dragged. He dragged with incredible speed and strength. Sparks flew from the charcoal. Flames leapt.

Leapt halfway to the ceiling. Red neon lit and re-lit the room. In minutest detail the faces of the watching Afghanis jumped into focus. Vanished. Re-appeared. vanished. This was no challenge – it was total victory.

'Jesus!' Jesse whispered.

Pleasure stood up. Now it was up to him. He knew the Canadians would not smoke. They wanted to keep their heads clear for bargaining. He understood their attitude. It wasn't his. Never had been. The pipe was as intrinsic a part of Afghan tradition as the hand pressing. This was the romance: travelling three thousand miles to sit at night surrounded by cloaked tribesmen in a small smoky room in Kandahar or Mazar-i-Sharif.

Here this pipe was equivalent to the Spanish macho: the masculinity test of a primitive male society. IF you passed, the Afghanis were your friends for ever. If you failed, you were too unimportant even to be mocked. To come this far and then not enter into their way of life seemed not only idiotic to Pleasure but also to deny the romance. And without the romance you were just one more Western businessman plundering the East for profit.

Here was his test. He smiled, first to himself, then to the watching tribesmen. He didn't try for a bugle note. Failure would have been too silly. One flame was his ambition, and then to get out of the room on his own two feet. He emptied his lungs as Hassan had done – squeezed them empty and slowly inhaled, on and on with his eyes on the bowl. Almost at the end of that inhalation he saw the first spark jump. He hit instantly and fast. *Drag Drag Drag In – Out In – Out In – Out.* The heat of the smoke seared his lungs. There were tears in his eyes. He knew he had to fall or stop. But the flames caught. The room leapt into light. Faces opened to him: smiling faces that egged him on. He hit twice more. Crazy conceit, he knew, even as he dragged but the flames danced and the Afghanis clapped. He had to. Then he was through. He smiled again and sank back on to his heels, shoulders against the wall.

'Still alive?' Jesse asked.

He hit instantly and fast. Drag Drag Drag In-Out In-Out In-Out

Pleasure waved the question aside. He was far too involved with waiting to talk. Then the hash struck. It came in on him in rolling waves that cast him back against the wall. He could feel his head being pushed deep into the clay brick – so deep that his ears were spread from his head like pinned-out butterfly wings. That was his body's feeling. His mind was clear. He felt everyone in the room watching him. This was the familiar paranoia of an overdose – something he'd long ago learnt to deal with.

There is nothing to fear, he whispered to himself – nothing to fear but fear itself. What was the worst that could happen? He could pass out. He could vomit. Neither mattered. The Afghanis might laugh at him. He let this picture drift on to the screen. He lay on the floor with his head lolling over a pool of sick. The Afghanis were standing. They were pointing at him. Laughing at him. Laughing and laughing. He started to laugh at himself. He looked so totally ridiculous lying there. Casualty of pride.

The screen cleared. The Afghanis were laughing. And he was laughing. Suleman had the pipe again. Flames danced and danced until finally the factory owner's lungs erupted.

'Easy,' he cautioned as he swung the mouthpiece to the American. 'Easy.'

The flames had leapt as high as his face and only now, a minute later, could he get his lungs back together so he could speak – and then only one word. Easy! Before he was off coughing again; coughing and crying and smiling all at the same time and his teeth so white, his whole face softening as Pleasure watched, losing his businessman's keenness, losing everything but laughter. Both of them laughing and laughing.

'Eee. . . ' he went.

'Eee . . . '

And they slapped their right hands hard together with joy of sharing this moment. Total mirth – nothing held back..

Something dragged at Pleasure's sleeve. He turned. Uri leant across his partner.

'How much?' he wanted to know. His voice seemed petulant. The ignored outsider.

What a crazy question, Pleasure thought. How much for heaven?

He shrugged helplessly as renewed laughter hit him. Hit him so hard his solar plexus ached with strain.

'Ask him,' he gasped. 'It's your shit.'

Coffeeshop AMSTERDAM

by Lee Harris

Amsterdam has a tradition of tolerance that dates way back and is a haven for radicals, expatriates, and outsiders of all kinds. It offers the wayfarer the freedom to partake in a particular activity without necessarily coming into contact or infringing on someone else's and so caters for separate needs on many levels. One of the most interesting examples of this tolerance at work is the rise and growth of the dope coffee shops that have opened up in various parts of the city over the last few years, where you can sit in congenial surroundings and buy hash or grass from a house dealer at set prices and know you aren't being ripped off. There are twenty such coffee shops scattered throughout the city, each in turn catering for a particular and regular clientele. The coffee shop dealers have taken cannabis out of the black market, which involves other illicit drugs like heroin and cocaine, and into a legitimate business setting as is the way with alcohol, or tea and coffee consumption, and ply their trade in an orderly and contained environment. It is the principle of de facto decriminalisation put in practice, and the nearest thing to legalisation to be seen in the western world, and could well serve as a working model to other enlightened societies.

* * * * * * * * * * * * * *

It was late July and Amsterdam was in the full-swing of its tourist season, bustling with young foreigners in search of a high time in this city of dope dreams. The Orange Full Moon Affair was on and the followers of "the God that fled" could be seen wandering around in couples entwined in their bright robes, that seemed to dance in the soft wind and glow in the sunshine. Walking across the Dam Square I could hear the street hustlers hissing the word 'hash' to the dreamy denizens ensconced in small groups around the embankments of the ornate fountain. In the red light district I stood on a canal bridge watching a party of middle-aged tourists being guided past The Sex Theatre, 'live' performances since 'Anno 1969', and on down the street where they viewed the seductive sirens who sit motionless in their beguiling lingerie, staring out of their windows like display dummies. As I walked on, I noticed a gay couple ambling by arm in arm, a member of the mackintosh brigade intensely engaged in the contents of a porno sexshop window, and then I came across a coffee shop with loud music blaring from its speakers, and on entering saw that the clientele sitting at the bar or on tables were all skinning up joints or leisurely passing them on to their companions.

> **Cannabis is now one of Holland's biggest tourist attractions and a large earner of foreign currency**

* * * * * * * * * * * * * * *

It is a beautiful Summer evening, and as I stroll about aimlessly dreaming in the moving light reflections glimmering in the water of a canal, a group of newly-arrived young German tourists stop me. "Can I ask you two questions?", begins the spokesman for the four of them in English, "Where is the Milky Way, and where can I buy some hash?"

The Melkweg (Milky Way), a multi-media youth centre, was one of the first places to have a house dealer, in the heyday of flower power when Amsterdam was a mecca for the stoned hippie. Last year it celebrated its tenth year and is attracting more foreign visitors than ever before with its mixture of rock music fringe theatre, cinema, wholefood, and good dope. The house dealer rents a table in the market-place, selling nuts and raisins as well as dope, displaying his list of goodies and their price per gram, on the table in front of him; there are four varieites on sale already weighed and packed in small plastic bags costing from ten to twenty-five guilders (£2 or £5 deals). As he opens shop and prepares his table for the evening a queue has already formed and from then on he will be busy supplying these small amounts to a steady

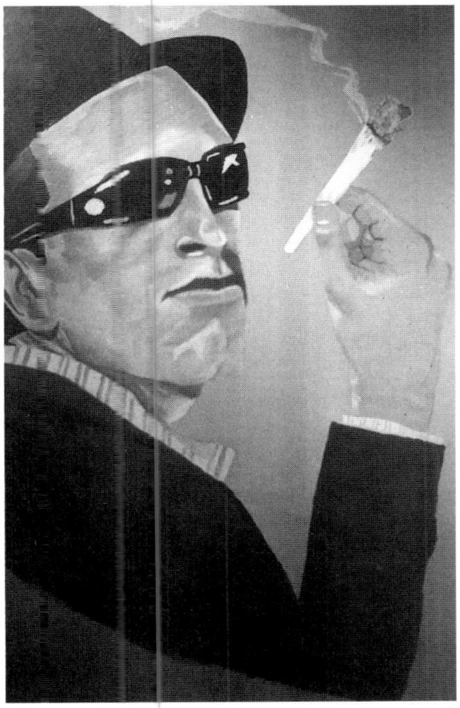

and a continuous flow of customers. No one would say how much money he makes and it's a closely-guarded house secret how much he pays the centre to rent the table. In the market-place you can buy a chillum, hand-made jewellery, a book or magazine, or a juicy slice of watermelon and pineapple if you've got the munchies. In the tea house upstairs, a large high-ceilinged room, serving herbal teas and chocolate and spice cake, the place is packed with young people from all over the world rolling joints and smoking them while a singer-guitarist fills the smoke-laden atmosphere with a hauntingly sad song. From the large high windows of the tea house you can see inside the brightly lit rooms on the first floor of the police station just across the street. It slowly dawns on you that the selling and smoking of cannabis this way has got nothing to do with crime any more.

* * * * * * * * * * * * *

"About the necessity to fight as much as possible the international trafficking in opiates like heroin almost everyone agrees. Because the police lack the capacity to do so, one cannot afford the luxury of powerful action against the users of cannabis."

H.P. Wooldrik, Public Prosecutor of Amsterdam.

It is this sort of pragmatic approach which has characterised the change in attitudes of the lawmakers in Holland. The law divides forbidden drugs into two categories. List 1 contains assorted substances such as heroin, cocaine, Lsd, and the amphetamines, and carries stiff sentences, the maximum being twelve years for large amounts. In List 2 there are only two substances, hashish and marijuana, and the maximum sentence for big consignments is four years. On the 19th August 1976 a user of cannabis was defined as a person with no more than 29 grams in his possession, and the offence was treated as a misdemeanour. If apprehended a ticket is handed out like a traffic offence, but if you don't pay up they can put you in jail for a month or fine you a maximum of £100. So a move was made to liberalise the law and shift the emphasis between hard and soft drugs still further apart.

> **"... one cannot afford the luxury of powerful action against the users of cannabis"**

* * * * * * * * * * * * *

"You're sitting in this coffee shop, your hand under your chin, feeling a little clammy in your Smoke The Russians Out of Afghanistan tee-shirt. Your tea has long gone cold, you ask yourself if you put sugar in it. You look at the sugar bowl, you see a stoned fly circling the sugar pot as if it's a fly-heaven. You are not aware of other people, the music blasts in your ears, it is hot, my God, it is hot. You dream of a freshly-juiced orange drink. You watch a group of punks leaving – their lunch break is over – and two school-types take their place. The fly is lost in a world of sugar and can't keep still. The last of the smoke? And while all this is going through your head the door opens, and you hear a voice say, 'Stay Where You Are' . . . and that is enough. Suddenly there are eight policemen, your heart starts to pound, you swallow hard, a cold sweat on your forehead, you think, think, you must immediately get rid of your dope, you rummage wildly through your pockets and throw away the plastic bag and by mistake your library card. Bad luck. Thy come further in, asking questions here and there, it's quiet, an eerie silence, you are aware that the music has stopped, that you're sitting still. The drug squad have got you in their grip, they've seen that your hands are shaking, that it was you who had thrown the piece away. But what can the police do? And you laugh? At the same time you feel cross, What Are They Doing Here? There lies this hash and grass on the floor. They search your pockets while they hold your arms above your head against the wall. How long in the nick, a few hours? a day? And all this for a few joints of hash or grass . . . "

I was at the office of the newly-formed Cannabis Union, an amalgam of two organisations, surrounded by index filing cards and reams of broadsheets ready to be mailed out, watching Koos Swart enacting the bust. For after rive years without any trouble the coffee shops have experienced a series of raids these last few months. About twenty shops were raided about thirty-six times in all, and the Cannabis Union was coming to the rescue, collating the busts, how much was taken, how many officers took part and how many man hours were spent on these actions. They had shown that during the same period only a couple of places were busted for heroin. They had maps pinpointing the coffee shops that had been raided and by which police districts, which were on display at most of the coffee shops. Usually very little was found, the dealer taken away for a few hours, and it was business as usual. I heard at one place that a counter-hand was knocked out, and saw at another shop that they'd ripped open the bar stools, ostensibly looking for hard drugs, and yet at another one they came in, looked around, couldn't find anything and walked out. The house dealer told me that he had put his leather satchel with the dope in it on top of one of the speakers and they just didn't see it.

So here was a joint action between the coffee shop owners and the Union of cannabis users, who put out a newsletter called Own Grown, and whose envelopes bear the slogan, 'Don't Pay The dealer, Grow Your Own'. On joining the Union a member is sent a large foolscap envelope containing seven varieties of seed packets

with instructions on how to grow them, recipes, and a list of standard works to read up on. Seeds are perfectly legal and can be distributed freely. The Union has branches in other cities and towns and its members come from all walks of life. The coffee shop action was undertaken by the Amsterdam branch and is a unique example of the cooperative growers working with the commercial dealers together for the benefit of the cannabis consumer. It also marks the emergence and recognition of the coffee shops as part of the business community. The Peoples Party for Freedom and Democracy and the Labour Party took up the issue of the raids in the council chambers and in a series of written questions to the mayor, wanted to know who supervised the destruction of the confiscated cannabis, and informing them of the police districts involved. It was not long before the raids stopped and the coffee shops were left in peace once more.

* * * * * * * * * * * * *

He was lean, wiry man aged about thirty, with an abundance of nervous energy, speaking rapidly in fluent English, as we walked through the Zeedijk, the old red light quarter, seedy and run-down. The area is now the territory of the newer immigrants, Surinamese, Turks and Chinese. In the one street there are forty six places where they sell heroin. The man I was walking with pointed to a building and said, "I was born there, brought up in this street. I know the area very well." He then greeted someone who was waving to him from the top floor window of an old house. "You see that man there, in the old days he was a big dealer importing from the Lebanon. Made a lot of money, runs gaming houses in the street. But he still lives in the same two rooms with his wife."

"I started my coffee shop five years ago in a business way with plastic bags. Before it was under the table and weighed to make it efficient."

His is a local boy makes good story. He was selling porno magazines in a basement in the red light district when he suddenly got sick of it and threw the whole lot in the canal after an English tourist asked to see even more lurid stuff than he had to offer, and started his coffee shop in the same premises. He now has another one in The Hague.

"My name and everything I started was bad, my name doesn't matter, but the name of my coffee shop matters. With every guilder you make, you make an enemy", he says philosophically.

The success of the coffee shops lies in their wise decision to keep cannabis as far removed from heroin and cocaine as they possibly could.

"Sometimes you get young policemen eager to try their luck. They come inside and wish and hope to find heroin, they search the place, take the dope off the dealer and walk out, and that's the last you hear of it."

We were now sitting on the wooden bench outside his coffee shop which overlooks a canal. He took a cigarette from his packet, mixed the tobacco with some resinous double-zero Moroccan, and kneaded it in the palm of his hand for some while before making a short, fat joint.

"It's better to eliminate the street-seller and know where it's happening. That way they can control it. The coffee shops have already cornered the market, local and tourist, now that it's taken off the streets."

But how do you turn black money into white money? First you start a business, pay rent and rates, hire staff, and then you reach the point where you have to declare your income and pay taxes. Like all businesses, you have an accountant and lawyer who deal with these problems, advising you and negotiating with the authorities to assess the amount you will have to pay.

The coffee shop dealers have taken cannabis out of the black market, and into a legitimate business setting.

"The market has now reached saturation point. You can only come into it if you have a lot of money to finance the thing. It's more like a machine, it's so busy you can't really speak to the customers."

From inside the coffee shop I could hear the incessant, pounding beat of the non-stop music as I watched the casual comings and goings, with the pleasant aroma of good coffee and dope wafting by in the late afternoon air.

* * * * * * * * * * * * *

One coffee shop is the headquarters of the local chapter of the Hell's Angels, whose leader, Jack, had recently died in a motorway collision while doing a ton on his bike. At a table stood an artist fervently painting a portrait of Jack from a photograph, etching the lines and furrows on his beaming face with great love and intense concentration. The bar assistant was a wee Scotsman whose tee-shirt brandished the words Fuck Off. Heavy metal emanated from the sound system as the Angels rapped about Jack's funeral procession which included a guard of honour of 140 bikers.

I'm sitting in a Space-O-Theek in a quiet street in the old Jewish quarter of the city. It is early on a Saturday evening and the place is calm and relaxed. A couple of neighbourhood youths are playing Space Invaders near the door. Sitting at the counter besides me is an attractive middle-aged lady sipping herbal tea, while watching the young people coming in to buy their weekend supply of hash or grass from the counter, then going to the rear disco room with its mirrors and coloured lights, to skin up and listen to the rhythmic sounds. It has the appearance of a modern youth club and is a focal point for the neighbourhood teenagers. The lady next to me treats it as her 'local', finding it a pleasure to see young people in an alcohol-free environment with no need to hang out on street-corners. the Space-O-Theek is unique in that it doesn't sell coffee, but boasts a variety of [illegible]8 herb teas. The young owner, who was brought up in the neighbourhood and used to work in a bank, was looking for a place where he and his friends could go and have a smoke together, when he saw

Photos by Koos Swart

this empty shop, and now he has been in operation for just on a year and it has become a popular local haunt.

* * * * * * * * * * * * * * *

The success of the coffee shops lies in their wise decision to keep cannabis as far removed from heroin and cocaine as they possibly could.

The latest addition to the coffee shops had just opened for the Summer season, its blue and white decor carefully chosen to appeal to the affluent young tourists who flock to Amsterdam from all over the world to smoke cannabis in a relaxed and easy atmosphere, often far removed from their paranoic home ground. Cannabis is now one of Holland's biggest tourist attractions and a large earner of foreign currency. But the coffee shop, teahouse and smoking room have long been an established part of European culture and to frequent them at one time or another was thought to be daring or even outrageous. They were often the haunts of artists, painters and poets, and revolutionaries spent hours plotting the overthrow of the state while puffing cigarettes and drinking coffee. There is no reason at all why the buying and smoking of cannabis should not become a part of this culture and just blend into the social scene. After all, Amsterdam has a long tradition of trading in exotic herbs and spices from the East. Long may the dope coffee shops reign.

* * * * * * * * * * * * * * *

THE PAPER PRINCE'S GUIDE TO THE COFFEE SHOPS

Coffeeshop	Address	Comment
BULLDOG	O.Z.Voorburgwal 90	For Jokers & Smokers, a haven in the heart of the red light district. Established around 5 years.
BUDDHA'S JOINT PARADISE	Nieuwmarket	Just opened. Really smart inside, no tourist marks yet, pay a visit, and relax in comfort.
BALLONNETJE	Roetersstraat 12	Not yet visited. Est. summer 1978.
GLORY'S	Ruysdaelstraat 48	Kick back & relax, inside, or laze in the sun outside, away from the bustling "Centrum". Est early 1978
de HAASJES	Hazenstraat 19	Not yet visited. Est. early 1980.
HIGH SOCIETY	Hieuwe Kerkstraat 67	Customers ages range from teenaged to pension-aged. The Lawmakers could learn from this example. Est. early 1980.
PASCHA	Marnixstraat 86	Not yet visited.
LAURIER 33	Ie Laurierdwarsstr't	Not yet visited. Recently busted for 20,000 grams assorted grass & hash — still open. Est. summer 1978.
RUSLAND	Rusland 16	One of the busiest coffee shops, meet people from all over the world, they sell interesting pancakes. Est. early 1977.
SCREEN	Da Costastraat 68	Split level, becoming very popular. The stairs are much steeper going down. . . good value. Est. 1980
SMOESIE	Waterlooplein 115	60's milk-bar type clientele, young dutch "punk's" "mod" looking . . . good atmosphere, not many tourists. Est. early 1979.
SMOKIE	Admiraal de Ruyter-weg 56	Unusual in that beer is served on the premises, in separate part downstairs. Videotheek. Tourist's welcome. Est. summer 1979.
STASH	Overtoom 255	Finds most of their trade comes in from the nearby Vondelpark . . . clean, good value. Open six months.
LIBERTAD	Jan Van Galenstraat	Potted plants galore, Videotheek, excellent racial harmony. It felt good just to be there.

L.S.D. AND THE MIND ALCHEMYST

BY MICHAEL HOLLINGSHEAD, DESIGN BY HAMISH.

There was a time in the late fifties and early sixties when dope was something that the 'beats' and 'spades' took. 'Taking acid' had not become the popular pastime of a turned-on youth, for they didn't exist.

It was in this rather drab and dreary period, which suffered from the after-effects of the Cold War, that L.S.D. first emerged on the social scene in America. Such writers as Aldous Huxley and Gerald Heard had used it with quite astonishing results, for in those days it was legal, though not easily available.

In 1960 a young Englishman, Michael Hollingshead, who happened to be living and working in New York at the time, telephoned Huxley at his home in Los Angeles to inquire about obtaining some mescaline. During the conversation, Huxley mentioned L.S.D. and a caution: "It is much more potent than mescaline." Huxley's information included the name of Dr. Albert Hoffman, the Swiss bio-chemist working at the Sandoz Pharmaceutical Laboratories in Basel, who discovered L.S.D. 25 – by chance – in 1943.

Michael simply asked an English doctor friend to write the order on a New York hospital letterhead, saying he needed the ergot-derivative as a 'control-drug' for a series of bone marrow experiments.

A LOVIN' SPOONFUL

A small package from Switzerland arrived in his mail one morning containing one gram of Dr. Hoffman's acid and a bill for 285 dollars. It was in a small dark jar marked "Lot no. H-00047" and looked a bit like malted milk powder. Michael poured some distilled water in a bowl, then dissolved the acid into it, adding icing sugar into the mixture to make a thick paste. He then transferred his 'divine confection' spoon by spoon into a large mayonnaise jar. By some alchemic process the stuff measured exactly 5,000 spoonfuls. Like all good chefs, he'd tasted the preparation with his fingers and absorbed about the equivalent of five heavy doses before he had finished. What followed, lasting perhaps some 15 hours, was an experience that would change Michael's life, and that of countless others with far-reaching effect.

After that first 'trip', Michael once more phoned Huxley to discuss his visionary experience. Huxley called him back a few days later and suggested that he contact a Dr. Timothy Leary, a Harvard professor, who had recently presented a paper on induced visionary experience. "If there is any one single investigator in America worth seeing, it is Dr. Leary," said Huxley.

In September 1961, Michael met, and subsequently moved into the home of Timothy Leary in Boston. He had been living there a couple of weeks when Maynard Ferguson, a jazz musician and a close friend of Leary's, arrived with his wife, Flo. At that time Leary didn't smoke marijuana as it was illegal, and took nothing stronger than a few micro-grams of psilocybin, and wine and whisky, which he believed were "indispensable luxuries". When Ferguson heard that Michael had some acid, he suggested they all have a session together. Leary excused himself, as he had papers to mark, but said they could take it if they so wished. Michael, Maynard and Flo took a spoonful each and settled down by the log fire. After about thirty minutes, Flo sat up suddenly, and with a huge smile on her face, waved at Leary: "You gotta try this Tim, baby. It's f-a-n-t-a-s-t-i-c."

Leary later wrote in his book *High Priest* about that experience: "It has been five years since that first L.S.D. trip with Michael Hollingshead. I have never forgotten it. Nor has it been possible for me to return to the life I had been leading before the session. I have never recovered from the shattering ontological confrontation, I have never been able to take myself, my mind and the social world around me seriously. Since that time five years ago, I have been acutely aware of the fact that I perceive everything within the world around me as a creation of my own consciousness."

Since then, Michael has turned-on and guided many a great man through their first trip. In his book *The Man Who Turned On The World*, published by Blond & Briggs, 1973, he gives a lucid and well-written account of his part in the early days of the psychedelic era, both in this country and America.

It is now over fifteen years since those embryonic sessions that helped change the life-style of a whole generation. HOME GROWN asked Michael Hollingshead, who lives in London, to give us some of his thoughts on acid as he views it today.

There are things of which it has been said the truly wise never try to conceptualise. Is L.S.D. one of them?

I think one can talk about L.S.D. in a non-psychological way, because it is something anyone can experience. Anyone, provided he has his heart and head in the right place, has the right to take L.S.D. as much or as little as he wants. It is Man's Fifth Freedom – the freedom to 'turn on' his own nervous system and on his own terms. Alas, it is a freedom that is severely curtailed at this time in our history. On the other hand, L.S.D. is something at which, as at holy springs, one does not drink habitually nor lightly.

Is it dangerous?

L.S.D. is a dangerous three-letter word. Say it to the average lawyer, churchman, clubman, and it will produce serious side-effects – they grow red in the face, shake, get high blood pressure, become incoherent. The stuff itself isn't dangerous. Nobody has ever died of it, if that is what you mean. One of the riddles of L.S.D. is that the user never has to increase the dose. There is no slavery to L.S.D. – it is, on the contrary, a liberation. There are those who would have you believe that L.S.D. is an escape from life and that it takes away one's sense of values. But if L.S.D. takes away the old life and the old scale of values from under our feet it sets up another for us, superior and more delicate.

The L.S.D.-user has a third-eye view of himself. One of the interesting things about getting 'high' via L.S.D. – getting in touch with your own inner processes, if you like – is that it gives you, albeit only for a 6–8 hour stretch at a time – a chance to see for yourself the many different motives which seem to underly all one does, thinks, feels. This is seeing yourself a little more consciously than before; the psychedelic experience is not so much a kind of *being* as a kind of *knowing*. And the memory lingers. This is why people who have taken L.S.D. often change in quite dramatic ways. They have discovered a new kind of truth about themselves, if by truth we mean to 'come to', to awake to an inner self who is palpably more real. It is one thing to live out your simple life or death as a programmed robot, which one does as the result of a most profound ignorance about the nature of man and his potential. But when one is in possession of all the facts, the 'nothing-but-the-truth' knowledge about oneself, it is impossible to live the shuttered life of the closed mind and eye.

There is really nothing arbitrary in suggesting that people extend themselves a little via a psychedelic experience. It is the last chance we shall have in life. It helps us feel the tender, know the irrational, feel the invisible and so forth. On the other hand, it takes a lot of L.S.D. to gain even a tiny bit of consciousness.

In what way do people change after an acid session?

They become aware of this tension between, on the one hand, the flowing process and, on the other, the fixed structure. Leary has written at length about expansion-contraction, that which gets you high and that which brings you down, and suggested that human life is better suited to getting high. I think that the human mind, like human history, is made for change, is part of the natural flowing process of the universe. And if contracted by societal 'man-made' systems we will lose whatever capacity it is in the human mind for growth, creativity and ultimately of course, happiness.

The real gulf today in our thinking is not, as C.P. Snow spoke about in the fifties, between science and art, but between those who are 'high' and those who are 'down'. When one can see through or beyond the imprinted symbols of a received culture it is to perceive a world in which there has been a fundamental change in men's minds. I remain convinced, despite my failures, that L.S.D. can be good and that it is entirely up to the individual to make it well disposed. We must first learn to handle it. Man's need to get in touch with the source of his being is something some of us feel is infinitely desirable – and knowable. It is also a certain disposition to act, to act in some primordial and metaphysical way, form an alliance of the mind with the soul, a disposition each time we take L.S.D. L.S.D. is the need to emerge from oneself – with flying colours.

Can you tell us something about the Harvard Psychedelic Project which you participated in, between 1960–63? How do you think L.S.D. affected the lives of those who took part in those early sessions? Was the d-LSD-25 that you were using then different in any way from today's 'street acid'?

It was an officially-sponsored research project by Harvard University, run under the aegis of the Social Relations Department, and headed by Timothy Leary. Our thesis – subsequently proved – was that L.S.D. and similar agents such as mescaline and psilocybin, may at times produce rapid personality changes of a long-lasting nature in normal people even when no psychotherapy is intended. We ran about 3,000 sessions for graduates and faculty, and about another 1,000 for artists, musicians, writers, poets, actors; and for prisoners in a maximum security prison at Concord, Massachusetts. And the great majority of these, something like 96%, reported major life changes of a positive kind. As for members of the research team, they were all third-year graduate students in Behaviourism, that is, with the exception of Leary, Richard Alpert and myself. We were faculty. On average, I think, each member of the project took L.S.D. in excess of one hundred times, some of us about three hundred times.

It is difficult to say why there should be so many beneficial claims for L.S.D. Some people have likened the L.S.D.-induced rapid personality change to the naturally occurring mystical or religious conversation experiences described by such thinkers as William James, Gerald Heard and Aldous Huxley. There is certainly a lot of evidence around to observe a positive correlation between people who have L.S.D.-mystical experiences and those claiming lasting benefits. People at Harvard were reporting for instance, that the L.S.D. experience gave them better understanding of themselves and others, and a high proportion claimed improved personal relationships, more tolerance of others and their viewpoints, and changes of values in several areas. They claimed they were less dogmatic in their thinking and beliefs, that the L.S.D. experience had made them more 'flexible'.

We found at Harvard that most of the bizarre, psychotic-like behaviours, and so forth, stressed by the media can be eliminated or greatly minimised by replacing the cold, impersonal 'clinical' approach with a supportive, 'natural' and protective environment. We also found that the attitude and the beliefs of the person giving the L.S.D. is almost as important as the state of mind of the person taking it. These are conditions not normally to be found in clinics; hence the number of reports of 'bad' sessions conducted in such places, for which the public turns for information about the subject. I don't think that it is possible to conceptualise the mode of action in terms of existing psychological theory. Religious metaphors are much closer as descriptions of what happens during an L.S.D. session.

But it is a fact of life at this present time that the phenomenon L.S.D. is beset with considerable resistance not encountered since the days of the Red Star Chamber. L.S.D. is the new heresy, it seems. People go to prison for it – so much for our Western ideas of personal freedom. The fact is that L.S.D. is completely outside our current cultural concepts. Thus, to a person who has not thoroughly experienced the effects of L.S.D. on himself, the literature is understandably confusing and contradictory.

As for what has happened to the other members of the Harvard Psychedelic Project, I can report that they are all alive and healthy and very much involved in the 'flowing processes'. Dr. Timothy Leary is out of jail and working on his Starseed project; Dr. Richard Alpert has become a Hindu monk, changed his name to Baba Ram Dass, and heads the Hanuman Foundation in New York; Dr. Ralph Metzner lives in California and also heads a foundation concerned with various forms of psychic healing; Dr. Gunther Weil, who edited *The Psychedelic Reader,* helps to run the American Gurdjieff group; Dr. Al Cohen heads the American Mehar Baba group; Dr. George Litwin heads up the Crossett Hill Learning Community in Vermont; Dr. Richard Katz has recently published a book, *Preludes to Growth: An Experiential Approach* and is now living with the Zu/wasi tribe in the Kalahari; Dr. David Kolb is lecturing and writing at M.I.T.; Dr. Rolf Von Ekartsberg runs the 'Open Door' group in Philadelphia; and I am being interviewed by 'Home Grown'!

As for your last question, about the L.S.D. we were using. Yes, I believe there is an important, if little understood, difference between what we used at Harvard and what is available on the streets, as it were. d-LSD-25, to give it its full title, is a *semi*-synthetic substance, that is, it requires ergot for its synthesis. Now large amounts of clandestine ergot are simply not available, so underground manufacturers have had to use a synthetic ergot such as ergotomine to produce the synthesis. And the subjective effects are really very different from those reported at Harvard. The street stuff may even be harmful on account of impurities. It is a difficult situation and I don't know what one can do about it. It seems unlikely, given the climate of the world at the moment, that any government would release a new batch of ergot-based acid for non-clinical purposes. Though, paradoxically, the government that did would force everyone to get smarter. But, like everything else I've said, it is my own private opinion.

Should one take acid?

As the old alchemists said, "You need a bit of light to find the light," and that pretty well sums up *why* acid.

Healing of the Nations.

"The greatest service which can be rendered to any country is to add a useful plant to its culture." Thomas Jefferson.

Meanwhile, I could hear the conference coordinator, Bob Pisani on the video giving an historical overview of international cannabis control. To refresh myself I had a mu tea and some carrot cake and sat down again. I looked around the lounge and there was all these people from all over the place gathered together here to change the cannabis laws. A momentous occasion.

During these three days, some three hundred of us from twenty different nations came together to exchange ideas and to talk about our experiences in our particular homelands. It was the public inauguration of ICAR, an alliance of legalisation organisations from most of the Western nations, who will lobby the United Nations to remove cannabis from the Single Convention Treaty – the international treaty that forbids governments from legalising public production, distribution and sale of cannabis.

On a high plane, it was a coming together of the cannabis cognoscenti from many different cultures, languages and backgrounds, learned in diverse disciplines from medicine, law, penal reform, ethno-botany to poetry, music, anarchy and high-culture. They were all there, the law reform campaigners and direct-activists, the home-growers and cultivating tipsters, the historians, scientists and other pundits, and the media people who would spread the word far and wide.

Cannabis – the drug, plant, herb, known in many tongues as grass, marijuana, hashish, ganja, bhang, dagga, hemp etc, this ageless weed, plant of the Gods – had brought together emissaries from many of the different cultures that co-exist on this planet Earth. An eclectic body of people from a wide spectrum of human activity, encompassing various spiritual beliefs and political ideologies. It was this cultural diffusion that gave the occasion an extra dimension.

Where else would you find an Episcopalian priest from Philadelphia, an Iberian anarchist, a Polish psychiatrist, a scaffolder from Brixton, a Japanese lawyer, a businessman from Chicago, a Rastafarian doctor, and a mystical and high lady just back from the East, all gathered together with others for three days in mutual harmony and respect?

We had come to Amsterdam to discuss strategies and means of removing cannabis from the prohibitions on its social and medical use. A long and difficult task by any standards. Anti-cannabis laws violate our basic human rights and perpetuate social lies to the detriment of societies as a whole. All sorts of areas are brought into play if you mention cannabis, from the plight of prisoners in foreign jails to the repression of minorities that don't adhere to the cultural norms of the conglomerate state. Attuned to the times and with growing conviction, a dissident voice is striving to be heard amidst the scientific half-truths and media misrepresentation that masquerades as "informed opinion".

A generation has grown up immersed in the multi-facets of their favourite high.

There are the logically-minded, adepts at drafting constitutions and framing statutes, looking for loopholes in the morass of legal jargon that binds us to outdated laws. They are the scientists and legal beavers that burrow through the mass of conflicting data that has amassed over recent years, steadily seeing through the contradictions that riddle the law and science. In the process they are discovering flaws in the very nature of scientific analysis and legalistic procedures. They will deal with the echelons of power, using their highly-educated minds and skills, that are rooted in Western culture, to play them at their own game.

Then there are the liberators of cannabis, those that want to free the weed. They are the cultivators of plants, the guerrilla growers using halide lamps and hydroponics, the botanists and taxonomists of the species of cannabis-indica, sativa and ruderalis. To them the outlawing of one of nature's oldest plants is beyond comprehension, an absurd quirk in the mind of rational men. Their noble task is to see forbidden fruit flowering freely in variable climes. The seeds have already been sown.

There are those who raise the cannabis flag at the barricades, who see it as their right and duty as citizens to defy an unjust law. They are aware that direct action and civil disobedience are often the only methods of effecting change in a pluralistic system. The repeated violation of a law obviously diminishes its effectiveness and practicality. If the process of changing an unworkable law is blocked, usually because the body politic is too cumbersome and stultified to read the writing on the wall, direct actions and symbolic gestures have a way of influencing these processes and speeding up the necessary steps towards change. Where would the liberation movements of women, blacks, gays etc be today without their direct-activists pushing for social acceptance and creating attention with their "street theatre" antics?

There are the mystics and mendicants who see cannabis as a gift of the Gods, a sacrament given to man so that he may commune with nature and live in harmony on this planet. There is no doubt that the whole Oriental spiritual trip that has surged through the consumer paradises of the West, was helped along its way by the seminal influence of this conscious-altering substance. It was no coincidence that the conference should take place in a meditation centre, with wholefoods and herbal teas to nourish the body. At one time during a lengthy discourse on a legal issue, this beatific lady, blissfully spaced out, sat on the platform in the lotus position, her arms carving the air with flowing mudras, and confounded the gathering by serenely stating that "cannabis is lingam" (the phallus). Here was Kali, the mother of creation and destruction, of darkness the Moon and emotion, balancing the logic intellect and brightness of Shiva.

**" . . . and the leaves of the tree were for the healing of the nations."
Revelations 22**